WORLD OF ANIMALS

9

MAMMALS

INSECTIVORES AND BATS

Hedgehogs, Moles, Anteaters, Bats ...

PAT MORRIS, AMY-JANE BEER

GROLIER

Species of tree shrews: common tree shrew (1); pen-tailed tree shrew (2); pygmy tree shrew (3); northern smooth-tailed tree shrew (4).

Published 2003 by Grolier,
Danbury, CT 06816
A division of Scholastic Library Publishing

This edition published exclusively for the school and library market

Planned and produced by
Andromeda Oxford Limited
11–13 The Vineyard,
Abingdon, Oxon OX14 3PX

www.andromeda.co.uk

Copyright © Andromeda Oxford Limited 2003

Project Director: Graham Bateman
Editors: Angela Davies, Penny Mathias
Art Editor and Designer: Steve McCurdy
Cartographic Editor: Tim Williams
Editorial Assistants: Marian Dreier, Rita Demetriou
Picture Manager: Claire Turner
Picture Researcher: Vickie Walters
Production: Clive Sparling
Researchers: Dr. Erica Bower, Rachael Brooks, Rachael Murton, Eleanor Thomas

Origination: Unifoto International, South Africa

Printed in China

Library of Congress Cataloging-in-Publication Data

Morris, Pat.
    Mammals / [Pat Morris, Amy-Jane Beer, Erica Bower].
        p. cm. -- (World of animals)
    Contents: v. 1. Small carnivores -- v. 2. Large carnivores -- v. 3. Sea mammals -- v. 4. Primates -- v. 5. Large herbivores -- v. 6. Ruminant (horned) herbivores -- v. 7. Rodents 1 -- v. 8. Rodents 2 and lagomorphs -- v. 9. Insectivores and bats -- v. 10. Marsupials.
    ISBN 0-7172-5742-8 (set : alk. paper) -- ISBN 0-7172-5743-6 (v.1 : alk. paper) -- ISBN 0-7172-5744-4 (v.2 : alk. paper) -- ISBN 0-7172-5745-2 (v.3 : alk. paper) -- ISBN 0-7172-5746-0 (v.4 : alk. paper) -- ISBN 0-7172-5747-9 (v.5 : alk. paper) -- ISBN 0-7172-5748-7 (v.6 : alk. paper) -- ISBN 0-7172-5749-5 (v.7 : alk. paper) -- ISBN 0-7172-5750-9 (v.8 : alk. paper) -- ISBN 0-7172-5751-7 (v.9 : alk. paper) -- ISBN 0-7172-5752-5 (v.10 : alk. paper)
    1. Mammals--Juvenile literature. [1. Mammals.] I. Beer, Amy-Jane. II. Bower, Erica. III. Title. IV. World of animals (Danbury, Conn.)

QL706.2 .M675 2003
599--dc21

2002073860   Set ISBN 0-7172-5742-8

About This Volume

This volume groups together many species that feed on insects and other small invertebrates. However, both hedgehogs, shrews, and moles (Insectivora) and the bats (Chiroptera) have evolved a wider range of diets, including fish, fruit, and blood in the latter. Since insects are small, insectivorous mammals tend to be small as well. The aardvark is the largest, about the size of a pig. Moreover, since ants and other tiny insects are often exceedingly abundant, they need not be chased and attacked individually, but can be scooped up in masses using a sticky tongue. Aardvarks, anteaters, and pangolins feed in this way. The tiny insect prey are small enough that they do not need chewing, so these creatures have reduced teeth or none at all. By contrast, bats and smaller insectivores, like shrews, are quite tiny in comparison to many insects and, indeed, may actually be smaller than certain beetles and moths. They need relatively large teeth to tackle their prey, behaving like minicarnivores as they attack worms, beetles, and moths. Bats constitute nearly a quarter of all mammal species. They are the only mammals capable of sustained flight, rivaling the birds with their aerial capabilities. Some of the other insectivorous mammals are rare and localized in their distribution. None of these creatures offer a significant threat to the human economy (although some fruit bats can be quite destructive). In fact, many perform important ecological functions, such as reducing insect numbers or pollinating flowers.

Contents

How to Use This Set	4
Find the Animal	6
INSECTIVORES	8
THE HEDGEHOG FAMILY	12
Western European Hedgehog	14
African Pygmy Hedgehog	20
Greater Moonrat	22
THE TENREC FAMILY	24
Common Tenrec	26
THE SHREW FAMILY	28
American Short-Tailed Shrew	30
Eurasian Common Shrew	34
American Water Shrew	36
Grant's Golden Mole	56
TREE AND ELEPHANT SHREWS	58
Common Tree Shrew	60
Golden-Rumped Elephant Shrew	62
ANTEATERS, ARMADILLOS, AND PANGOLINS	64
Giant Anteater	68
Three-Toed Sloth	72
Nine-Banded Armadillo	74

Aardvark	78
BATS	80
Indian Flying Fox	88
Egyptian Rousette Bat	92
Vampire Bat	94
False Vampire Bat	98
Mexican Free-Tailed Bat	100
Little Brown Bat	104
Lesser Horseshoe Bat	106
Fisherman Bat	108
Long-Eared Bat	110
List of Genera	112
Glossary	114
Further Reading and Websites	117
Set Index	118
Picture Credits	128

The delicately built lesser horseshoe bat is found throughout southern Europe.

Various species of hedgehogs and moonrats: greater moonrat (1); short-tailed gymnure (2); North African hedgehog (3); long-eared hedgehog (4); desert hedgehog (5); shrew gymnure (6).

How to Use This Set

World of Animals: Mammals is a 10-volume set that describes in detail mammals from all corners of the earth. Each volume brings together those animals that are most closely related and have similar lifestyles. So all the meat-eating groups (carnivores) are in Volumes 1 and 2, and all the seals, whales, and dolphins (sea mammals) are in Volume 3, and so on. To help you find volumes that interest you, look at pages 6 to 7 (Find the Animal). A brief introduction to each volume is also given on page 2 (About This Volume).

Article Styles

Articles are of three kinds. There are two types of introductory or review article: One introduces large animal groups like orders (such as whales and dolphins). Another introduces smaller groups like families (The Raccoon Family, for example). The articles review the full variety of animals to be found in different groups. The third type of article makes up most of each volume. It concentrates on describing individual animals typical of the group in great detail, such as the tiger. Each article starts with a fact-filled **data panel** to help you gather information at-a-glance. Used together, the three article styles enable you to become familiar with specific animals in the context of their evolutionary history and biological relationships.

Data panel presents basic statistics of each animal

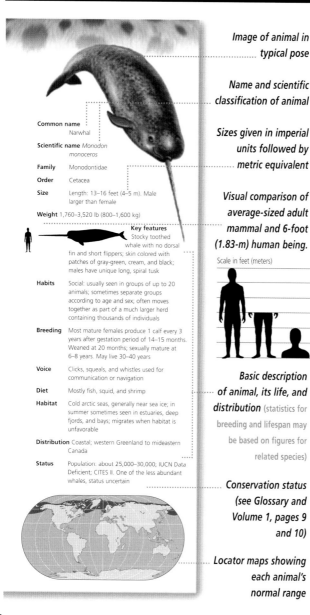

Image of animal in typical pose

Name and scientific classification of animal

Common name Narwhal

Scientific name *Monodon monoceros*

Family Monodontidae

Order Cetacea

Size Length: 13–16 feet (4–5 m). Male larger than female

Weight 1,760–3,520 lb (800–1,600 kg)

Key features Stocky toothed whale with no dorsal fin and short flippers; skin colored with patches of gray-green, cream, and black; males have unique long, spiral tusk

Habits Social: usually seen in groups of up to 20 animals; sometimes separate groups according to age and sex; often moves together as part of a much larger herd containing thousands of individuals

Breeding Most mature females produce 1 calf every 3 years after gestation period of 14–15 months. Weaned at 20 months; sexually mature at 6–8 years. May live 30–40 years

Voice Clicks, squeals, and whistles used for communication or navigation

Diet Mostly fish, squid, and shrimp

Habitat Cold arctic seas, generally near sea ice; in summer sometimes seen in estuaries, deep fjords, and bays; migrates when habitat is unfavorable

Distribution Coastal; western Greenland to mideastern Canada

Status Population: about 25,000–30,000; IUCN Data Deficient; CITES II. One of the less abundant whales, status uncertain

Sizes given in imperial units followed by metric equivalent

Visual comparison of average-sized adult mammal and 6-foot (1.83-m) human being.

Scale in feet (meters)

	6 (1.83)
	5 (1.5)
	4 (1.2)
	3 (0.9)
	2 (0.6)
	1 (0.3)

Basic description of animal, its life, and distribution (statistics for breeding and lifespan may be based on figures for related species)

Conservation status (see Glossary and Volume 1, pages 9 and 10)

Locator maps showing each animal's normal range

Article describes a particular animal

Scientific name of animal

Captions to photographs provide additional information about each animal's lifestyle

Common name of animal

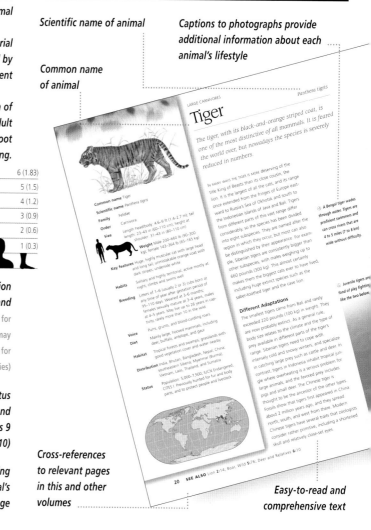

LARGE CARNIVORES

Panthera tigris

Tiger

The tiger, with its black-and-orange striped coat, is one of the most distinctive of all mammals. It is feared the world over, but nowadays the species is severely reduced in numbers.

IN MANY WAYS THE TIGER IS MORE deserving of the title King of Beasts than its close cousin, the lion. It is the largest of all the cats, and its range once extended from the fringes of Europe east-ward to Russia's Sea of Okhotsk and south to the Indonesian islands of Java and Bali. Tigers from different parts of this vast range differ considerably, so the species has been divided into eight subspecies. They are named after the region in which they occur, but most can also be distinguished by their appearance. For exam-ple, Siberian tigers are consistently bigger than other subspecies, with males weighing up to 660 pounds (300 kg). This almost certainly makes them the biggest cats ever to have lived, including huge extinct species such as the saber-toothed tiger and the cave lion.

Common name Tiger

Scientific name *Panthera tigris*

Family Felidae

Order Carnivora

Size Length head/body: 4.6–9 ft (1.4–2.7 m); tail length: 23–43 in (60–110 cm); height at shoulder: 31–43 in (80–110 cm)
Weight: Male 200–660 lb (90–300 kg); female 143–364 lb (65–165 kg)

Key features Huge, highly muscular cat with large head and long tail; unmistakable orange coat with dark stripes; underside white

Habits Solitary and highly territorial; active mostly at night; climbs and swims well

Breeding Litters of 1–6 (usually 2 or 3) cubs born at any time of year after gestation period of 95–110 days. Weaned at 3–6 months; females sexually mature at 3–4 years, males at 4–5 years. May live up to 26 years in cap-tivity, rarely more than 10 in the wild

Voice Purrs, grunts, and blood-curdling roars

Diet Mainly large, hooved mammals, including deer, buffalo, antelope, and gaur

Habitat Tropical forests and swamps; grasslands with good vegetation cover and water nearby

Distribution India, Bhutan, Bangladesh, Nepal, China; southeastern Siberia, Myanmar (Burma), Vietnam, Laos, Thailand, and Sumatra

Status Population: 5,000–7,500; IUCN Endangered; CITES I. Previously hunted for fur and body parts, and to protect people and livestock

A Bengal tiger wades through water. Tigers are proficient swimmers and can cross rivers that are 4 to 5 miles (7 to 8 km) wide without difficulty.

Juvenile tigers are fond of play fighting like the two below.

Different Adaptations

The smallest tigers came from Bali and rarely exceeded 220 pounds (100 kg) in weight. They are now probably extinct. As a general rule, body size relates to the climate and the type of prey available in different parts of the tiger's range. Siberian tigers need to cope with intensely cold and snowy winters, and specialize in catching large prey such as cattle and deer. In contrast, tigers in Indonesia inhabit tropical jun-gle where overheating is a serious problem for large animals, and the favored prey includes pigs and small deer. The Chinese tiger is thought to be the ancestor of the other types. Fossils show that tigers first appeared in China about 2 million years ago, and they spread north, south, and west from there. Modern Chinese tigers have several traits that zoologists consider rather primitive, including a shortened skull and relatively close-set eyes.

20 SEE ALSO Lion **2**:14; Boar, Wild **5**:76; Deer and Relatives **6**:10

Cross-references to relevant pages in this and other volumes

Easy-to-read and comprehensive text

A number of other features help you navigate through the volumes and present you with helpful extra information. At the bottom of many pages are **cross-references** to other articles of interest. They may be to related animals, animals that live in similar places, animals with similar behavior, predators (or prey), and much more. Each volume also contains a **Set Index** to the complete *World of Animals: Mammals*. All animals mentioned in the text are indexed by common and scientific names, and many topics are also covered. A **Glossary** will also help you if there are words used in the text that you do not fully understand. Each volume ends with a list of useful **Further Reading and Websites** that help you take your research further. Finally, under the heading "List of Species" you will find expanded listings of the animals that are covered in each volume.

Introductory article describes family or closely related groups

The Raccoon Family

SMALL CARNIVORES

Raccoons are medium-sized, long-bodied mammals with a long tail. Although there are only 19 different species in the family Procyonidae, its members display a remarkable diversity in their appearance and ecology. Only the kinkajou has a uniform body color. The rest have distinctive coats with various facial markings and ringed (banded) tails.

Various members of the raccoon family: a ring-tail eating a lizard (1); a coati sniffing for insects (2); a kinkajou licking nectar from a flower while gripping a branch with its prehensile tail (3).

Detailed maps clarify animal's distribution

At-a-glance boxes cover topics of special interest

The Disappearing Tiger

Meticulous drawings illustrate a typical selection of group members

Tables summarize classification of groups and give scientific names of animals mentioned in the text

Who's Who tables summarize classification of each major group and give scientific names of animals mentioned in the text

Introductory article describes major groups of animals

WHALES AND DOLPHINS

Whales, dolphins, and porpoises all belong to a major group of mammals known as cetaceans. The word cetacean comes from the Greek word *ketos*, meaning "whale." The great size of whales, their eerie calls, and mysterious lifestyles are the basis for many legends about sea monsters. Today whales are popular animals, especially because of their social behavior and highly developed intelligence.

Graphic full-color photographs bring text to life

Detailed diagrams illustrate text

Find the Animal

*W*orld of Animals: Mammals is the first part of a library that describes all groups of living animals. Each cluster of volumes in *World of Animals* will cover a familiar group of animals—mammals, birds, reptiles and amphibians, fish, and insects and other invertebrates. These groups also represent categories of animals recognized by scientists (see The Animal Kingdom below).

The Animal Kingdom

The living world is divided into five kingdoms, one of which (kingdom Animalia) is the main subject of the

World of Animals. Also included are those members of the kingdom Protista that were once regarded as animals, but now form part of a group that includes all single-cell organisms. Kingdom Animalia is divided into numerous major groups called Phyla, but only one of them (Chordata) contains those animals that have a backbone. Chordates, or vertebrates as they are popularly known, include all the animals familiar to us and those most studied by scientists—mammals, birds, reptiles, amphibians, and fish. In all, there are about 38,000 species of vertebrates, while the Phyla that contain animals without backbones (so-called invertebrates, such as insects, spiders, and so on) include at least 1 million species, probably many more. To find which set of volumes in the *World of Animals* is relevant to you, see the chart Main Groups of Animals (page 7).

Rodents (Order Rodentia): **squirrels, rats, mice Volume 7; cavies, porcupines, chinchillas Volume 8**

Lagomorphs (Order Lagomorpha): **rabbits, hares, pikas Volume 8**

Tree shrews (Order Scandentia): **Volume 9**

Insectivores (Order Insectivora): **shrews, moles, hedgehogs Volume 9**

Colugos, flying lemurs (Order Dermoptera): **Volume 8**

Primates (Order Primates): **lemurs, monkeys, apes Volume 4**

Pangolins (Order Pholidota): **Volume 9**

Carnivores (Order Carnivora): **raccoons, weasels, otters, skunks Volume 1; cats, dogs, bears, hyenas Volume 2**

Seals and sea lions (Order Pinnipedia): **Volume 3**

Odd-toed ungulates (Order Perissodactyla): **horses, rhinoceroses, tapirs Volume 5**

Even-toed ungulates (Order Artiodactyla): **pigs, camels Volume 5; deer, cattle, sheep, goats Volume 6**

Whales and dolphins (Order Cetacea): **Volume 3**

Bats (Order Chiroptera): **Volume 9**

Xenarthrans (Order Xenarthra): **anteaters, sloths, armadillos Volume 9**

Elephant shrews (Order Macroscelidea): **Volume 9**

Aardvark (Order Tubulidentata): **Volume 9**

Hyraxes (Order Hyracoidea): **Volume 8**

Dugongs, manatees (Order Sirenia): **Volume 3**

Elephants (Order Proboscidea): **Volume 5**

Marsupials: **opposums, kangaroos, koala Volume 10**

Monotremes (Order Monotremata): **platypus, echidnas Volume 10**

Mammals in Particular

World of Animals: Mammals focuses on the most familiar of animals, those most easily recognized as having fur (although this may be absent in many sea mammals like whales and dolphins), and that provide milk for their young. Mammals are divided into major groups (carnivores, primates, rodents, and marsupials to name just

The chart shows the major groups of mammals in this set arranged in evolutionary relationship (see page 10). The volume in which each group appears is indicated. You can find individual entries by looking at the contents page for each volume or by consulting the set index.

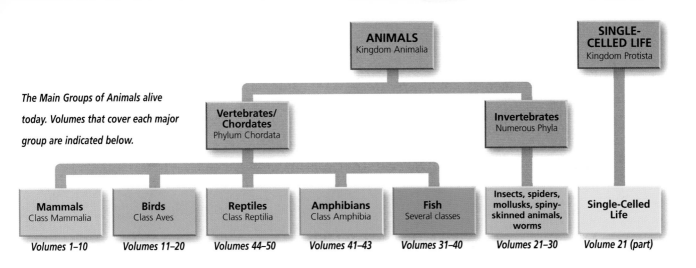

The Main Groups of Animals alive today. Volumes that cover each major group are indicated below.

| ANIMALS Kingdom Animalia | | | SINGLE-CELLED LIFE Kingdom Protista |

Vertebrates/ Chordates Phylum Chordata

Invertebrates Numerous Phyla

Mammals Class Mammalia	**Birds** Class Aves	**Reptiles** Class Reptilia	**Amphibians** Class Amphibia	**Fish** Several classes	**Insects, spiders, mollusks, spiny-skinned animals, worms**	**Single-Celled Life**
Volumes 1–10	Volumes 11–20	Volumes 44–50	Volumes 41–43	Volumes 31–40	Volumes 21–30	Volume 21 (part)

a few). All the major groups are shown on the chart on page 6. To help you find particular animals, a few familiar ones, such as sheep, goats, cats, and dogs, have been included in the chart.

Naming Mammals

To be able to discuss animals, names are needed for the different kinds. Most people regard tigers as one kind of animal and lions as another. All tigers look more or less alike. They breed together and produce young like themselves. This popular distinction between kinds of animals corresponds closely to the zoologists' distinction between species. All tigers belong to one species and all lions to another. The lion species has different names in different languages (for example, *Löwe* in German, *Simba* in Swahili), and often a single species may have several common names. For example, the North American mountain lion is also known as the cougar, puma, panther, and catamount.

Zoologists find it convenient to have internationally recognized names for species and use a standardized system of two-word Latinized names. The lion is called *Panthera leo* and the tiger *Panthera tigris*. The first word, *Panthera*, is the name of the genus (a group of closely similar species), which includes the lion and the tiger. The second word, *leo* or *tigris*, indicates the particular species within the genus. Scientific names are recognized all over the world. The scientific name is used whatever the language, even where the alphabet is different, as in Chinese or Russian. The convention allows for precision and helps avoid most confusion. However, it is also common for one species to apparently have more than one scientific name. That can be because a particular

species may have been described and named at different times without the zoologists realizing it was one species.

It is often necessary to make statements about larger groups of animals: for example, all the catlike animals or all the mammals. A formal system of classification makes this possible. Domestic cats are similar to lions and tigers, but not as similar as those species are to each other (for example, they do not roar). They are put in a different genus (*Felis*), but *Felis*, *Panthera*, and other catlike animals are grouped together as the family Felidae. The flesh-eating mammals (cats, dogs, hyenas, weasels, and so on), together with a few plant-eaters that are obviously related to them (such as pandas), are grouped in the order Carnivora. These and all the other animals that suckle their young are grouped in the class Mammalia. Finally, the mammals are included, with all other animals that have backbones (fish, amphibians, reptiles, and birds) and some other animals that seem to be related to them, in the Phylum Chordata.

Rank	Scientific name	Common name
Phylum	Chordata	Animals with a backbone
Class	Mammalia	All mammals
Order	Carnivora	Flesh-eaters/carnivores
Family	Felidae	All cats
Genus	*Panthera*	Big cats
Species	*leo*	Lion

The kingdom Animalia is subdivided into phylum, classes, orders, families, genera, and species. Above is the classification of the lion.

INSECTIVORES

The order Insectivora covers over 400 species with an almost worldwide distribution. Most of the species actually eat insects, but many are carnivorous in a broader sense, including worms and other small animals in their diet. All living members of the Insectivora are small; few are larger than a hedgehog, and the smallest, the Etruscan or pygmy white-toothed shrew, is the smallest living mammal, weighing only 0.07 ounces (2 g). Most of the Insectivora have a long, narrow snout that is usually very mobile. Almost all have tiny eyes and relatively poor vision; most also have small ears, but good hearing and an acute sense of smell. Although many are considered "primitive," since they resemble early mammal types now extinct, insectivores have adapted to fill a wide range of ecological niches and show diverse and sometimes very specialized features.

Primitive Features

The Insectivora are generally considered to be the most primitive of the living placental mammals. They share many characteristics with ancestral mammals, including primitive teeth. Many species have a cloaca—a single opening into which the genital, urinary, and fecal passages empty, instead of having separate openings to outside the body. The males of most species hold their testes inside the body, instead of hanging in a scrotal sac. They have primitive features in their ear structures and collar bones, and walk with the heels and soles of their feet flat on the ground (called "plantigrade" locomotion).

Insectivores have relatively small brains, with few surface wrinkles. The brain has a low surface area for processing information, so the animals are generally not very intelligent. However, the olfactory lobes of the brain are relatively large, emphasizing the importance of the sense of smell. These are all features that have been modified in more advanced mammals, and their retention is evidence of primitiveness among the Insectivora.

Superimposed on the basic body plan are some very specialized characteristics, including adaptations for

⤊ *A greater white-toothed shrew dines on a grasshopper. Shrews have huge appetites—some species will even starve to death if they do not eat every couple of hours.*

burrowing or swimming. The poisonous saliva of solenodons and some shrews, and the spines of hedgehogs and tenrecs are further examples of advanced specializations superimposed on otherwise simple creatures. Some shrews and tenrecs are also thought to be able to use a form of echolocation—another advanced feature seen elsewhere in bats and whales.

Insectivores show a diverse range of lifestyles, from the terrestrial shrews and hedgehogs that run along the ground, to the tunneling moles and the semiaquatic desmans, water shrews, and aquatic tenrec.

True to their name, most insectivores feed on insects and other invertebrates such as millipedes and earthworms, while the aquatic species eat mollusks, crabs,

and probably fish. Most species are opportunists and will eat almost anything they find or catch, but few eat much vegetable material. Some are capable of catching reptiles or mammals, even ones larger than themselves. The poisonous saliva of solenodons and certain shrews may help immobilize prey.

Solitary and Secretive

Although members of the Insectivora are widespread, and often abundant, they have not been intensively studied because almost all are secretive and nocturnal. They are generally solitary, with males and females only associating for breeding. Some species such as the shrews are strongly territorial and aggressive when they meet.

Insectivores show a wide range of breeding strategies. The most prolific are members of the *Tenrec* genus, which can have up to 32 developing embryos—at least half may survive to birth. Other tenrecs, moles, hedgehogs, and shrews have a litter size of between two and 10, while solenodons have only one or two young that stay with the mother for many months. At birth young insectivores are usually small, blind, and hairless.

Members of the Insectivora are widely distributed and are found across Africa, much of Asia, most of the Northern Hemisphere (apart from the colder extremes), and northern South America. However, that broad spread is mainly accounted for by only three of the six families: Erinaceidae (hedgehogs and moonrats), Talpidae (moles and desmans), and Soricidae (shrews). The other three families have more limited distributions. Solenodontidae (solenodons) are now found only on two Caribbean islands, the Tenrecidae (tenrecs) are mostly confined to Madagascar, and the Chrysochloridae (golden moles) are only found in the drier parts of southern Africa.

The Insectivora has often been treated as a "rag bag" group for any small, insectivorous animal with a pointy

nose that cannot be classified as anything else. There have been many attempts at subdividing the order into logical groupings. In 1866 Ernst Haeckel divided them into two groups: the Menotyphla (those with a cecum as part of the digestive system), containing tree shrews and elephant shrews, and the Lipotyphla, with no cecum. Others have used the shape of the upper molars and various other characteristics in attempts to organize this complicated set into sensible subgroups.

Origins

By classifying animals, scientists aim to reflect their evolution. A "good" group should contain members that all evolved from a single ancestor and share many similar features. New theories now question this assumption for the insectivores. When mammals began to diversify in the late Cretaceous period, there were just two major land masses—Gondwana in the south and Laurasia in the north. It is now thought that animals on each of these supercontinents evolved separately, but their adaptations to similar lifestyles led to striking parallels in their appearance—a process known as convergent evolution. Golden moles and true moles are a

A Probing Nose

A characteristic feature of solenodons and shrews (and to a lesser extent moles and other insectivores) is the long snout, which extends beyond the jaws. It is made of cartilage, not bone, and is extremely flexibile. The long, bendy nose is perfect for probing under stones or in soil and leaf litter for invertebrates. Many Insectivora also scavenge carrion, and some may even catch prey assisted by producing toxic saliva that helps immobilize victims.

good example. Although not closely related, they look alike and have similar burrowing habits. Hedgehogs and many tenrecs have bodies covered in spines for defense and can curl into a ball, yet they are not closely related.

Recent DNA studies confirm these theories of separate ancestry. If widely accepted, a new "supergroup" called the Afrotheria will be established for a diverse group of mainly African animals from elephants to hyraxes to tenrecs. It will alter our current classifications for a huge swath of mammals, including the insectivores. Meanwhile, zoologists have adopted a simple system of dividing the group into six distinct families, shown below, avoiding the question of how closely they are actually related to each other.

Tenrecs

The family Tenrecidae includes tenrecs and otter shrews. There are 24 species in 10 genera. Tenrecs live in Madagascar, and many look similar to hedgehogs. Others are smooth-coated and more shrewlike. The otter shrews are aquatic and live in central Africa. They are so different from tenrecs in their lifestyle, distribution, and habitat that they have often been put into a separate family— the Potamogalidae.

Solenodons

Solenodons are strange, primitive insectivores that resemble giant shrews. The two species live in Cuba, Haiti, and the Dominican Republic and are almost identical to fossilized solenodons that lived around 30 million years ago. They are among the largest living insectivores, with a head-body length of around 12 inches (30 cm) and a tail almost as long again.

They are nocturnal, generally solitary, and noisy compared with most insectivores. They are long-lived—up to 11 years in captivity—and breed slowly, having only one, or rarely two, young at a time. Unusually for insectivores, the young stay with the mother for several

⬅ *The most distinctive feature of solenodons is their elongated snout. In the Hispaniola solenodon the snout is connected to the skull via a ball-and-socket joint, making it very flexible.*

months. She carries them around attached to her teats. Solenodons were once common, but introduced predators such as cats, dogs, and mongooses have driven at least one species to extinction in the recent past and seriously threaten the remaining two.

Hedgehogs and Moonrats

The family Erinaceidae includes the spiny hedgehogs and hairy moonrats. There are 22 species in seven genera, with a wide distribution over much of Eurasia and Africa. However, wild hedgehogs and moonrats do not live in the Americas or Australia.

Shrews

The shrews form the most successful insectivore family, with over 300 species in 23 genera. They are found throughout North and Central America, Europe, Asia, and most of Africa. All are mouselike animals with a long tail and a long, pointed nose. Their eyes and ears are tiny, often hidden by fur. They have an unpleasant smell, and some species also have poisonous saliva.

Moles and Desmans

There are 42 species of moles and desmans in 17 genera. The moles are burrowing animals that live almost entirely underground. By contrast, desmans are semiaquatic and are good swimmers. There are only two species, each in its own genus.

Golden Moles

Golden moles are similar to true moles in body form and burrowing lifestyles, but are only distantly related. The 21 species in nine genera are only found in Africa.

➡ *The Pyrenean desman is one of only two species of desmans. Desmans are adapted for swimming, with a long, flat tail like a rudder, semiwebbed hands, and webbed toes.*

The Hedgehog Family

The family Erinaceidae includes hedgehogs, moonrats, and gymnures—a group of 22 species that have a wide distribution throughout Europe, Asia, and Africa. The hedgehogs are the most familiar and distinctive, with their spiny coats and defensive habit of rolling into a ball. Because of their spines they have little to fear from predators and tend to be bold in character. The western European hedgehog can often be seen in urban habitats and is a popular garden visitor.

The moonrats and gymnures are native to China and Southeast Asia. They lack spines, and their vulnerability causes them to be shy and elusive. Often called hairy hedgehogs, they look more like rats, but have a totally different dentition. They can run faster than hedgehogs, but do not roll into a defensive ball and are less adept at burrowing. All species have anal glands that release a strong smell, described as being like rotting garlic.

The smallest of the family is the lesser moonrat, with a head and body length of just 4 inches (10 cm) and a weight of 1.4 ounces (40 g). The largest is the greater moonrat. At 18 inches (46 cm) long, plus a tail of 8 inches (20 cm) and a weight of 9 pounds (4 kg), it is about the size of a cottontail rabbit. The hedgehogs, on the other hand, are all intermediate in size.

Hedgehogs and moonrats share many features with other members of the order Insectivora. They have an elongated head and snout and a small braincase. They walk in a plantigrade fashion, with the entire sole of the foot touching the ground. They are also nocturnal and tend to be solitary, except in the breeding season.

Adaptable in Diet and Habitat

Hedgehogs and moonrats are adaptable animals that have often responded well to agricultural and other environmental changes. Their flexibility probably accounts for their wide distribution. Most species eat invertebrates such as worms, beetles, earwigs, slugs, and caterpillars. They also sometimes eat seeds and fruit, and supplement their diet with carrion and small prey, including occasional birds and their eggs or chicks. African and Asian hedgehogs eat more vertebrates than those in Europe, with the diet of the collared hedgehog consisting of up to 40 percent meat from vertebrate prey.

Hedgehogs and moonrats can be found in habitats as diverse as desert and dry steppe farmland, tropical and temperate forest, grassland, cities, and montane areas. The greater moonrat has even been seen in mangrove swamps, where it catches crabs, mollusks, and fish.

Hedgehogs also demonstrate their adaptability in their response to changing seasons, sleeping when food is in short supply or when temperatures are extreme. The

---

Family Erinaceidae: 2 subfamilies, 7 genera, 22 species

SUBFAMILY Erinaceinae (hedgehogs): 4 genera, 15 species

Erinaceus 3 species, including western European hedgehog (*E. europaeus*); eastern European hedgehog (*E. concolor*)

Atelerix 4 species, including African pygmy hedgehog (*A. albiventris*); North African hedgehog (*A. algirus*)

Mesechinus 2 species, Daurian hedgehog (*M. dauricus*); Hugh's hedgehog (*M. hughi*)

Hemiechinus 6 species, including desert hedgehog (*H. aethiopicus*); long-eared hedgehog (*H. auritus*); collared hedgehog (*H. collaris*)

SUBFAMILY Hylomyinae (moonrats and gymnures): 3 genera, 7 species

Echinosorex 1 species, greater moonrat (*E. gymnura*)

Hylomys 4 species, including Hainan gymnure (*H. hainanensis*); short-tailed gymnure (*H. suillus*); shrew gymnure (*H. sinensis*)

Podogymnura 2 species, Dinagat moonrat (*P. aureospinula*); Mindanao moonrat (*P. truei*)

⬆ *A desert hedgehog. Hedgehogs are not generally threatened in the wild, but increasing desertification is leading to fragmentation of populations of this species.*

such as carrion or even scented soap. The animal sniffs and often chews the object. Drooling copiously, it works the saliva into a froth, then spreads it onto the spines of the shoulders and back. Nobody knows why the animals salivate in this way, and not all individuals perform the ritual. Because it is difficult for hedgehogs to groom themselves, fleas, ticks, and other small bloodsuckers are an irritating problem for them. Self-anointing may help clean the spines, possibly acting as an insecticide. However, skin parasites remain a characteristic feature of the animals, so it cannot be particularly effective.

western European hedgehog is one of the species that regularly hibernates during the cold season. Other species that live in desert regions may sleep through the hottest and driest periods of summer (called estivation). Moonrats and hedgehogs that inhabit the tropics do not need to hibernate, since there is plenty of food all year round.

Some hedgehog species use burrows or natural hollows and crevices for day-to-day resting; others use such hideaways only for nursing young or during periods of hibernation. A few hedgehogs build quite large nests by carrying leaves and other material in their mouth, not on their spines as is widely believed.

Hedgehogs often anoint their spines with saliva. The behavior seems to be triggered by contact with strong-smelling substances

Hedgehog Defense

With their strong spines hedgehogs are safe from almost all predators, even lions. When threatened, they simply curl up, nose to tail, contracting a well-developed band of skin muscle around the edge of the body. Rather like pulling on a drawstring bag, the action brings the spiny skin over the vulnerable face and underbelly, forming a dense ball of protective spikes. Other special muscles then cause the spines to bristle in all directions.

Threatened Species

Hedgehogs do no harm, so they are not persecuted; nor are many eaten by people today. They have no commercial value, except perhaps as pets: African hedgehogs have become popular household animals in the United States. Hedgehogs are not generally threatened in the wild, but habitat loss is always a danger. Hugh's hedgehog from central China is considered to be at risk. Five species of moonrats and gymnures are also threatened by habitat destruction and fragmentation, especially where species already have only a limited geographical range.

⬅ *Some representative species of hedgehogs and moonrats: shrew gymnure (Hylomys sinensis) (1); short-tailed gymnure (H. suillus); long-eared hedgehog (Hemiechinus auritus) (3); North African hedgehog (Atelerix algirus) (4); Hainan gymnure (Hylomys hainanensis) (5); Mindanao moonrat (Podogymnura truei) (6).*

4

5

6

Common name Western European hedgehog (European hedgehog, urchin)

Scientific name *Erinaceus europaeus*

Family Erinaceidae

Order Insectivora

Size Length head/body: 6–10 in (16–26 cm); tail length: 0.5–1 in (1.5–3 cm)

Weight Up to 1–2.2 lb (0.5–0.9 kg), normally 17–28 oz (480–800 g)

Key features Spiny animal that rolls into a ball when alarmed; short tail; 5 long claws on each foot; general color grizzled brown and cream

Habits Nocturnal; normally lives alone; does not defend territory

Breeding Usually 4–6 (up to 8) young born in early summer after gestation period of 32–34 days (late litters born August–September). Weaned at 4–6 weeks; sexually mature at 1 year. May live up to 7 years in the wild, perhaps 10; fewer in captivity

Voice Snorts and grunts; piglike squeal if attacked

Diet Almost anything edible found at ground level, including beetles, worms, caterpillars, eggs, slugs, and occasional soft fruit

Habitat Farmland, short grass areas, hedges, woodlands, town parks, and gardens

Distribution Western Europe from Britain and southern Scandinavia to the Mediterranean east to Romania

Status Population: several million. Widespread and fairly abundant, especially in suburban areas

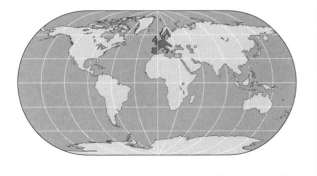

Western European Hedgehog

Erinaceus europaeus

The hedgehog is Europe's only spiny mammal. It is widespread, familiar, and most easily seen by flashlight in gardens or in areas of short grass, where there are plenty of earthworms.

THE HEDGEHOG IS ONE OF Europe's favorite mammals, yet it is not at all cuddly and can be rather smelly. It is common in parks and gardens and is completely unmistakable. It is particularly well known because of its trusting nature and willingness to share parks and gardens with people. Hedgehogs will become tame, attracted to suitable food put out by householders who welcome the animal's bold and regular appearances. Few people realize that they are watching one of the most ancient types of animal still alive today. Hedgehogs evolved long before mammoths and saber-toothed tigers, yet while those creatures are now extinct, hedgehogs potter on into the 21st century.

Settled in New Zealand

Hedgehogs are found over most of mainland Europe up to the limit of tree growth. At higher altitudes and higher latitudes there are few leaves with which to build their vital winter nests. In more extreme conditions there are also fewer worms and other invertebrates on which to feed. Hedgehogs have been transported (deliberately or accidentally) to many offshore islands, and several batches of hedgehogs were taken to New Zealand in the 19th century. Settlers wanted to feel at home with familiar animals around them. Hedgehogs were also thought to be useful in controlling the grubs that damage sheep pasture. In a century or so hedgehogs have prospered in their new home. They are now more common in some parts of New Zealand than in most of Europe.

The hedgehog's spines are immediately obvious, but they make it hard to examine

details of the rest of its body, especially when it rolls up. The spines are only on the animal's back and sides. The belly is covered by long, sparse hair. The covering offers little insulation or protection, but soft, fine fur would get wet and matted as the hedgehog trundles around in dewy grass seeking food. The legs are surprisingly long and enable the animal to run quite fast, up to about 6 miles per hour (10 km/h). The hedgehog's tail is about half an inch (1.5 cm) long, but is normally hidden by its overhanging spiny coat. The five toes are each furnished with a long claw. The claws are not particularly sharp and are used mainly for scraping away soil and leaves in search of food.

⊖ The spines of hedgehogs play host to many blood-sucking parasites, since their impenetrability makes it difficult for hedgehogs to groom themselves.

Protective Spines

There are about 5,000 spines on an adult. They are modified hairs, which bristle aggressively in all directions when the animal is threatened or attacked. Rolled up and encased in its spiny skin, the animal is so well protected that few predators will even touch one. Foxes, polecats, owls, and eagles may take the odd baby hedgehog, but adults have little to fear. Badgers are the exception. They are strong, and their powerful claws can get in between the protective spines and rip apart a hedgehog. Cars are another danger and probably kill several hundred thousand hedgehogs every year. The hedgehog's defense of rolling up in its spiny skin is no match for heavy traffic. Hedgehogs are also at risk from mowing machines, another new threat in the 20-million-year history of the species.

Large numbers of hedgehogs escape death but nevertheless suffer serious injuries. Many of the animals are rescued by kindly people and taken to animal hospitals to be nursed back to health. Because hedgehogs do not bite or run away like most other animals, people can pick them up easily and rescue them. Baby hedgehogs are often victims, and those born late in the year often find it difficult to fatten up enough to hibernate properly. They can be found wandering around in daylight during the fall. Many thousands of hedgehogs are taken into care each year to be restored to the wild later. Fortunately, the animals adjust to treatment very well and cope well with being released again, even young ones who have had no previous experience of life in the wild.

Hedgehogs are mostly active after dark, although in midsummer, when nights are short, they may come out early and will still be active around dawn. At night they are more likely to find their favorite foods, which include beetles, caterpillars, slugs, and worms. The hedgehog

has lower front teeth that point forward, making an efficient scoop with which to seize smaller prey such as spiders. However, the lower teeth bite into a gap between the upper ones, reducing the effectiveness of the bite if they attempt larger animals. The teeth are quite blunt, too, especially in older hedgehogs that have been chewing a lot of gritty earthworms.

Apart from invertebrates, hedgehogs will eat the chicks of ground-nesting game birds. Birds' eggs are also taken, making hedgehogs unpopular where they have been introduced to islands that were previously a secure home for nesting bird colonies. The hedgehogs can then become a serious problem, causing severe losses. Hedgehogs are reputed to attack and eat snakes, but that probably does not happen often, since snakes are normally not active at night. However, the hedgehog does have special immunity to adder venom, and it is not understood how or why that evolved.

Apple Gatherers

A widespread folktale is that hedgehogs collect apples on their spines by rolling on them, then carry the fruit to their nest. Although hedgehogs will sometimes eat soft fruits, the story seems far fetched. Rolling on apples is unlikely to pick up more than one at a time, and anyway hedgehogs do not normally carry food of any kind, nor do they store it in their

⮝ ⮕ *A European hedgehog feasts on a snail. Hedgehogs will devour virtually anything edible found on the ground, including beetles, birds' eggs, and fallen fruit. They are even known to kill and eat snakes (above).*

bizarre behavior. Sometimes the activity is triggered by chewing on leather or some other sharp-tasting substance. At other times it is not clear what sets it off. It is not known why some hedgehogs perform the strange ritual.

Wandering Far and Wide

Normal behavior for the hedgehog involves traveling more than half a mile (1 km) each night. Males are especially active, scurrying here and there in search of food and mates. In the breeding season some may clock up 2 miles (3 km) before retiring to a nest at dawn. A different nest may be used each day or two, with homes scattered over a wide area, perhaps as much as 140 acres (60 ha). By contrast, females occupy a much smaller area and often use the same nest every day for a couple of weeks before moving on.

Although its ears are not particularly large, the hedgehog relies a lot on its sense of hearing. It reacts immediately to a sharp noise by "freezing" and bristling its spines. It can probably hear many of its potential prey victims because the ear is so close to the ground. At such close proximity even worms and beetles can seem noisy. Eyes are less important to hedgehogs. In thick vegetation the animals would not be able to see far anyway. Hedgehogs cannot distinguish between colors and are probably not much better at night vision than humans. By contrast, smell is extremely important, and the hedgehog has an efficient nose. The animals can easily follow scent trails and probably use smell to detect and recognize each other.

Hedgehogs can live up to seven years, perhaps even 10 occasionally. However, the majority will probably live only about three years. Many will die young, especially during their first winter if they have failed to gain sufficient fat reserves. Offspring are normally born about May or June, but there are many late births in August and September. The latecomers will be lucky to survive because they will need a couple of months to fatten up before hibernating. Rapid weight gain may be

nests. Despite such doubts the story has persisted for centuries and turns up in the folklore of many different countries. Another folktale suggests that hedgehogs take milk from cows, even though they are too short to reach the udder. Even so, hedgehogs are fond of milk and may be attracted by its smell.

Self-anointing is an even more unlikely behavior, but it actually does happen. A hedgehog will suddenly start to produce a lot of frothy saliva in a most alarming way. The animal then twists and turns to spread the foam all over its body using its tongue. The contortions continue for 20 minutes or more, with the animal apparently engrossed in its

⤒ *A hedgehog's first set of spines, which emerge within hours of birth, are white. Darker ones grow among them later.*

possible in some years when there is a mild fall; but if cold weather comes early, the unprepared young will probably die. Over half of all hedgehogs die before their first birthday.

Hedgehogs in Hibernation

The hedgehog is a true hibernator. Its body shuts down from about October to March to save energy when food is short. Younger animals may still be active as late as Christmas as they try to fatten up. Winter is passed in a nest made of leaves. These are gathered at night and thrust into a heap below a bush or pile of brushwood. The hedgehog then burrows inside. The leaves offer protection from the cold and wet. Young animals are not so good at making nests and often need several attempts. It is important to get it right, since the nest needs to remain intact and weatherproof for at least five months. Hibernation normally ends in about April. However, if there is a cold snap, the animals will reenter hibernation and wait for better weather. In the warmer parts of New Zealand the animals may be active at almost any time of the year.

⊖ *As it rolls up, the hedgehog tucks its feet inside the spiny part of its skin, which is brought around to cover the animal's face and belly.*

Fleas

The hedgehog is famously flea ridden. Sometimes over 500 can be taken off a single animal. That is probably no more than from a rabbit or other animal of similar size, but the fleas are easier to see among the hedgehog's spines than in the deep fur of a more typical mammal. Consequently, hedgehogs are often blamed when pets pick up fleas.

In fact, the hedgehog has its own special species of flea adapted to the peculiar living conditions among the spines. The flea species is rarely found on other mammals. Cats and dogs have their own fleas and get them from each other, not from hedgehogs.

African Pygmy Hedgehog

Atelerix albiventris

African pygmies are neat little hedgehogs that are fairly uncommon in their natural habitat. However, large numbers are bred in captivity as novelty pets.

Common name African pygmy hedgehog (four-toed hedgehog, dwarf hedgehog, white-bellied hedgehog)

Scientific name *Atelerix albiventris*

Family Erinaceidae

Order Insectivora

Size Length head/body: 6–8 in (15–20 cm); tail length: 0.5–1.5 in (1.5–4 cm)

Weight 8–21 oz (230–600 g)

Key features Small spiny animal with short furry legs and white belly; white spines with sharply contrasting black band near tip

Habits Nocturnal; normally solitary; uses burrows and rock crevices for daytime dens; hunches or rolls into a prickly ball if disturbed

Breeding Up to 10 (usually 4–5) young born after gestation period of 35 days. Weaned at about 6 weeks; sexually mature in captivity at 9 weeks, in wild probably about 1 year. May live about 5–7 years in captivity, probably about 4–5 years in the wild

Voice Normally silent, except for quiet puffing and grunting during foraging activity; may scream if alarmed

Diet Small invertebrates, especially beetles; also lizards and almost anything else that can be caught and eaten easily; occasionally fruit

Habitat Grassland, scrub, savanna, and gardens

Distribution Southern fringe of the Sahara south to Zambezi River

Status Population: unknown. Not very common in the wild

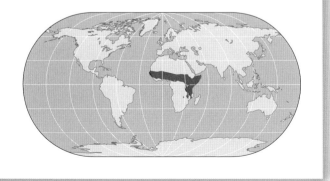

AFRICAN PYGMY HEDGEHOGS live in a wide variety of habitats, including scrub and suburban gardens. However, they appear to avoid marshes, dry deserts, and dense forests. They seem to be most at home in heavily grazed grassland, where nibbling by large numbers of antelope and cattle keeps the grass short. Here the hedgehogs come out at dusk to forage in the cool of the night, under cover of darkness.

Unfussy Foragers

Pygmy hedgehogs will eat almost anything edible that they can catch on the ground, particularly invertebrates of all kinds. They will even eat millipedes despite the distasteful chemicals that many produce. They will tackle small vertebrates too, including small frogs, lizards, and tiny snakes. They will occasionally catch mice or find birds' eggs. Vegetable matter does not feature frequently, but they sometimes eat fungi or fallen fruit. Often the fruit attracts invertebrates, so the hedgehogs will visit fruiting trees as a source of various foods. Food is located by scent and also by the sound that small animals make rustling through the soil or grass. Pygmy hedgehogs have strong claws and often dig in the earth to extract prey.

During the day they sleep safely in a rock crevice or burrow, which is often lined with dry leaves or grass. Except when raising a family, they do not use these refuges for long periods and move on from place to place each night. That enables them to exploit a wider area in the search for food. In some parts of their range food is difficult to find during the dry season, and pygmy hedgehogs will enter a state of torpor similar to hibernation. Technically, it is not real hibernation because it does not take

SEE ALSO Hedgehog, Western European **9**:14

place in the winter. Instead, it is known as estivation, but its effect is the same: The body processes slow down, economizing on energy expenditure until the next rains come, and food becomes plentiful once again. Like their European cousins, African pygmy hedgehogs will perform self-anointing, covering their spines with frothy saliva.

Extended Breeding Season

Pygmy hedgehogs live solitary lives, only coming together to mate. They have an extended breeding season that allows for two litters per year. The young are born in a leafy nest. Births occur in the wetter months of the year. The young are born blind; their eyes do not open for about two weeks. When they are about a month

A captive African pygmy hedgehog with young in Tampa Bay, Florida. The species has become a popular pet in the United States. In 1992 the North American Hedgehog Association was founded, bringing together breeders and fanciers of the species.

old, the babies begin to accompany their mother on foraging trips. They are weaned at about six weeks, and the family then disperses.

Since the late 1980s African pygmy hedgehogs have been bred in large numbers as novelty pets in both Europe and the United States. However, concern for the welfare of animals in transit and possible health risks led the U.S. Department of Agriculture to ban further imports in 1990. There is also a potential danger to wild populations if too many are captured. Already the numbers of a closely related species, *Atelerix frontalis* from southern Africa, had declined, and the status of pygmy hedgehogs in the wild is poorly known.

Pygmy hedgehogs have done very well in captivity. They seem to be better suited to captivity than European hedgehogs, being able to eat dry foods. They are also less messy to keep. If they are well looked after, pygmy hedgehogs can become sexually mature at 61 to 68 days old and can give birth several times a year. That means that the captive population can increase very rapidly. It is unlikely that numbers can grow so fast in the wild, since the animals cannot remain so well fed throughout the year, especially in the northern parts of their range, where the dry season may be both harsh and prolonged. By contrast, captive hedgehogs can become overfed and rather obese.

Common name Greater moonrat

Scientific name *Echinosorex gymnura*

Family   Erinaceidae

Order   Insectivora

Size   Length head/body: 10–18 in (26–46 cm); tail length: 6.5–12 in (16.5–30 cm)

Weight 1–4.5 lb (0.5–2 kg)

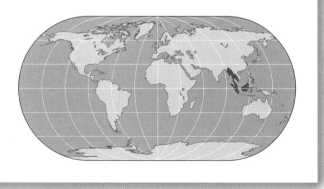

Key features Thin, rat-sized animal with pointed snout; tail scaly with sparse hairs; fur dark; head and rear half of tail pale; black facial "mask"

Habits   Nocturnal and solitary; little known of general activity patterns

Breeding   Two young born twice yearly after gestation period of 35–40 days. Probably weaned at about 1 month; sexually mature at probably 6–12 months. May live up to 4.5–5 years in captivity, probably similar in the wild

Voice   Generally silent, but sometimes hisses and puffs

Diet   Insects, worms, small mollusks, and other invertebrates; sometimes fish, frogs, and fruit

Habitat   Lowland tropical forest, mangroves, rubber plantations, and cultivated areas

Distribution From Myanmar (Burma) and Thailand south through Malaysia to Sumatra and Borneo

Status   Population: unknown

Greater Moonrat

Echinosorex gymnura

Moonrats are actually hairy hedgehogs and have nothing to do with either rats or the moon! They are animals of tropical Asia, and this is the best-known species.

THE MOONRAT HAS A SCALY, RATLIKE TAIL, but there the similarity with the rat ends. It has a long, pointed face rather like a giant shrew, and its 44 teeth are completely different from those of rats and all other rodents. The basic anatomy, especially the skeleton, is actually similar to that of typical hedgehogs. However, instead of having a spiny coat, the moonrat has a coat of dense fur with long, coarse hairs overlying it. Like hedgehogs, the animals walk with the soles of their feet flat on the ground, a condition known as "plantigrade." Moonrats are primitive mammals, resembling the very earliest types that evolved millions of years ago.

Rare and Threatened

There are seven species of moonrats and their close relatives, the gymnures, distributed widely across Southeast Asia. All are rare, and some are seriously threatened. The greater moonrat is the best-known species; but although it was officially discovered in 1821, it has been little studied since. That is because all moonrats live in small numbers and inhabit dense undergrowth in thick tropical forests. They are hard to find at all and almost impossible to study in detail.

Moonrats live mainly on the forest floor, but they can climb quite well and have been seen in trees. This would provide a way of escaping from predators and also allow access to birds' nests and other sources of food. Moonrats can run quite fast, and their long, thin body is highly suitable for squeezing through small spaces and dense vegetation.

An unusual all-white version of the greater moonrat. The species is normally black with a whitish head and shoulders.

seeking food. They poke their long noses into every likely place, sniffing out worms, mollusks, and large insects. They happily enter water to catch frogs and small fish. Their dense underfur is covered by a layer of long coarse hairs from which the wet can be thrown off with a quick shake. That way the animal can keep dry despite moving around in wet undergrowth. Moist places are preferred because such areas are particularly rich in large-bodied invertebrates. Moonrats will also live in mangrove swamps—a difficult habitat for many mammals to inhabit because of the dense tangle of tree roots. However, they are rich in crabs and other suitable food for the moonrats. Greater moonrats will live in rubber plantations, although the way they are managed must make it hard to find much food there.

Cool and Damp

The continued spread of cultivation, at the expense of natural forests, is a serious threat to moonrats. Dense forest casts a deep shadow throughout the year, protecting the ground from the heat of the tropical sun. The trees also trap humid air, creating a moist but cool environment ideal for large numbers of sensitive invertebrates. Once the trees are removed, or even just thinned out, the wind and sun quickly cause the soil to dry up, reducing the quantities of invertebrates on which moonrats feed. Opening up the habitat also exposes animals like moonrats to predators, such as dogs and birds of prey. Forest clearance is therefore a major threat to moonrat populations, which are now reduced and badly fragmented as a result. Fortunately, greater moonrats seem to be fairly adaptable and are able to survive on certain types of cultivated land, at least for a while. Some wildlife reserves have been established, but they are difficult to protect, and the distribution of moonrats among them is poorly known. At least they are safe from hunting, since they are no use as food. Nor are they used in traditional Oriental medicines—a major threat to many other rare animals in Asia.

They worm their way into crevices, among tree roots, and into small holes and hollow logs in order to nest and hide away during the day. They are active under the cover of darkness, when they potter around

The Tenrec Family

Tenrecs and otter shrews (the family Tenrecidae) show the widest diversity in body form of all the families that make up the order Insectivora. Some resemble hedgehogs, shrews, or moles, while the otter shrews look like miniature otters. Their coats are soft-furred or spiny and range in color from a uniform brown or gray to contrasting streaks.

The smallest species is the pygmy shrew tenrec, which weighs around 0.18 ounces (5 g) and is only 1.7 inches (4.3 cm) long. The largest, and the largest of all insectivores, is the common tenrec, which can weigh up to 3.3 pounds (1.5 kg).

All tenrecs live in Madagascar. One species, the common tenrec, is also found on the nearby Comoro Islands and has been introduced to other Indian Ocean islands, including Mauritius and the Seychelles. Otter shrews are found in West and central Africa. They live in a wide range of habitats from semidesert areas to rain forest, mountains, and even near human settlements, but are normally associated with slow-flowing waters.

Like many insectivores, tenrecs are opportunists. They eat a wide range of invertebrates, plus some plant matter, including fruit, and also small vertebrates. Common tenrecs are large enough to catch reptiles, amphibians, and even small mammals or ground-nesting birds. Some species are specialists, for example, the streaked tenrec concentrates on earthworms, and otter shrews prey on freshwater crabs.

Primitive Temperature Regulation

One of the many characteristics that tenrecs probably share with the early placental mammals is a limited ability to control their body temperature. It is low, ranging between 86 and 95°F (30 and 35°C) when active. Some species go into dormancy, or torpor, during the dry season. Others, including the giant otter shrew and some rice tenrecs, save energy all year round by letting their body temperature fall close to that of their surroundings when they sleep during the day.

Family Tenrecidae: 4 subfamilies, 10 genera, 24 species

Subfamily Tenrecinae 4 genera, 4 species

   Setifer 1 species, greater hedgehog tenrec (*S. setosus*)

   Echinops 1 species, lesser hedgehog tenrec (*E. telfairi*)

   Tenrec 1 species, common tenrec (*T. ecaudatus*)

   Hemicentetes 1 species, streaked tenrec (*H. semispinosus*)

Subfamily Oryzorictinae 3 genera, 16 species

   Limnogale 1 species, aquatic tenrec (*L. mergulus*)

   Oryzorictes 3 species, including four-toed rice tenrec (*O. tetradactylus*)

   Microgale 12 species, including pygmy shrew tenrec (*M. parvula*); long-tailed tenrec (*M. melanorrachis*)

Subfamily Geogalinae 1 genus, 1 species

   Geogale large-eared tenrec (*G. aurita*)

Subfamily Potamogalinae (otter shrews) 2 genera, 3 species

   Potamogale 1 species, giant otter shrew (*P. velox*)

   Micropotamogale 2 species, Ruwenzori otter shrew (*M. ruwenzorii*); least otter shrew (*M. lamottei*)

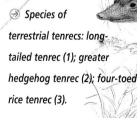

⊙ *Species of terrestrial tenrecs: long-tailed tenrec (1); greater hedgehog tenrec (2); four-toed rice tenrec (3).*

SEE ALSO Weasel Family, The **1**:32; Hedgehog Family, The **9**:12; Tenrec, Common **9**:26

⬅ *The streaked tenrec has stripes from the nose to the body and flanks.*

⬇ *Representative species of otter shrews and tenrecs; aquatic tenrec (1); giant otter shrew (2); Ruwenzori otter shrew (3).*

Like most insectivores, tenrecs tend to be solitary. They communicate primarily through scent. Tenrecs scent-mark by dragging their hind end on the ground. They also rub secretions from eye and neck glands onto stones and logs. Otter shrews deposit feces in or near burrows and under banks to mark their territory. Breeding is usually seasonal, with most births in the wet season, when invertebrate numbers are highest. Litter sizes range from two up to 32 in the common tenrec.

Early Arrivals

Tenrecs are thought to be among the first mammals to arrive on Madagascar. Without competition from others they adapted to fill most of the available niches, resulting in a wide range of body forms and lifestyles. The spiny tenrecs ("Madagascan hedgehogs") pursue a lifestyle similar to true hedgehogs. They are mainly terrestrial, although the lesser hedgehog tenrec can climb well and spends some of its time in trees. The greater and lesser hedgehog tenrecs have spines over the upper surface of their bodies. The streaked and common tenrecs have a mane of stiff spines at the nape of the neck that they can erect for defense. Spiny tenrecs roll into a ball when alarmed like true hedgehogs.

The shrewlike tenrecs are soft furred. They include the long-tailed and large-eared tenrecs. They tend to live in Madagascar's evergreen forests, and they are both terrestrial and semiarboreal. Some climb trees; others jump or run along the ground.

Rice tenrecs occupy the "mole" niche. Like true moles, they are burrowers with velvety fur, small ears and eyes, and relatively large forefeet. They live in tunnel systems at the side of paddy fields.

Aquatic species include the otter shrews and the aquatic tenrec. They have a sleek, streamlined body and a flattened head, enabling the ears, eyes, and nostrils to project above the water. Some have webbed toes and a slightly compressed tail, which acts as a rudder.

Common name Common tenrec (greater tenrec, tailless tenrec)

Scientific name *Tenrec ecaudatus*

Family   Tenrecidae

Order   Insectivora

Size   Length: 10–15 in (26–39 cm); tail length: 0.4–0.6 in (1–1.5 cm)

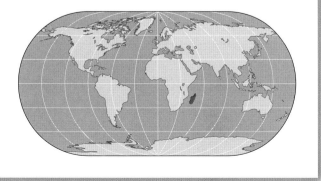

Weight 3.5–5.3 lb (1.6–2.4 kg)

Key features Buff, grayish, or reddish-brown animal with hairs and spines; crest of long, rigid spines at nape of neck; long snout and extremely wide gape; short legs and tail

Habits   Generally solitary; peaks of activity in the early and late parts of the night; shelters during the day in a burrow, hollow log, or under rocks; hibernates underground

Breeding   Litters of up to 32 (usually about 15) young born December–January after gestation period of 56–64 days. Weaned at 6–8 weeks; sexually mature at 6 months. May live over 6 years in captivity, probably fewer in the wild

Voice   Squeaks and squeals; low hissing noise when aggravated

Diet   Mainly invertebrates, plus fruit, vegetation, and occasional small reptiles, amphibians, and mammals

Habitat   Areas with brush or other cover near water, from sea level to about 2,900 ft (900 m)

Distribution Madagascar; introduced to Mauritius, Réunion Island, and the Comoro and Seychelles archipelagos

Status   Population: unknown, but probably many thousands (including introduced populations)

Common Tenrec

Tenrec ecaudatus

Like large, thin-spined hedgehogs, common tenrecs have the size, strength, and sharp teeth to eat other animals as well as insects. They have larger litters than any other mammalian species.

THE COMMON TENREC IS THE largest member of the tenrec family, and at about the size of a rabbit it is the largest living member of the order Insectivora. It is also known as the greater tenrec and tailless tenrec, although it does have a short, stubby tail. Its body shape is like that of a hedgehog, with a long snout, short limbs, and large, flattened claws on all four feet. The coat is a mixture of bristly hairs and thin spines, with stronger spines concentrated on the nape, behind the head. The animal does not roll into a ball like some of the spikier hedgehog tenrecs. Instead, the nape spikes are raised in threat or alarm. The common tenrec, like all other tenrecs, lives in Madagascar; but people have introduced it as a means of controlling pests on other Indian Ocean islands. They include Réunion and the Comoro Islands, Mauritius, and the Seychelles.

Insect Hunters

Tenrecs scurry around at night under the cover of scrub and woodland, digging through leaf litter and soil with their snout in search of invertebrates. They also use their strong claws to break open rotting wood and turn over stones. They will happily scale quite steep rocks, but are rarely seen in trees. Like most insectivores, they are omnivorous, even eating fallen fruit when available. Their large size means they can also eat reptiles, amphibians, and even small mammals. They will also attack ground-nesting birds and their eggs. They therefore pose a threat to rare species, especially on islands where tenrecs have been introduced. Foraging tenrecs can cover 1.2 to 5

acres (0.4 to 2 ha) per night, but adult females tend to stay in a smaller area. During the day tenrecs usually rest in burrows. They are dug specially, often with two exits. Tenrecs collect leaves and other nesting materials, and carry them by the mouth to line their nest.

Tenrecs are generally solitary, foraging and hibernating alone or, in the case of nursing mothers, in the company of their many offspring. Adults tend to fight if they meet. They are muscular and powerful creatures, and fights can cause serious injury. Fighting tenrecs open their mouths in an extremely wide gape, exposing long canine teeth, and slash sideways at their opponent. They will also raise the spines on the neck, then drive them into their opponent with a swift buck of the head.

During the dry season (the southern winter) from May to October food is often in short supply, so tenrecs hibernate to reduce their energy expenditure. They sleep in burrows with a single entrance that they plug with soil before going to sleep. Like other mammals in hibernation, their breathing rate and other metabolic processes slow right down. Their

⊕ The common tenrec has been a source of food for the people of Madagascar since ancient times, but such traditional hunting has not threatened the species.

body temperature drops close to that of the surroundings, so the animal feels cold to the touch and is incapable of rapid movement. On waking, tenrecs begin their breeding cycle within a few days.

Spiky Babies

Mating takes place in October to November, but it is not a romantic occasion. There is no elaborate courtship, and there is only a brief encounter between the male and female. Common tenrecs have huge litters of up to 32 young, the largest family size of any mammal. The average brood size is 15, but varies depending on the type of habitat. In stable rainforest habitats litters are smaller than in seasonal woodland or savanna. To match their huge litter sizes, female tenrecs have more nipples than any other mammal—usually 24.

Newborn tenrecs are blind and hairless, but develop relatively quickly. They can see within a week or two, and from three to six weeks the babies start to forage with their mother. Feeding so many offspring is hard work, and the mother has to forage during the day as well as at night in order to find enough food.

Young tenrecs have longitudinal stripes of white spines down their back, which help camouflage them during the daytime on the woodland floor. They also have a group of specialized spines on the center of the back: By twitching a muscle, young tenrecs can rub the spines together, making a rattling noise known as stridulation. They do this when they are alarmed or to keep in touch with their mother or siblings while foraging. They lose the quills when they molt into an adult coat.

By March or April the brood is fully grown, and the young tenrecs have molted their striped coats. When the mother leaves them, the siblings may stay together briefly, but they soon separate to lead solitary lives.

The Shrew Family

Shrews have a reputation for being vicious, bad-tempered, and cunning—hence the word "shrewd." They are fierce fighters for their tiny size and seem to exist by the motto "live fast, die young."

What Is a Shrew?

Shrews are mouselike creatures, but with a longer, more pointed nose and completely different dentition. Their fur is velvety and grayish or brown, and their eyes and ears are tiny. A shrew's eyesight is poor, but its hearing is good, and the long, sensitive whiskers help with groping around in confined spaces. Many shrews have large scent glands in the skin that produce a foul smell that deters predators. However, owls, which have a poorly developed sense of taste, often include large numbers in their diet.

Over three-quarters of the 400-odd species in the order Insectivora are shrews, making them the most successful family of all the insectivores. They are distributed throughout North and Central America, Europe, Asia, and most of Africa. They live in a wide range of habitats from desert to grassland and forest. Despite their primitive structure and appearance, shrews are a relatively modern group. The earliest fossil shrews date back to the middle Eocene, some 45 million years ago.

The smallest member of the family is the Etruscan white-toothed shrew, which at 0.07 ounces (2 g) is the smallest land mammal. The largest species of shrew is the rat-sized African forest shrew, weighing 1.2 ounces (35 g). Generally, shrews do no harm to humans, carry no serious diseases, and have no commercial value. However, the Indian house shrew does make itself a nuisance by contaminating houses and food stores with its droppings and pungent scent. The species has become widely distributed throughout many parts of Asia by being transported accidentally with trade goods.

Noisy Loners

Most shrews are solitary and territorial. They lead secretive lives, sleeping in burrows and foraging out of sight in and under litter in forests and grassland. However, some species are semiaquatic. Stiff fringes of hair on the feet and tail help propulsion in the water. The Tibetan water shrew even has webbed feet.

Shrews are very vocal in encounters with each other, squealing and twittering noisily. Some species make ultrasound noises (so high pitched as to be beyond human hearing) and may use echolocation.

Most shrews live on a diet of worms, insects, and other invertebrates. Generally, shrews eat any invertebrates they come across. Aquatic shrews may catch frogs and fish. There are some even more carnivorous species, such as the piebald shrew, which eats lizards. A few species also have poisonous saliva that allows them to attack and subdue quite large prey, but the poison is too weak to affect humans.

Family Soricidae: 2 subfamiles, 23 genera, at least 312 species

Subfamily Crocidurinae (white-toothed shrews) At least 200 species in 12 genera, including

Diplomesodon, including piebald shrew (D. pulchellum)

Myosorex, including forest shew (M. varius)

Suncus, including Etruscan white-toothed or pygmy shrew (S. etruscus); Indian house shrew (S. murinus)

Scutisorex, including armored shrew (S. somereni)

Subfamily Soricinae (red-toothed shrews) At least 112 species in 11 genera, including

Blarina, including American or northern short-tailed shrew (B. brevicauda)

Sorex, including Eurasian pygmy shrew (S. minutus)

Nectogale, including Tibetan water shrew (N. elegans)

Neomys, including Eurasian water shrew (N. fodiens)

 SEE ALSO Mouse and Rat Family, The **7**:64; Shrew, Eurasian Common **9**:34; Shrew, American Water **9**:36

⊕ *One of the oddest of all mammalian activities, a Eurasian pygmy shrew performs refection. It pushes out the end of its rectum and nibbles and licks at it, probably to obtain nutrients from partially digested food.*

⊖ *Surrounded by air bubbles, a Eurasian water shrew dives downward on an underwater hunting trip. The animals feed on aquatic invertebrates, small fish, and amphibians.*

ceaseless activity of these animals. Heart rates of 1,000 beats per minute have been recorded, more than 10 times the pulse rate of a human. Because their small bodies do not have enough reserves to last a whole night, shrews tend to have alternating periods of activity and rest throughout the day and night. They will starve if they get no food for more than a couple of hours. Such frenetic activity cannot be sustained indefinitely, and most shrews live only a few months, dying literally "worn out." Few adult shrews survive long into their second year.

A few species, such as the desert shrews, are able to go into torpor during the hottest times of the day when they are not able to feed, although none are known to hibernate. In several northern species the skull, skeleton, brain, and some other internal organs shrink during winter, apparently helping reduce energy demands.

The spine of the armored shrew is unique. It has more lumbar vertebrae than other shrews, and they are large and have many criss-crossing spikes that form a girderlike structure. It is so strong that an armored shrew is reported to have withstood a man standing on it.

A strange habit seen in many shrews is rectum licking. Immediately after defecating, the shrew pushes out the last half an inch (1 cm) of its rectum, then nibbles and licks it. This is probably to obtain droplets of fat, minerals, and vitamins from partly digested food, but it may seem an odd and distasteful activity to us.

Shrews are very active and need large amounts of food for their size. They often consume more than their own body weight each day, and most need to eat every few hours to stay alive. This is linked to a very high metabolic rate, burning up energy all the time, fueling the

American Short-Tailed Shrew

Blarina brevicauda

Common name American short-tailed shrew (northern short-tailed shrew)

Scientific name *Blarina brevicauda*

Family Soricidae

Order Insectivora

Size Length head/body: 3.5–4 in (9–10 cm); tail length: about 1 in (2.5–3 cm)

Weight 0.6–1 oz (17–28 g)

Key features Typical red-toothed shrew with a distinctly short tail; general color slate gray to almost black; underparts slightly paler

Habits Burrows in soft soil and leaf litter; rarely found on the surface; active day and night, punctuated by short rest periods

Breeding Litters of usually 4–7 young born February–September after gestation period of 21–22 days. Weaned at 25 days; sexually mature at 47 days. May live up to 33 months in captivity, up to 30 in the wild

Voice Quiet twitter; aggressive squeaks and shrieks if attacked

Diet Soil invertebrates, including small worms, insect larvae, and beetles; some plant material and occasional vertebrate prey

Habitat Dense ground cover in woodland and thick grassy areas

Distribution Much of northern-central and northeastern U.S.; southern regions of adjacent Canadian provinces

Status Population: unknown, likely to be millions. Abundant

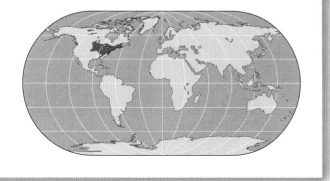

The American short-tailed shrew is one of the common small mammals of the northeastern United States, easily recognized by its long, pointed nose, red teeth, and noticeably short tail.

ALL THREE SPECIES OF SHORT-TAILED shrew forming the genus *Blarina* have a tail that is only about one-third the length of the head and body. This contrasts with the various species of long-tailed shrews, whose tail is about half the length of the body or longer. The American short-tailed shrew is also larger than any other shrew found in the northeastern United States and adjacent parts of Canada. The other two species of short-tailed shrews—the southern and Elliot's short-tailed shrews—occupy geographically separate areas of the United States and also have different numbers of chromosomes.

Burrowing Shrew

The short-tailed shrew is one of the common species of small mammals found in woodland and old grassland. It prefers habitat where there is dense ground cover, and it is rarely seen out in the open. The short-tailed shrew actually spends most of its time underground, often using the tunnels excavated by moles and other small mammals. But the species also digs its own burrows, and it is the most fossorial of the American shrews. Its tunnels may honeycomb large areas of soft soil and collapsed tangles of grass and weeds. The tunnels are generally within 5 inches (12 cm) of the surface, and like those dug by moles, they act as traps into which soil invertebrates fall. They will then be found and eaten by the shrew as it patrols its tunnel system. Digging shrews use their front feet for excavating, and the dirt is kicked away with the hind feet. Nests are built underground, usually of shredded grass and leaves, but they sometimes incorporate fur. The short-tailed

 SEE ALSO Shrew, Eurasian Common **9:34**

shrews do not hibernate and are active all winter, often using burrows under snow. At that time their food requirements increase substantially to over half their body weight daily.

The shrews forage for soil invertebrates, particularly small worms, millipedes, spiders, mollusks, and insect larvae. However, they will kill larger things, assisted by their ability to deliver a poisonous bite. The poison is useful in paralyzing large invertebrates, allowing them to be saved and eaten later. Surplus food is cached in the shrew's burrow, and the animal will return repeatedly to its store to consume what is there and to replenish supplies. The behavior is most common in winter, but also occurs in summer.

Plant material has sometimes been found in the stomachs of short-tailed shrews, but it may have been eaten accidentally along with animal prey, rather than deliberately consumed. For example, shrews attracted to rotting fruit or mushrooms for the maggots they contain would find it difficult to extract the animal food without swallowing some of the vegetable matter. They probably do not need to drink, since their food, particularly juicy earthworms, contains a lot of water. The shrews also lick

⬆ *The short-tailed shrew can deliver a poisonous bite. The venom is strong enough to kill small animals, which ordinarily would be too large for the shrew to prey on.*

shrew can also climb well and may occasionally be found up in trees. Here it may perform a useful service by eating forest pests such as larch sawflies and other destructive insects.

Ravenous Appetites

Short-tailed shrews starve if they do not feed frequently. As a result, they need to be active throughout the day and night to fulfill their high energy requirements. They are active in brief bursts averaging four to five minutes, followed by rest periods lasting about 20 to 25 minutes. They seem to be busier in the early morning and also more active on cloudy days than in sunny or rainy weather. Short-tailed

dew off the vegetation. Moreover, living in the humid air of tunnels in damp soil, and among moist grass, the shrews are likely to lose less water by evaporation from their body and lungs than if they lived out in the open.

Shrews have large scent glands on their flanks and bellies. They produce a strong odor that marks out their tunnels. The size of the glands and production of scent vary with the sex and reproductive status of the individual. Breeding males have the largest glands and produce the greatest amount of scent. The short-tailed shrew is said to use vocal clicks to detect objects by echolocation. That ability might help compensate for the fact that its eyes are smaller than pinheads and barely able to distinguish light from dark. In any case, eyes are of little use in underground burrows. Echolocation by shrews is not sufficiently sophisticated to detect small objects the way that bats can, but it should help locate tunnel openings and tell the difference between those that are blocked and routes that are accessible.

Young Wanderers

While adults seem to have a fixed home range averaging about 5 to 6 acres (2 to 2.5 ha), the younger animals may be nomadic until they find a place for themselves. Short-tailed shrews are solitary animals—particularly the males and

Toxic Saliva

The saliva of the short-tailed shrew is poisonous and contains chemicals that paralyze the nervous system (neurotoxins) and damage blood cells (hemotoxins). It is not dangerous to large animals such as humans, although a bite can remain painful for several days. The toxic saliva is similar to the venom produced by some snakes. However, unlike snakes, which have hollow fangs, the shrew cannot inject the poison. Instead, it is chewed into the wound at every bite. The toxin is sufficiently effective that it will kill mice and other large prey, enabling the shrew to prey on larger animals than would be expected. The saliva will also paralyze invertebrates such as mollusks, preventing their escape and allowing them to be eaten later.

older individuals who tend not to be sociable at all. Population densities vary from year to year and range from less than one to 50 per acre (120 per ha). Dense populations may crash late in the year and take several years to recover. Winter mortality may reach 90 percent, especially in bitterly cold weather.

Rough and Tumble

The breeding season begins in early February (later farther north) and lasts until September, with the females tending to come into breeding condition earlier than males. Mating is a rough and tumble affair, with the shrews joined together for several minutes. During that time

family then disperses. The juveniles are capable of breeding when they are under two months old. Adult females can give birth to as many as three litters in a season, so the shrew population often builds up rapidly and reaches high numbers by the end of the breeding season in September.

Natural and Man-Made Perils

The short-tailed shrew, like many other small mammals, faces a wide range of predators. Owls are a particular threat, since they have a poorly developed sense of taste and are not put off by the shrew's strong-smelling skin glands. Consequently, the short-tailed shrew is a frequent victim. Shrews are also highly inquisitive animals and will push into small spaces to seek food. As a result, they often fall victim to discarded bottles and drink cans, unable to escape having squeezed inside.

A subspecies of the short-tailed shrew, found only at one place in southwestern Florida, may have been wiped out by development of its habitat and predation by domestic cats. The many threats faced by shrews ensure that only 11 percent live more than one year, and very few reach two years old. That is partly because their gritty food, such as earthworms, wears down their teeth, which do not grow continually like the incisor teeth of rodents. As a result, old shrews are less able to chew their food properly, even though they have 32 teeth. The animals are also likely to get worn out by having to be active day and night throughout their lives. Average survival is only about four or five months.

In October and November the shrews shed their summer coat and replace it with longer winter fur. The winter molt begins on the tail and moves forward toward the head. The spring molt begins in about February, but can take place any time up until the early summer. The dark-gray winter coat is then replaced by shorter, slightly paler fur. This time the molt starts at the head and proceeds toward the tail. Why the molt should go in different directions at different seasons is a mystery.

the female continues to move around, dragging the male behind her. Females seem to need several matings in a day in order to induce their ovaries to release eggs that are then fertilized and develop directly into embryos. Gestation lasts for three weeks, after which the young are born blind, pink, and helpless. The normal family size is between four and seven. The newborn young are hairless except for their whiskers. They take 25 days to be weaned and are fully independent within four weeks. The

ⓐ *A short-tailed shrew feeds on the carrion of a meadow vole. The shrews need to hunt for prey at all times of day and night, only stopping to rest for brief periods.*

Common name Eurasian common shrew

Scientific name *Sorex araneus*

Family	Soricidae
Order	Insectivora
Size	Length head/body: 2–3 in (5–7 cm); tail length: about 1 in (2.5 cm)

Weight 0.2–0.5 oz (5–15 g)

Key features Small mammal; brown all over, paler below; long, pointed nose, small ears and tiny eyes; tail about half the length of head and body

Habits	Active day and night; rushes around constantly; solitary and aggressively territorial; lives in shallow burrows and tunnels in soil and leaf litter
Breeding	About 6 (but as many as 10) young born April–September in up to 4 litters per season after gestation period of 22–25 days. Weaned at 3–4 weeks. May live a maximum of 23 months in captivity, similar in the wild, but average life span less than 1 year, and half die within 2 months
Voice	Loud piercing shrieks and squeaks when angry or alarmed
Diet	Mostly insect larvae and soil invertebrates; small worms
Habitat	Woodland, farmland, hedgerow, and tundra; especially abundant in damp places
Distribution	Most of Europe from Mediterranean to Arctic and from Britain to western China
Status	Population: many millions. Very common animal

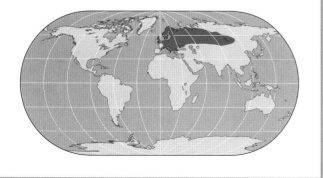

Eurasian Common Shrew

Sorex araneus

A common and widespread creature across Europe and northern Asia, the Eurasian common shrew occurs in many habitats. It is constantly active and breeds rapidly, but has a short life span.

SHREWS ARE UNMISTAKABLE. They are tiny and have a distinctive long, pointed snout that is constantly in motion. Shrews use the snout to seek out smells and to poke around under stones. They have small ears that are almost hidden in their fur, and their eyes are minute—about the size of pinheads. They are not much use anyhow, since shrews normally live in burrows or hide away under rocks or logs. The sense of smell is much more important.

Frenetic Pace of Life

Shrews are incredibly active little creatures, rushing constantly here and there. They must eat almost continuously to supply the energy for all their charging around. They are active day and night, with alternate bouts of frantic activity and comparative calm at about two-hour intervals. Throughout their life they are hardly ever still for more than a few minutes. Rest periods are normally spent in the safety of the nest, and active times are spent searching for food. They do not have far to look: The soil is teeming with small worms, beetles, caterpillars, and other tiny creatures that make up their diet.

Most prey items are tiny, but sometimes a large worm may be tackled by attacking the head end first to paralyze it. Larger items like grasshoppers may have the legs bitten off first. Shrews can locate food more than 4 inches (10 cm) deep in the soil: Their sensitive whiskers detect movements of prey, and their ears are sensitive too. Much of their food consists of the indigestible outer coverings of insects—even worms are full of water and dirt. As a result,

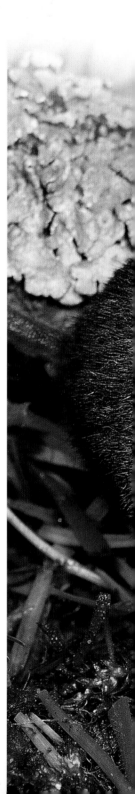

SEE ALSO Shrew, American Short-Tailed **9:**30; Shrew, Etruscan White-Toothed **9:**38

shrews need to eat large quantities to get enough nourishment and energy to power their high-speed lifestyle. They eat about 90 percent of their own body weight daily—equivalent to an average man consuming an entire sheep.

Shrews are solitary animals and highly belligerent toward each other. They make piercing shrieks if they meet in the undergrowth, and a noisy standoff results. Often they will rear up on their hind legs and scratch at each other, squeaking violently. Sometimes they grapple together, rolling over and over. When one runs away, the other may pursue it, biting at the retreating rump and tail.

A single shrew occupies a home range of about 500 square yards (420 sq. m). Most of it is fiercely defended through fighting and scent-marking. Each shrew normally remains in its own area throughout its life, although in spring males start to expand their range, and females become temporarily more tolerant of visitors. Males are nevertheless usually rebuffed by the females. There is no real courtship and the two animals separate immediately after mating. They probably never meet again. During mating the male often grasps the female by the scruff of the neck, using his teeth to get a better grip. Hairs are pulled out, and those that grow in their place are sometimes white. Adult females often bear a tuft of white hair as a souvenir of such brief encounters.

Females sometimes give birth to as many as 10 young, but more usually it is five or six. The offspring are born pink, blind, and furless, but by a fortnight their eyes are open. At birth the whole family weighs almost as much as the mother (in humans even twins are rarely equivalent to more than about 10 to 15 percent of their mother's weight). Baby shrews grow so fast that in two weeks the family is double the weight of their mother. She feeds the babies on her own milk, which requires tremendous effort on her part. To do so, she must consume more than her own weight of food every day.

An Exhausting Task

Breeding is a huge task for a mother; yet once the family is independent, she will start over and have another litter as many as four times in one summer. By about September the females are completely exhausted and soon die. Only a tiny percentage of the shrews live to be one year old, and very few exceed 14 months. In fact, most shrews die young, and only about one in four survives to breed. Nonetheless, summer population densities can reach about 20 per acre (50 per ha) in good habitat.

Juvenile shrews are pale brown all over. In the fall they molt out of their short-haired summer coat, and a darker coat of long, sleek fur develops. The molt begins on the rump and moves forward. By November the change of coat is complete, and the animal is dark chocolate brown, with paler fur on the belly. Their body weight also changes; but instead of fattening up for winter, as so many other mammals do, shrews shrink by a quarter. Even their skulls and bones get smaller, only to regain full size the following year.

⊕ A Eurasian common shrew in Surrey, England, showing the long, probing nose and miniscule eyes that are typical of shrew species.

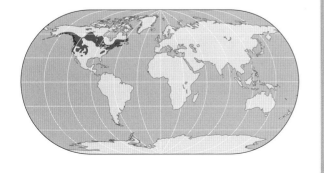

Common name
American
water shrew

Scientific name *Sorex palustris*

Family Soricidae

Order Insectivora

Size Length head/body: 3–4 in (7.5–10.5 cm); tail length: 2.5–3 in (6–7.5 cm)

Weight 0.3–0.5 oz (8.5–14 g)

Key features Relatively large shrew; blackish-gray coat sometimes becoming browner in summer, pale to dark-gray underside; 2-colored tail; distinctive fringe of stiff white hairs on sides of feet; tiny eyes and ears; red tips to teeth

Habits Solitary; active day and night but mostly just after sunset and before dawn; hunts in water

Breeding Litters of 3–10 young born late February–June after gestation period of about 21 days. Weaned at 28 days; sexually mature at 2 months in early-born young, 10 months in late-born young. May live about 18 months in captivity, similar in the wild

Voice High-pitched squeaks during territorial disputes and habitat explorations

Diet Aquatic invertebrates such as caddis fly larvae and insect nymphs; occasionally small fish; on land takes flies, earthworms, and snails

Habitat Waterside habitats from bogs to fast-flowing mountain streams, especially in northern forests; prefers humid conditions

Distribution Canada; southeastern Alaska; mountain regions of U.S. into Utah and New Mexico, Sierra Nevada to California

Status Population: unknown, but likely to be millions. Widespread and abundant

American Water Shrew

Sorex palustris

The American water shrew can actually walk on water, helped by stiff hairs that trap bubbles of air under each foot, allowing the shrew to run quickly over the surface of a pool.

WHEN FORAGING FOR PREY underwater, the American water shrew's body fur traps a layer of air. This helps keep it warm in the water, but also gives the shrew extra buoyancy. The shrew requires more effort to prevent itself bobbing to the surface, and it has to swim vigorously to keep itself submerged. The shrew has special stiff hairs on its feet that increase the resistance to water, making them more efficient as paddles. The water shrew will swim, dive, float, and run along the bottom of a stream in its search for food. The animals are also able to hunt and catch small fish, demonstrating their remarkable agility in the water.

Once they have captured their prey, it is held in the forepaws and torn to pieces using the shrew's sharp teeth and upward-tugging motion of the head. Vegetation found in the stomachs of some water shrews may have been eaten accidentally with the usual insect prey.

Regulating Their Temperature

The American water shrew has the ability to control the way blood flows around its body so that it can even dive during the winter. It keeps from freezing to death by diverting blood away from the surface of the skin, where it would quickly get cold. Each dive can last for up to 48 seconds—a very long time for such a tiny creature to hold its breath.

The shrew manages this feat by using its oxygen supply to power the muscles and slowing down other body processes such as the heartbeat and digestion. Immediately after swimming, the shrew dries off its coat, using its hind feet to brush away water from its fur.

 SEE ALSO Shrew, American Short-Tailed **9**:30; Bats **9**:80

It has been suggested that water shrews may be able to echolocate as bats do, since they make constant high-pitched squeaks as they explore their territory. However, there is little evidence to support this, and they certainly cannot use sound in such a precise way as bats. They probably mainly use their sense of smell to locate prey on land and their whiskers to detect movements of prey when underwater.

Never Satisfied

American water shrews can go without food for up to three hours, but they usually feed far more frequently—every 10 minutes on average during active periods. Every day they must eat at least five to 10 percent of their body weight. To find enough food, shrews hunt over territories of up to 1 acre (0.4 ha).

Water shrews are very aggressive toward any other shrews of either sex. When two shrews meet, they will squeak a warning and stand on their hind legs to show their pale-colored stomachs. If neither shrew backs down, there will be a fight in which the shrews wrap up into a tight ball, biting each other. Tail and head injuries are common from such encounters.

The only time a shrew will tolerate another is to mate; although once mating has taken place, the female will chase off the male and raise her family alone. It is thought that mates may be attracted by the strong, sometimes nauseatingly powerful odor emitted by the shrew. The water shrew's nest is about 6 to 8 inches (15 to 20 cm) in diameter, built under a boulder, inside a hollow log, or in a tunnel dug by the shrew. Shrews dig as a dog would, scraping at the soil with their front feet and pushing it back with their hind feet. The nest of shredded grass, leaves, and dried vegetation is then pushed into place with the muzzle.

The scientific name of the American water shrew comes from the words *soric,* meaning "shrew-mouse," and *paluster,* meaning "marshy"—a good description of where it normally lives at the water's edge. It particularly favors mountain streams up to 4,000 feet (1,200 m) above sea level. Here the water is cool, has plenty of dissolved oxygen, and therefore supports abundant aquatic invertebrates on which the shrew can feed. The American water shrew is a relatively large, typical long-tailed shrew. The tail is longer than the body, which is unusual in the shrew family. It probably helps the water shrew in steering when it swims. It has many predators, which on land include owls, hawks, opossums, foxes, bobcats, weasels, and skunks. In the water it faces another range of hungry attackers, including large fish such as trout, and garter snakes. The water shrew must often use its swimming ability to escape from such predators.

⊖ *An American water shrew on the shore of a Colorado creek. The species' scientific name literally means "marshy shrew-mouse."*

Common name Etruscan
white-toothed shrew

Scientific name *Suncus etruscus*

Family Soricidae

Order Insectivora

Size Length head/body: 1.4–2 in (3.5–5 cm); tail
length: 0.9–1.2 in (2.4–3 cm)

Weight 0.05–0.09 oz (1.5–2.5 g)

Key features Minute shrew with large protuberant ears;
fur short and soft, black or grayish-brown,
with pale-gray underside; long hairs scattered
through coat give a "frosted" appearance

Habits Most active at night, but bouts of activity
during day; males in breeding condition
develop large flank glands that give off
strong musky smell

Breeding Litters of 2–5 young born in March–April and
September–October after gestation period of
27–28 days. Weaned at 20 days; sexually
mature after winter, but do not reproduce in
year of birth. May live 26 months in captivity;
probably up to 18 in the wild

Voice Shrill cry; male squeaks, female chirps

Diet Insects and other invertebrates up to
grasshopper size

Habitat Moist habitats: open terrain, grassland, scrub,
deciduous woodland, and gardens up to
3,280 ft (1,000 m) above sea level

Distribution Southern Europe around Mediterranean,
including many islands; Morocco to Arabia

Status Population: abundant, but isolated
populations thought to be threatened

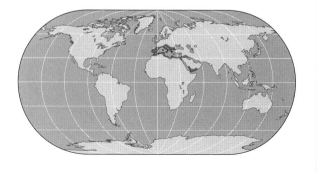

Etruscan White-Toothed Shrew

*Suncus
etruscus*

*The Etruscan white-toothed shrew is the
smallest land mammal in the world and is
not even the size of many beetles.*

EVERYTHING THAT GOES ON in our own bodies—the
circulating blood, breathing lungs, beating
heart—also happens inside this minute animal,
smaller than one joint of our little finger. The
Etruscan shrew is almost the smallest mammal
alive, with Kitti's hog-nosed bat (*Craseonycteris
thonglongyai*) from Thailand only marginally
smaller. Both animals weigh just one-twentieth
of an ounce (1.5 g).

Easily Missed

The Etruscan shrew is often overlooked in the
wild, and very little is known about it. Being so
small causes many problems for warm-blooded
animals. They lose heat so quickly from their
body surface that they have to eat constantly to
get enough energy to keep warm. They lead
such a high-speed lifestyle that their hearts can
beat at a rate of up to 1,300 beats per minute.
They breathe amazingly fast too, but rapid
panting means they also lose a lot of moisture
through their lungs. The tiny animal seems to
be confined to places where the average July
temperature is 68°F (20°C) or higher, and it
avoids the cool floor of dense forests and dry
areas such as sand dunes. Such behavior assists
in reducing heat and water loss.

To help cope with periods when food is not
readily available, the Etruscan shrew can go into
a state of torpor to conserve energy. Bats and
dormice also do this at times when they are not
active. While in torpor, the animal's heart rate
and body temperature drop. The shrew takes
several minutes to recover from this state and
become active again. If disturbed from torpor,
the shrew will utter a harsh shrieking sound to
surprise any predators and hopefully put them
off for long enough to allow it to wake up and

escape. Etruscan shrews will also share nests to keep warm. Survival rates of nest-sharing shrews are significantly higher than for those sleeping alone. Even so, their frantic lifestyle means that not many of these tiny shrews live more than a few months.

Etruscan shrews are not very strong and cannot burrow to find food as some of the larger shrews do. However, they can fit into tiny crevices where others cannot and hunt for prey there. They are even tiny enough to run along tunnels used by large earthworms. Usually, however, they stick to surface foraging, picking up invertebrates from among plants and leaf litter. Every day they must consume at least twice their own body weight of invertebrates in order to survive. Like all shrews, they are aggressive hunters and can kill insects and worms that are almost their own size, using poisonous saliva to help subdue their prey.

Shrew Caravans

Newborn Etruscan shrews are only half the size of a coffee bean and grow so quickly that they can double in size in just four days. If a nest is disturbed, the mother will move her family to a new home by "caravaning." This method is used because shrew's eyes do not open until they are 14 to 16 days old. To form a caravan, each youngster grips the base of the tail of the shrew in front, and the mother leads the way. They hold onto each other so tightly that even if a shrew at one end is lifted off the ground, the others will not let go. It is thought that caravans are also used so that the mother shrew can guide her litter on a tour around their habitat in order to teach them about their surroundings.

The shrew's constant search for food often brings it out into the open and within view of predators. The main killers are owls and other birds of prey that are not put off by the shrew's distasteful skin glands. Mammal predators, having a better sense of taste, probably catch more shrews than are actually eaten. The shrew produces a strong-smelling musk from its flank glands: A discerning mammal will generally drop the shrew uneaten, although Etruscan shrews are taken by snakes. Another possible predator is the preying mantis.

⊕ *An Etruscan white-toothed shrew eating a locust. The shrew is a ferocious predator, capable of killing creatures much larger than itself. It is often found under logs or rocks and in crevices, stone walls, and ruins.*

Moles, Desmans, and Golden Moles

Moles, shrew moles, desmans, and golden moles are all rather elusive burrowing and swimming insectivores. Moles live underground and are rarely seen at the surface. Their presence is usually only revealed by the mole hills and ridges of soil they push up in their frequent digging activities. The two species of desman are even more obscure. One lives in the mountain streams of the Pyrenees, the other in lakes and rivers of the former Soviet Union. They are semiaquatic, good swimmers, and look rather different than moles. What unites this group is similarities in their teeth and other aspects of their anatomy.

The smallest members of the family are the shrew moles, with a head-body length of just under 1 inch (2.5 cm), a tail of the same length, and a weight of under 0.4 ounces (12 g). The largest member of the family is the Russian desman, which is about the size of a rat and weighs 19.5 ounces (550 g).

The earliest fossil moles and desmans are found in Europe and are around 45 million years old (from the mid-Eocene period). From Europe moles spread throughout much of Asia and North America, but they never reached Africa. Here golden moles, whose fossils are also known from the Eocene, occupy their ecological niche.

In Africa the golden moles evolved in complete isolation from true moles. Although they are not closely related, they have developed very similar adaptations due to their similar lifestyles—a process known as convergent evolution. Most burrow in sand dunes and deserts, and today they are distributed from the equator throughout southern Africa. They are named for their fur, which is usually a shade of brown, but has an iridescent gold or bronzy sheen of green, violet, yellow, or red.

Family Talpidae (true moles): 3 subfamilies, 17 genera, 42 species

Subfamily Talpinae (true moles) 14 genera, 36 species, including

Talpa, including European mole (*T. europaea*); Persian mole (*T. streeti*)

Condylura, star-nosed mole (*C. cristata*)

Euroscaptor, including small-toothed mole (*E. parvidens*)

Parascalops, hairy-tailed mole (*P. breweri*)

Scapanus, including coast mole (*S. orarius*)

Subfamily Uropsilinae (Asiatic shrew moles) 1 genus, 4 species

Uropsilus, including inquisitive shrew mole (*U. investigator*)

Subfamily Desmaninae (desmans) 2 genera, 2 species

Desmana, Russian desman (*D. moschata*)

Galemys, Pyrenean desman (*G. pyrenaicus*)

Family Chrysochloridae (golden moles): 9 genera, 21 spcecies, including

Chrysospalax, including giant golden mole (*C. trevelyani*)

Neamblysomus, including Juliana's golden mole (*N. julianae*)

Eremitalpa, Grant's golden mole (*E. granti*)

Tunneling Machines

Most moles are perfect tunneling machines. Their bodies are long and cylindrical, the front legs are broad and powerful, and the spadelike hands are permanently turned outward. In the European mole the humerus (one of the arm bones) is short and wide, and the sternum (chest bone) is enlarged, giving a large area of attachment for the strong pectoral muscles used for digging.

Shrew moles are less well adapted for burrowing. Although they do tunnel, they also forage above ground in the leaf litter. Their forefeet are relatively narrow, although the claws are well developed.

The limbs of desmans are adapted for swimming rather than burrowing. The legs and feet are relatively long and powerful, the toes are webbed, and fingers are half-webbed. All are fringed with stiff hairs, like the flat tail. Unlike moles, the hind legs are the strongest and provide most of the propulsion. Desmans can close their ears and nostrils underwater. Their snout is long, flattened, highly mobile, and used as a snorkel for breathing above the surface.

Golden moles, like true moles, are adapted for burrowing. The forelimbs are powerful, and the hands have four digits, the central two being large with huge pointed claws. They have fewer finger bones than most mammals, so the claws seem to be directly attached to the hand. The hind feet are small, with five toes. Golden moles have no external tail.

True moles have a gray or brownish-black coat of dense, velvety fur. It can be brushed in both directions, handy for reversing in tunnels. In shrew moles the coat has guard hairs and underfur that lies flat. Desmans also

⊕ A coast mole among dead leaves. Moles are rarely seen on the surface, preferring to spend their lives underground. Their bodies have many adaptations for a burrowing lifestyle.

have double-layered fur, with long, shiny guard hairs covering a short, dense, waterproof underlayer. In golden moles the fur also lies front to back, and although not as velvety as in the true moles, it is dense, with a soft underfur and metallic sheen.

Moles' teeth are unspecialized—typical of insectivores—while those of golden moles are rodentlike, with small canines and large first upper and second lower incisors. In young golden moles the teeth do not emerge until the animal is almost fully grown.

Sensing the World
Moles' and desmans' senses are also shaped by their underground or watery lives. Eyesight is not much use underground, so moles have very small eyes, almost hidden by fur, and are virtually blind. They can tell light

41

from dark, but probably not a lot more detail than that. In golden moles the eyes are rudimentary and covered by skin. Moles have some sense of hearing, although the ears are little more than fur-covered holes. Only the Asiatic shrew moles have ears that stick out.

Moles' sense of smell is good. As they tunnel, they rub scent-coated fur onto the walls, leaving a signal that warns other moles away. However, the predominant sense is touch. Moles have sensitive whiskers on a long, mobile snout, together with small bumps called Eimer's organs on the bare skin of the nose. A mole's snout is extremely sensitive, and the star-nosed mole has 22 delicate fleshy protuberances on the end of its snout to enhance its detection skills. Moles also have sensory whiskers on other parts of the body, including the tail, helping them feel their way when they run backward along their tunnels. The desmans have sensitive whiskers on their legs instead.

Pitfall Traps

Moles do not burrow through the soil in pursuit of worms and other prey. Instead, most of their food consists of what drops through the roof of their permanent tunnels. The burrows are therefore not the result of underground

Running through Sand

Golden moles dig differently than true moles. With their large claws they use a scraping, "running" motion, compared to the "swimming" movement of true moles. They tend to make ridges close to the surface, rather than heaps. They have an amazing sense of direction underground. If part of their burrow system is damaged, the mole will dig a new tunnel that exactly meets the end of the existing one.

⊙ *A ridge in the sand indicates a golden mole foraging tunnel. The moles make ridges close to the surface, but most species also dig deeper nesting burrows.*

chases, but effectively form permanent pitfall traps into which worms, beetles, and insect larvae fall. The mole simply patrols its tunnels eating whatever it finds, including slugs, snails, and spiders. Many species store earthworms, semiimmobilizing them with a bite to the head. Some moles eat plant matter too, and certain western American moles can cause problems by eating bulbs and garden crops.

Desmans eat aquatic insects, water snails, crustaceans, and in the case of the Russian desman, fish and amphibians. Golden moles eat earthworms, insect larvae, termites, and millipedes. One species catches legless lizards that burrow in the soil.

Moles are very active and need to eat frequently. Like shrews, they need to consume large quantities because earthworms and other invertebrates are mostly water, with a relatively low nutritional content. European moles spend about four hours eating, then four hours resting, day and night, for most of the year. Digging also uses a lot of energy.

⊙ *A hairy-tailed mole from the United States and Canada. The hairy-tailed is a typical mole with enlarged forefeet for digging, tiny eyes, and a long, sensitive nose.*

Golden moles reduce their energy requirements, and hence their food intake, by not controlling their resting body temperature. They go into torpor daily or in response to cold, saving energy needed to keep warm.

Going Underground

Moles dig by bracing themselves with their back legs, then, pushing their hands into the soil, they scoop it sideways and behind, almost in a breaststroke motion. When they dig deep tunnels, they make "mole hills" by periodically making a vertical shaft and pushing the soil up from below with the palm of one hand. Some species do not burrow deeply and just make subsurface runs, raising earth into a continuous ridge, rather than heaps.

For moles the breeding season is short and marked by intense activity. As the season approaches, the sex glands and reproductive tracts of both sexes enlarge, then swiftly shrink again as soon as the season passes.

Moles are seen as pests by farmers, gardeners, and golf greenkeepers, since their tunneling can disturb and kill young plants and leaves unsightly molehills. Moles are usually controlled using poisoned worms inserted into the tunnels. In the past European moles were trapped to supply a huge trade in moleskin fur. Professional mole catchers earned their living by ridding fields of moles and selling millions of skins into the fur trade for use mainly in trimming hats, coat cuffs, and collars.

The Russian desman is highly valued for its fur. Because of widespread trapping, the species is now rare and listed by the IUCN as Vulnerable. Five other species are Endangered, and two species (the small-toothed and Persian moles) are Critically Endangered. Over half of the 21 species of golden moles are threatened, mainly due to habitat degradation. The human population in Africa is encroaching on golden mole habitats through urbanization, mining, and poor agricultural practices. The animals are also preyed on by domestic cats and dogs.

⊖ *A Juliana's golden mole photographed in Pretoria, South Africa. Golden moles share many features with true moles, although the two families have evolved in complete isolation from each other.*

Common name European mole (moldewarp and want are two Old English names still occasionally used)

Scientific name *Talpa europaea*

Family Talpidae

Order Insectivora

Size Length head/body: 5.5–6 in (14–15 cm); tail length: 0.8 in (2 cm). Male usually somewhat larger than female

Weight 2.5–4.5 oz (70–130 g)

Key features Unmistakable, cylindrical black animal with enormous hands, pink snout, and no obvious ears or eyes

Habits Solitary; territorial; active at all times of day or night, mostly underground; makes heaps of soil ejected from tunnels; breeding nest is ball of grass, often below an extralarge molehill called a fortress

Breeding Three or 4 young born between March and June after gestation period of 28 days (sometimes second litter in same year). Weaned at 35–40 days; sexually mature at 11 months. May live up to 7 years in the wild, not normally kept in captivity

Voice Usually silent, but squeaks aggressively if attacked

Diet Worms, insect larvae, beetles, and other soil animals; occasional carrion

Habitat Fields, woodlands, and gardens; absent from sand dunes, mountainsides, and other places with barren soil

Distribution From Britain to central Russia south to the Mediterranean; absent from Ireland and many other islands

Status Population: abundant

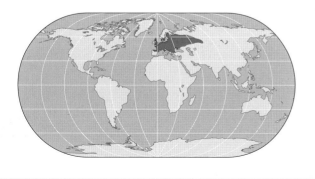

European Mole

*Talpa
europaea*

Moles live alone and are highly adapted for a subterranean burrowing existence. They are fascinating creatures, but generally unpopular with farmers and gardeners, despite all the soil pests they consume.

THE CHARACTERISTIC HEAPS OF SOIL pushed up by moles from their subterranean tunnels are a familiar sight in the countryside. However, relatively few people have ever seen a live mole because the animal spends almost all its time underground. Since it is hidden in its subterranean environment, people are largely unaware of what it does except when it ejects piles of soil onto prized lawns and flower beds. At such times gardeners become apoplectic, convinced that they are the victims of a mole conspiracy. Farmers curse the soil heaps and stones, since they blunt harvesting machinery. People will go to huge lengths to banish moles from their property, but their efforts are mostly in vain. The European mole is a fascinating and highly adapted mammal, but most people just want to know how to get rid of it!

Digging Muscles

The mole is a cylindrical creature whose head appears to be joined to the body with no neck. Big hands stick out from the shoulders as though the animals had no arms, giving moles powerful leverage in their forelimbs. The upper arm bone is short and almost rectangular, allowing a relatively enormous area for the attachment of massive digging muscles. Anyone who picks up a live mole is immediately astonished by how immensely powerful it is. The tiny creature is able to break a human grip, forcing fingers apart as though thrusting aside heavy soil. The hind legs are slender and used to propel the animal along its tunnels. They can be jammed into the burrow wall to steady the mole when using its front feet to dig. Since the animal's weight rests on its belly, not on its legs,

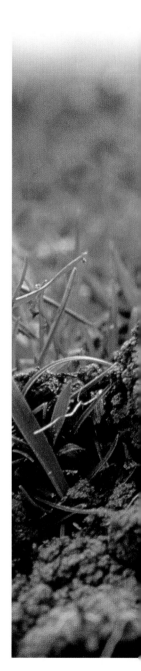

the skin of the underside is extrathick; in most mammals the belly skin is thinnest.

The head seems to have no ears, since they are tiny and hidden among the fur. There seem to be no eyes either, and moles are often said to be blind. In fact, the eyes are the size of pinheads and normally kept closed. Vision is not good, but moles can see movement and also tell light from dark, but they cannot distinguish colors. The mole's snout ends in a flat plate, like a pig's nose. This area of bare pink skin is highly sensitive to touch. Special pimples called Eimer's organs cover the surface and detect the tiniest movements, temperature changes, and perhaps other sensations too. The organs help the mole detect its prey in the underground darkness.

The tail is special, too, and carried pointing upward like a flagpole. Stiff hairs are linked to sense organs in the tail itself, and they help the mole detect obstacles. They are especially useful when the mole

travels backward, feeling its way as it goes along. Moles can run backward almost as fast as they go forward. A normal mammal's fur points backward and would poke into the tightly fitting burrow walls, causing the animal to become jammed in a tunnel. But the mole's fur does not have the characteristic "lie." Instead, the hairs can point either forward or backward with equal ease. In addition, the hairs are fine and silky, giving the mole a velvety feel. Mole fur was formerly valued for the making of moleskin waistcoats and coat collars.

The fur is longer in winter than in summer, and the hairs are unusual in being of almost uniform length over the whole body. Almost all moles are black, but gray, white, and even orange varieties occur. The mole's streamlined body and fur hide any obvious signs of sex organs, so there is little visible difference between males and females. Moles tell the difference by using scent, and the belly fur is often discolored by brownish secretions that are particularly noticeable in the breeding season. Scent is enormously important to moles.

⊕ A European mole emerges from a hole. The molehills created by the animal's industrious tunneling are the scourge of gardeners and farmers alike.

Worm Larders

Worms are essential to moles. A mole will collect surplus worms and bite their head ends, leaving the worms alive but unable to burrow. The paralyzed prey is stashed away in a small chamber off the main burrow, ready for future use. Some larders may contain over 450 worms. A mole needs to eat about half its own weight of worms per day. These and other prey are attacked ferociously with the mole's 44 sharp teeth. However, earthy food like worms cause the teeth to become worn down by the large amount of grit in their bodies. Despite wear and tear on their teeth, some moles manage to live for up to seven years. Blunted teeth would be an important factor in not surviving longer.

They leave scent on the tunnel walls, which is renewed every time the animal brushes by. The scent acts as a warning to others to stay away. It is an effective deterrent, since moles are almost never found occupying each other's tunnels. They live a totally solitary life, belligerently expelling intruders, except for a brief period of a few hours each year when the female will tolerate the presence of a male. Males must be checking on the females all the time, constantly waiting for a scent message to say that it is safe to approach.

Early Departures

Moles breed when they are one year old. The female gives birth to three or four young in about April or May (later in northern Europe). The babies weigh about one-tenth of an ounce each (3.5 g) and are naked and blind. Their fur grows when they are two weeks old, and they become independent about five weeks after birth. Juvenile moles soon leave their mother's tunnel system, or she drives them away. She will not tolerate lodgers competing for food, even her own family. Some females will have a second litter that season. The small litters seem to be just enough to maintain the population without large fluctuations in numbers, as seen so often among rodents.

⊕ *A mole eating a worm. Worms are a favorite food item, but the animals also take slugs and insect larvae.*

Although moles are supremely adapted to living in their burrows—where they spend most of their time—they are also sometimes active at the surface. Young moles need to find an unoccupied area in which to set up home. They can disperse faster by traveling on the surface than by burrowing underground and do so under cover of darkness. Shortage of food may also bring moles above ground. They emerge in dry summers when earthworms burrow deep in the soil, and the mole's normal supply dwindles dangerously. Many moles then venture to the surface at night to seek other food in the dew-dampened grass. Here they may get caught by owls or cats, but otherwise they have little to fear from predators for most of their life.

Woodland Habitats

The mole's main habitat is woodland. Its presence there is often unsuspected because the molehills are hidden by fallen leaves. Here they may live at a density of 1 to 2 per acre (2.5 to 5 per ha). They are more obvious in farmland, especially where the habitat is rich in food. Here there may be up to four times as many moles living in good pastureland. Moles also invade arable crops, but deep plowing makes life difficult for them at least once a year. Winter floods may force moles to retreat from low-lying areas, but their spread back is evident from the lines of molehills marching outward from hedge banks and higher ground. Moles also occur up to 3,000 feet (1,000 m) above sea level, but tend to be rarer at high altitudes. Their scarcity in such regions is partly due to the poor soil. Wet and cold moorland conditions also mean that vital worms are in short supply.

It is a popular misconception that moles dig through the soil to catch worms. Yet what the mole actually does is excavate a series of tunnels that serve as a giant pitfall trap for any worms, beetles, and other minibeasts that

happen to be wriggling through the soil. If they break into the tunnel or fall through the roof, they are exposed to a patrolling mole, which swiftly gobbles up the unlucky visitors. Where plenty of soil animals are present, a mole can get by with a fairly small tunnel system. In poor, sandy soils, where worms and other small prey are infrequent, each mole needs a more extensive burrow network, and the mole population density is lower.

The mole alternates between periods of activity (spent digging, feeding, and patrolling the tunnels) and rest periods when it returns to the nest to sleep. Moles usually start work each day at the same time. What influences their accurate timekeeping is a mystery, since it is always pitch black underground. In winter they may still start their activity periods at the same times, even though it is probably not yet dawn in the world above.

Each mole has its own private tunnel system spread over about 2,000 square yards (1,670 sq. m). Females tend to remain in the same area throughout their life, but males travel more widely. In the breeding season they can double the extent of their tunnel system in the hope of encountering female moles. If a mole is removed from its burrow system, its tunnels are swiftly occupied by other moles. Scent probably helps the moles know when there are vacant tunnels ready to be taken over. Perhaps underground vibrations also give clues to the presence or absence of a neighbor in nearby tunnel systems.

↑ *Four-week-old European moles in a nest. As soon as they are weaned, the mother expels them from her territory, and they start the perilous search for their own place to live.*

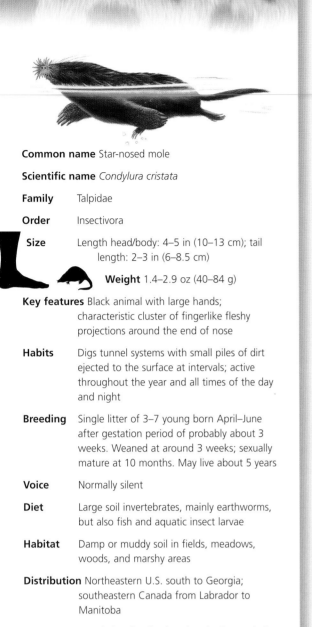

Common name Star-nosed mole

Scientific name *Condylura cristata*

Family	Talpidae
Order	Insectivora
Size	Length head/body: 4–5 in (10–13 cm); tail length: 2–3 in (6–8.5 cm)

Weight 1.4–2.9 oz (40–84 g)

Key features	Black animal with large hands; characteristic cluster of fingerlike fleshy projections around the end of nose
Habits	Digs tunnel systems with small piles of dirt ejected to the surface at intervals; active throughout the year and all times of the day and night
Breeding	Single litter of 3–7 young born April–June after gestation period of probably about 3 weeks. Weaned at around 3 weeks; sexually mature at 10 months. May live about 5 years
Voice	Normally silent
Diet	Large soil invertebrates, mainly earthworms, but also fish and aquatic insect larvae
Habitat	Damp or muddy soil in fields, meadows, woods, and marshy areas
Distribution	Northeastern U.S. south to Georgia; southeastern Canada from Labrador to Manitoba
Status	Population: locally abundant in the north, but scattered and less common in the south

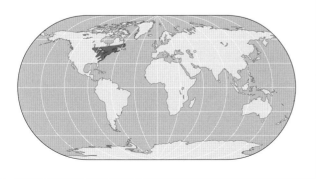

 SEE ALSO Mole, European **9**:44

Star-Nosed Mole

Condylura cristata

The star-nosed mole looks quite unlike any other mammal. It boasts a bunch of 22 fleshy projections encircling its nostrils, appearing like a pink flower at the end of the animal's nose.

STAR-NOSED MOLES LIVE IN DAMP and very wet soil, in contrast to other mole species that often prefer drier places. They create tunnels about 2 inches (5 cm) in diameter by compressing the earth to the sides or pushing it up as a ridge on the surface of the ground. They also dig burrows by scraping away earth with their very large, square hands and pushing it to the surface at intervals to form molehills. They are about 12 to 24 inches (30 to 60 cm) wide and can be up to 6 inches (15 cm) high. In wet ground the water table (the level at which the soil is completely saturated, and burrows will become flooded) is quite near the surface and limits how deep the mole can dig. Mostly the network of tunnels is just below the surface, but in drier ground burrows may be as much as 24 inches (60 cm) deep. The burrow system has a number of chambers, at least one of which will be furnished with a nest made of dry vegetation about 6 inches (15 cm) in diameter. It is normally constructed above the level at which the soil is saturated, sometimes even above the surface of the ground, but safely tucked away underneath a log or tree stump and linked by tunnels to the main burrow system.

The star-nosed mole patrols its network of tunnels in search of food in the form of soil invertebrates that fall into the underground passageways. They include earthworms, insect larvae, and small mollusks. Although most of its time is spent underground, the star-nosed mole

⊕ The star-nosed mole sometimes comes to the surface at night to forage for worms lying in the damp grass.

also comes to the surface at night and often forages extensively there, particularly in search of worms that lie around in damp grass on moist summer evenings.

Indigestible Diet

Many of the invertebrates that the moles eat have a high proportion of their body made up of indigestible materials such as shells and exoskeletons. Worms have a very high water content and also contain large amounts of dirt. Consequently, the star-nosed mole has to eat large quantities of that kind of food in order to get enough nourishment from its diet, which requires the mole to be active both day and night and also throughout the year.

During the winter it may construct a series of tunnels under the snow that enable it to forage on the ground surface without being exposed to predators. Part of the tunnel system is often

flooded, and there is usually at least one tunnel entrance that opens underwater. Living in such wet places, the mole needs its waterproof fur in order to keep warm. The star-nosed mole is at home in the water, and it is also a very competent swimmer, using all four feet to propel itself. In winter it will dive and swim under the ice. Diving enables the mole to obtain food from the bottom of ponds and streams. It can remain submerged for long enough to search for aquatic insects, small fish, and crustaceans. They represent an additional source of nourishment to food that the mole finds in its own tunnels. The peculiar fingerlike fleshy appendages at the end of the snout are used to feel for and recognize prey. These sensitive projections can be used to help manipulate food. They are constantly moving, except for the two middle ones on top of the snout, which point forward like fingers. These additional sensory structures on the snout of

Peculiar Projections

The star-nosed mole's scientific name, *Condylura cristata*, draws attention to the peculiar structures on the nose—*crista* meaning "crest" or tuft. The fleshy fingerlike projections are extremely sensitive and help the animal feel for its prey, both in the darkness of the burrow system and also underwater. The sensitivity is partly due to large numbers of so-called Eimer's organs, like microscopic goose pimples on the surface of the thin skin. The projections around the end of the snout are not just sensitive to touch, but may also be able to detect minute electrical disturbances in the water created by muscle and nerve activity in the mole's prey. The projections are also capable of being moved and can be used to help manipulate the mole's food. The name *Condylura*, meaning "lumpy tail," is a reference to an old illustration of the animal that showed a knobby tail. However, live animals do not have a lumpy tail, and it is possible that the drawing was made from a badly preserved animal in which the tail had dried into a lumpy condition.

the star-nosed mole must be very useful, since its eyes and ears are tiny and buried among the dense fur. Eyes especially are of little use underground—an enhanced sense of touch is much more help.

Shared Burrows

Moles are generally solitary animals, each one occupying a home range covering about 0.9 acres (0.4 ha). However, unlike most other species of mole, the male and female star-nosed mole may live together, sharing the same burrow system at least during the winter.

The summer coat is molted in September or October, and a dense winter coat replaces it. At this time of year the tails of both sexes become enlarged with stored fat. It probably serves as an energy reserve to help tide the animals over during periods of food shortage.

Litters are mostly born in May or June, but can be as early as March or as late as August. The young are born into a nest made of dry grass and leaves collected at the surface. Breeding nests are generally larger and more elaborate than those used at other times. At birth the young are naked except for a few short whiskers on the snout, but they soon grow a covering of fine hair. They produce their first young in the spring following their birth. Generally, the population density is about one per acre (2 per ha), but in good swampy habitats there may be five times that number.

The species spends more time on the surface than is usual among moles, exposing it to greater risk of predation. A variety of carnivores eat star-nosed moles, ranging from house cats to snakes, and even large-mouth bass. Generally speaking, star-nosed moles do not encroach on human activities. That is partly because their home, low-lying wet ground, is not an economically important habitat. However, where the moles invade golf courses or lawns, their molehills are unwelcome.

⊖ *The star-nosed mole's unique nose is divided into a number of fleshy tentacles that are used for locating prey both in the soil and underwater.*

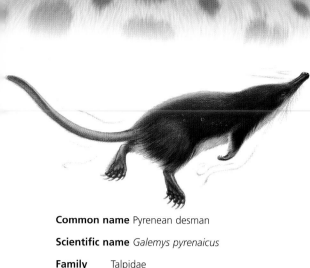

Common name Pyrenean desman

Scientific name *Galemys pyrenaicus*

Family Talpidae

Order Insectivora

Size Length head/body: 4–6 in (10–15 cm); tail length: 5–6 in (12–15 cm)

Weight 1.8–2.8 oz (50–80 g)

Key features Chubby animal with short neck and long, mobile nose; small eyes and ears; long tail whose tip is flattened from side to side; fur dark brown or black, with gray or brown belly

Habits Nocturnal; swims and dives, comes ashore to feed and to groom fur

Breeding Litters of 1–4 young born up to twice a year after gestation period of about 1 month. Weaned at 4–5 weeks; sexually mature at 1 year. May live up to 5 years in the wild, rarely kept in captivity

Voice Normally silent, loud shriek if attacked

Diet Freshwater invertebrates, including crustaceans and various insect larvae

Habitat Mountain streams, marshes, and other pollution-free waterside habitats

Distribution Pyrenees (France and Spain), small area of northern Spain, and Portugal

Status Population: unknown; IUCN Vulnerable. Small numbers in scattered localities; rare and declining

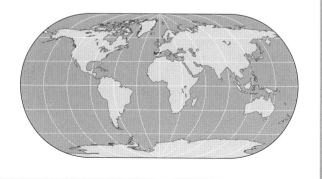

Pyrenean Desman

Galemys pyrenaicus

Desmans look more like giant shrews than moles. They are adapted for life foraging in water, but are critically affected by developments that reduce the supply of aquatic invertebrates on which they feed.

DESMANS ARE WELL ADAPTED to their life in water. Their long tail is partially flattened to form a rudder. The feet are fringed with stiff bristles to gain better propulsion in the water, and the hind feet are webbed. The toes of the front feet are partially webbed and bear strong claws for getting a grip on slippery rocks and stones. The fur is very soft and dense, with long glossy hairs that glint like metal in the light and shed water readily when the animal shakes itself. Desmans have poor vision, but good hearing and an acute sense of smell.

Pair Bonds

The animals are generally intolerant of each other, but live in stable pairs, defending a shared territory. They are mostly nocturnal, but often come out briefly during the day. They spend their active time hunting for food in the water, swimming and diving rapidly, investigating every nook and cranny among the stones and underwater vegetation using their long, flexible nose. They bring food ashore to eat and need to find up to half their own body weight of food every 24 hours. They also spend a lot of time constantly grooming their fur to ensure that it does not lose its key warmth-retention and waterproof qualities. The day is spent safely asleep in a burrow above the water level. Desmans defend their territory by driving off intruders and by leaving scent marks. Each occupies a range of about 300 yards (270 m) of stream, but may need more if food is scarce.

The animals live in the cold waters of fast-flowing mountain streams in the Pyrenees. On the French side of the mountain range they

⊕ *The Pyrenean desman lives in waterside habitats in the Pyrenees, northern Spain, and Portugal. Water quality is very important to desmans, and increasing pollution is threatening their survival.*

The Russian desman is the only other species of desman that exists today. Desmans were once widespread across Europe, with fossils being found as far west as Britain. Both desman species are classified as Vulnerable by the IUCN.

occur in nine river systems, but on the Spanish side their distribution is less precisely known. Desmans also occur in northern Portugal and a small area of northern-central Spain. They are sometimes found in marshes and beside lakes and slow-flowing waters such as canals. Desmans eat a variety of freshwater invertebrates, particularly small shrimp and the larvae of various aquatic insects such as stoneflies and caddis flies. Tiny fish may also be on the menu occasionally. The food is not chewed, but rapidly crushed by the desman's 44 sharply pointed teeth, then swallowed swiftly before the animal sets off to find more.

The invertebrates on which desmans feed are very abundant in the cold, well-oxygenated water of mountain streams, but they are very sensitive to pollution. Water quality is therefore of vital importance to desmans, and increasing levels of pollution pose a serious threat to their continued survival. Moreover, many fast-flowing streams and rivers are dammed to create opportunities for the generation of hydroelectricity. This represents a major transformation of the natural freshwater ecosystem. Below the dam water flow is much reduced and may stop altogether during periods of low rainfall in the summer. Above the dam fast-flowing water is replaced by a static lake, whose waters may become quite warm, especially at the edges. Warm water carries less oxygen and supports fewer of the desman's prey, which are very sensitive to oxygen levels in the water.

Tourism Threats

Further threats come from the development of water-based tourism that affects the composition of waterside vegetation. It is especially significant where fishermen operate or boats are pulled in and out of the water, which interferes with the places that desmans make their burrows. Clearance of fringing plants also exposes the animals to greater risk of predation. Desmans are regarded with suspicion by some fishermen, who fear that they may eat trout. A developing threat comes from the escape of American mink from fur farms in central Spain. If the animals spread widely, desmans are likely to suffer severely from increased levels of predation caused by these voracious carnivores as they spread into their habitat. Many of the areas where desmans live lie within protected parks, but that is still a weak defense against pollution and predators that come in from outside.

The mating season lasts from January until May. Sometimes a second litter is produced in the same season. The young are born with fur already grown. The offspring swiftly disperse once they are weaned, with the young males going farther away than females. Although desmans can sometimes live to be as much as five years old, few actually do so because of the many threats that they face.

Common name American shrew mole (Gibb's shrew mole)

Scientific name *Neurotrichus gibbsi*

Family Talpidae

Order Insectivora

Size Length head/body: 2.5–3 in (6.5–8.5 cm); tail length: 1–2 in (2.5–4 cm)

Weight 0.2–0.4 oz (7–11 g)

Key features Black animal with long, pointed snout; resembles a mole, but without the enormously large front feet projecting to the sides; forefeet larger than in shrews

Habits Active by day and night underground and on the surface

Breeding At least 1 litter of 1–4 young born per year after gestation period of probably about 4 weeks. Weaned at about 3 weeks; sexually mature at about 1 year, perhaps less. Probably may live about 2 years

Voice Extremely quiet twittering noise

Diet Small invertebrates, particularly worms and insect larvae

Habitat Deep soil in mountain forests and shady ravines up to 8,200 ft (2,500 m) above sea level

Distribution Coastal range of central California, through Washington and Oregon to southwestern British Columbia

Status Population: unknown. Fairly abundant where it occurs

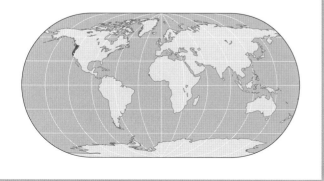

American Shrew Mole

Neurotrichus gibbsi

Not quite a mole, but bigger and more specialized than a shrew, the shrew mole is aptly named.

THE SHREW MOLE IS THE SMALLEST of the American moles, but has a distinctly longer tail. It is not so fully adapted for an underground existence as a true mole, but nevertheless has many appropriate modifications for that way of life. Its eyes are tiny, being little use underground, and they are buried in the fur of the face, protecting them from dirt. The shrew mole has no ears projecting from its smooth head, just minute holes that open deep within the fur. The nostrils open on the sides of the snout toward the tip, where they are less likely to become plugged with soil during burrowing.

The front feet are not enormously enlarged as they are in typical moles, but the three middle claws on each foot are lengthened to assist with digging. In contrast, the feet of shrews are not modified at all. The heavy head and powerful jaws are like those of true moles, but the fur is more like that of a shrew, being soft and dense with a slight gloss and varying from sooty black to dark gray. Curiously, the American shrew mole is more closely related to the two species of Japanese mole (*Urotrichus*) than to any of the American mole species that live much nearer.

Mountain Mole

The shrew mole lives at altitudes from sea level up to more than 8,200 feet (2,500 m). Its main home is on the Pacific slopes of the Cascade Mountains, although the shrew mole is also found occasionally on the eastern slopes and is widespread in the coastal range of northern California. The shrew mole prefers the moist, deep soil that forms a soft blanket on the mountain slopes under trees and shrubs. It forages on the surface of the ground, but mostly searches for prey in a complex system of

 SEE ALSO Shrew Family, The **9:**28; Mole Family, The **9:**40

runways excavated just below the surface and among the leaf litter. The shrew mole uses its special front claws to excavate true burrows about 1 inch (2.5 cm) in diameter in the top layer of the soil, rarely going deeper than about 12 inches (30 cm).

The burrows are formed by pushing aside and compressing the earth to make the tunnel walls—dirt is not pushed to the surface as molehills. The tunnel system is ventilated by small shafts opening at the surface.

The shrew mole is not entirely adapted for a life underground the way that true moles are, but still has a number of adaptations to a burrowing lifestyle.

Increased Agility

Unlike a true mole, the shrew mole can bring its front feet underneath the body instead of having them permanently stuck out to the sides. This makes it a more agile animal, and it will sometimes even climb into low bushes, presumably in search of food. It can also swim.

The shrew mole does not hibernate. It is active all year round and also during both day and night. It searches for various soil invertebrates, especially earthworms, but also eats large quantities of insects and their larvae. In fact, a shrew mole will consume up to one and a half times its own weight of food in a day, equivalent to a man eating a large barrowload of hamburgers.

Shrew moles tend to be patchy in their distribution, since mountain slopes are often too rocky or too dry to accommodate them. Where they occur, there are often about 5 or 6 shrew moles per acre (12 to 15 per ha). The animals seem to be relatively tolerant of each other's company and may even live in loose groups, rather than as solitary individuals the way that true moles do.

Year-Round Breeding

Shrew moles nest above ground, and they appear to breed throughout the year except during the midwinter period. Females probably produce more than one litter in a year. Litters are small, varying between one and four young. Newborn shrew moles are blind, pink, and helpless. Each measures about 1 inch (2.5 cm) long, and a whole family of four weighs only about one-tenth of an ounce (3 g).

Since it does not create molehills, the species is less of a nuisance than many other molelike animals. Indeed, the shrew mole is probably wholly beneficial because it destroys many insect pests and also helps aerate the soil.

Common name Grant's golden mole (desert golden mole)

Scientific name *Eremitalpa granti*

Family   Chrysochloridae

Order   Insectivora

Size   Length head/body: 3–3.5 in (8–9 cm)

Weight   About 0.5–1 oz (14–28 g)

       Key features Smallest of the golden
       moles, with pale silvery fur

Habits   Makes shallow burrows in sand; probably
       mainly forages on the surface at night

Breeding Probably gives birth in October or November;
       average litter size likely to be small, since the
       few pregnant females found so far contained
       only a single embryo each. Rate of
       development not known. Life span also
       unknown, but probably about 3 years

Voice   Normally silent

Diet   Insects; spiders; also small reptiles dug from
       shallow burrows in the sand or among grass
       roots

Habitat   Coastal sand dunes

Distribution Narrow fringe of southwestern Africa,
       including Cape Province and Little
       Namaqualand (South Africa) and part of
       Namibia

Status   Population: unknown. Rare

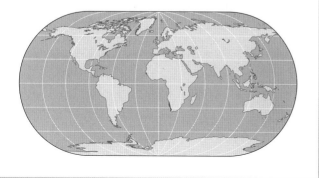

Grant's Golden Mole

Eremitalpa granti

The tiny and rare Grant's golden mole lives in the loose sands of the Namib coast, a remote area whose small mammals have been infrequently studied.

GRANT'S GOLDEN MOLE IS A desert species. It has long, silky fur, which varies in color from an elegant pale gray to creamy white. The fine hairs tend to turn yellow with increasing age, while the tips of the hairs glisten, giving the animal a silvery sheen. Superficially the species looks like other golden moles, with no visible ears, eyes, or tail. There is also a shiny pad on the nose. However, there are differences in the structure of the skull, and—unlike other golden moles—Grant's golden mole has three enlarged claws on its front feet, which are of similar length. There is also a prominent patch of thick skin on the heels of the hind feet. The head of Grant's golden mole appears disproportionately large for its short, fat body.

Shifting Sands

Grant's golden mole is named after Captain C. H. B. Grant, the man who discovered it while collecting specimens for the Natural History Museum in London. It is also known as the desert golden mole, although it does not occur widely in the deserts of southern Africa. Instead, it lives along the coastal strip of southwestern Africa. Here, there are hundreds of miles of white sand dunes with shifting, windblown sand facing the sea. Sparse vegetation helps keep the sand from blowing around, but the terrain is generally unstable. The area is the home of Grant's golden mole, rather than farther inland where the sand is stable and the soil more compacted.

    The animal lives a highly specialized existence, apparently forcing its way through soft sand that often collapses behind it. The golden mole's body is somewhat flattened, a

  SEE ALSO Mole Rat Family, The **8**:56; Mole, American Shrew **9**:54

feature that may help the animal push its way through loose sand. The snout and large claws are also useful for such tunneling activity. The claws are broad, curved, and hollowed out on the underside. They no doubt scoop away the loose sand more efficiently than if they were flat or rounded, as in other golden moles that tend to dig in more consolidated soils. Grant's golden mole forces the sand to one side or into a ridge on the surface as the animal moves along. It does not push the sand up into typical molehills. The tunnels are often quite extensive and can sometimes be traced for 50 yards (46 m) or more. The shallow surface burrows are not permanent, but sometimes they connect with deeper shafts that may go several feet down into the ground. It is possible that the young are born in deep chambers, rather than in the unstable surface tunnels.

⊕ *A Grant's golden mole feasts on a locust, a change from its usual diet of soft-bodied termites. The largest recorded prey item is the web-footed gecko, a kind of nocturnal lizard.*

Grant's golden mole does not need a permanent tunnel system to collect food the way true moles do. Instead, the golden moles venture onto the surface at night under cover of darkness. There they travel long distances: The tracks of a single animal have been followed for nearly 6,500 yards (5,880 m). The average home range extends over about 11 acres (4.6 ha), with the individual moles operating alone. They tend to avoid each other while foraging, but do not defend exclusive territories. The animals visit a different part of their home range every night as they forage for insects. They particularly favor termites, but also the larvae of small desert beetles. They sometimes catch spiders and crickets, and may forage in the dry riverbeds where there is a greater variety of food. Studies of the stomach contents of Grant's golden moles invariably reveal large quantities of sand, presumably taken in along with their prey.

At the end of the night the desert golden mole usually retreats underground. An ideal spot is a nest in a shallow burrow under vegetation, where roots and leaf litter have helped stabilize the shifting sand. Normally the animal uses different daytime shelters rather than returning to the same place day after day. It can therefore exploit a wide area when foraging—a useful strategy, since sand dunes rarely support a high density of invertebrate food.

TREE AND ELEPHANT SHREWS

Tree shrews and elephant shrews are small, lively animals that are predominantly insectivorous. However, most species in both groups will also eat a variety of plant matter.

Elephant shrews live in Africa in a range of habitats from forests to savannas and deserts. They are mouse- to rat-sized balls of fluff with long, skinny legs like a miniature antelope, a ratlike tail covered in small bristles, and a long, flexible snout that looks a bit like an elephant's trunk. They are much bigger than true shrews (family Soricidae). Although their shape and diet are similar, they are not related. Some people prefer to refer to them by their African name of *sengi*.

Tree shrews are even less appropriately named. They are squirrel-like animals that live in the rain forests of India and Southeast Asia. They do not look much like shrews, having a short snout and bushy tail, and most spend very little time in trees.

⬿ *Representative species of tree shrews: the largely arboreal pygmy tree shrew (1); the arboreal pen-tailed tree shrew holding an insect in its front paws (2); the Philippine tree shrew—the largest species of tree shrew (3).*

Classifying tree shrews and elephant shrews has always been a problem. Tree shrews share many characteristics with animals as diverse as squirrels and primates; elephant shrews have features that are also seen in true shrews, rabbits, and even hyraxes. Both groups of animals were once classified as members of the order Insectivora. Then the tree shrews were thought to be primitive primates, while the elephant shrews were believed to be distant cousins of ungulates. For a while they were put together in a group called the Menotyphla. Then elephant shrews were grouped with rabbits and hares. Recent molecular studies have shown that they are distinct from each other and from other groups of mammals. They have now each been given their own orders: Scandentia (meaning "climbers") for tree shrews and Macroscelidea for the elephant shrews.

Tree Shrews

Tree shrews look and act like long-nosed squirrels. Nearly all are active by day, but the pen-tailed tree shrew is nocturnal. It is also the smallest of all the tree shrews; and unlike the others, it has long whiskers and a tail that is bare except at the tip. It is so different from the other tree shrews that it is classified in its own subfamily.

Like squirrels, tree shrews dash up and down tree trunks and dart around on the ground, nosing through leaf litter. They are constantly on the go, trying to find enough insects, fruit, and seeds to meet the needs of their extremely rapid metabolism. Fruit bats are the only animals that digest their food more quickly.

Tree shrews live as pairs or in small, loose groups. Males may mate with more

⊖ *A checkered elephant shrew forages on the forest floor. Elephant shrews rely on camouflage to avoid being caught by a predator—if that fails, they use their long legs to outrun a snake or other carnivore.*

→ *Representative species of elephant shrews: North African elephant shrew (1); short-eared elephant shrew (2); four-toed elephant shrew (3); black and rufous elephant shrew tearing at prey (4).*

than one female. They can breed through most of the year and quickly colonize new areas. Litter size is one to three, usually matching the number of pairs of teats in the females, which differs between species.

Tree shrews pay less attention to their young than almost any other mammal, apart from some seals. Mothers park their babies in a nest and visit briefly once every two days, giving them fewer than 10 minutes to drink enough milk to last until the next visit. The milk has an extremely high fat and protein content. The protein helps the young grow quickly, and the fat provides energy for warmth, since the babies do not share their mother's body heat by sleeping with her.

Elephant Shrews

Like tree shrews, and unlike most other small mammals, elephant shrews are active during the day, foraging for insects, fruit, seeds, and leaves. At night most sleep in leafy nests or deserted rodent burrows. Some do not use a nest at all, but simply "lie low" like many antelope.

Elephant shrews are secretive and swift, bounding or running fast when alarmed. Many species make networks of trails, clearing paths of debris with a sweep of their forearms: Clear escape routes are vital when fleeing from predators. Monogamous pairs stay together for life, defending their shared territory against rivals.

The earliest fossil elephant shrews are from the Eocene epoch, 50 million years ago, but they reached their maximum diversity during the Miocene, 24 million years ago, when there were six subfamilies. Today only two subfamilies remain.

59

Common name Common tree shrew

Scientific name *Tupaia glis*

Family Tupaiidae

Order Scandentia

Size Length head/body: 5.5–6 in (14–15 cm); tail length: 6–6.5 in (15–16.5 cm)

Weight 3.5–7 oz (100–200 g)

Key features Small, squirrel-like animal with a sharply pointed nose; coat color olive to dark brown on back and flanks, creamy white to orange-red below; tail covered in long hairs like a squirrel; emits a distinctly musky smell

Habits Active during the day; forages on the ground or in low bushes; nests in tree roots and among fallen timber

Breeding Twins born after gestation period of 40–52 days. Weaned at 5 weeks; sexually mature at 4 months. May live 12.5 years in captivity, unlikely to survive as long in the wild

Voice Squeals, squeaks, hisses, and chattering alarm calls

Diet Insects, fruit, seeds, and leaves

Habitat Tropical rain forest

Distribution Southern Malay Peninsula, Sumatra, and surrounding islands

Status Population: unknown, but likely to be many thousands. Habitats threatened by deforestation, so numbers likely to be declining

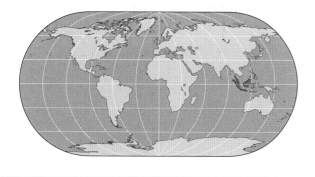

Common Tree Shrew

Tupaia glis

Resembling a squirrel with a pointed nose, the tree shrew is a lively creature, constantly on the move and foraging for food. All most people see of it is a flash of brown fur as it dashes up a tree or dives into a bush.

TREE SHREWS LOOK MUCH more like long-nosed squirrels than shrews. They have a long tail, about the same length as the body and covered in long hairs. The tails of most other tree shrews are only sparsely haired. However, squirrels are rodents with a completely different dentition. Tree shrews have numerous sharp, pointed teeth for snatching and chopping up insects— they do not gnaw as rodents do.

Tree shrews are incredibly lively animals. They are active during the day, spending most of their time in low undergrowth or on the ground. At night they nest among tree roots, fallen timber, or inside hollow bamboo stems. Like other tree shrews, the common tree shrew is omnivorous, eating a wide range of invertebrates, but also fruit, seeds, and leaves. When it feeds, it often sits on its haunches, holding food in its front paws like a squirrel.

Boundary Conflicts

Common tree shrews often form loose social groups of an adult pair together with their recent offspring. However, males will generally mate with more than one female. Common tree shrews are territorial, with each individual fiercely defending its patch against rivals. Boundary conflicts are always between the same sex; although the territories of males and females overlap, they do not fight each other when they meet. Territories are usually about

2.5 acres (1 ha) in size. Males have larger territories than females, which may overlap with areas used by more than one female.

The number of animals in an area depends on the quality of the habitat and the amount of food available. In Malaysia populations have been recorded at two to five animals per acre (5 to 12 per ha), while in Thailand populations can reach a relatively dense six to 12 animals per acre (15 to 30 per ha).

Tree shrews communicate using scent and vocalizations. They are more vocal than most other species and use at least five calls, including a chattering alarm call. The sound may encourage other group members to help mob a predator.

Scent is vital in communicating presence and identity. The adults have a strong musky smell, and females wipe scent from their chest glands onto their newborn offspring. If the smell is rubbed off, a mother will not recognize her babies and will eat them.

Common tree shrews can be prolific breeders. They are capable of reproducing throughout the year, but in some parts of their range seasonal changes in food supply mean that breeding is restricted to times of plenty. Soon after giving birth, females can ovulate and become receptive again. They may also be able to delay implantation, keeping a fertilized egg "on hold" before it begins development.

Neglectful Parents

Uniquely among mammals, it is the father that builds the brood nest. His duty done, he abandons his young family. The mother almost completely neglects her blind, hairless offspring. She leaves them in the brood nest, only visiting them for a brief feeding once every two days. She does not even groom them—the babies have to groom each other. What may seem like lazy parenting does have advantages. Time spent running to and from the nest is time that could be spent feeding. Also, by staying away, her musky smell does not attract predators.

Common name Golden-rumped elephant shrew

Scientific name *Rhynchocyon chrysopygus*

Family	Macroscelididae
Order	Macroscelidea
Size	Length head/body: 9–12 in (23.5–31.5 cm); tail length: 7–10 in (19–26.5 cm)

Weight 14.4–15.5 oz (408–440 g)

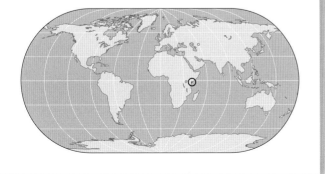

Key features	Size of a large rat, with elongated snout; coat dark reddish-black with yellow patch on rump; black ears, feet, and legs; fur fine, stiff, and glossy; male canine teeth are longer than those of female
Habits	Active during day, foraging in leaf litter; spends nights in leaf nests on forest floor; forms monogamous pairs, but they usually sleep and forage separately
Breeding	Single young born after gestation period of 42 days. Weaned at 2 weeks; sexually mature at perhaps 3–6 months. May live up to 4 years in captivity, similar in the wild
Voice	Range of squeaks and squeals
Diet	Wide variety of invertebrates, including grasshoppers, crickets, beetles, spiders, centipedes, worms, and termites
Habitat	Open coastal forest
Distribution	Kenya
Status	Population: may now be fewer than 5,000, perhaps a fraction of that; IUCN Endangered. Threatened by habitat loss

Golden-Rumped Elephant Shrew

Rhynchocyon chrysopygus

The golden-rumped elephant shrew is a large, fast-running insectivore with a bright-yellow rump. Its coastal forest habitat is being destroyed to make way for urban development and agriculture, so numbers are rapidly declining.

THE GOLDEN-RUMPED ELEPHANT shrew is the largest and most distinctive of all the elephant shrews. It is the size of a large rat, with a long mobile snout like other elephant shrews. The coat is dark reddish with a conspicuous straw-colored patch on the rump. The forehead is grizzled, and the ears, feet, and legs are black. The underparts are slightly paler, and the tail is usually tipped with white. An alert, nervous animal, the elephant shrew's nose, ears, and whiskers are constantly twitching.

Evading Predators

Golden-rumped elephant shrews make a meal for many predators, including black mambas, forest cobras, harrier eagles, eagle owls, local dogs, and even occasionally leopards. But instead of staying hidden as most small animals do, elephant shrews almost seem to demand attention. They are active by day, and the bright golden rump is eye-catching. However, by being alert and aware of the presence of a predator, they are able to judge when they have been spotted. As soon as the predator reveals its intentions, maybe with a slight turn of the head or body movement, the elephant shrew reacts. If the shrew is at a safe distance, it pauses, then repeatedly slaps the leaf litter with its tail. The action tells the predator that it has been spotted and does not stand a chance of catching its prey. The sharp cracking sound carries well through the forest and may also

serve to warn other elephant shrews in the area that a predator is close. If, on the other hand, a predator has been spotted a little too close for comfort, the elephant shrew dashes away, pounding its back legs on the ground as it flees. A golden-rumped elephant shrew can run quickly for its size. Its top speed is about 16 miles per hour (25 km/h), which is about as fast as a person. Its bounding gait enables it to leap over obstacles, usually leaving less agile predators far behind. It bounds away into dense undergrowth, where birds and larger animals cannot follow. The speed of its flight is much faster than any snake can manage in pursuit.

If an elephant shrew is caught, it has another strategy to avoid death. The conspicuous rump patch acts like a target and is usually the first place that a predator strikes. However, the rump skin is much thicker than elsewhere on the body. A bite here is not likely to do much damage, and the animal is far more likely to survive than if bitten on the more vital and vulnerable parts of its body.

⊕ A golden-rumped elephant shrew forages on the forest floor. Like typical shrews, it uses its long, whiskery, flexible nose to probe around in leaf litter, seeking insects and other invertebrates.

At night elephant shrews nest on the ground in hollows lined and covered with leaves. The mounds are 3 feet (1 m) across. Each shrew builds a new nest every couple of days. The process can take two hours. It is usually done in the early morning, when a layer of dew softens the leaves, reducing rustling and making them easier to pack together.

Faithful Pairs

Golden-rumped elephant shrews live in monogamous pairs that stay together for life. Each pair defends a territory averaging 4.2 acres (1.7 ha). Any rival trying to cross a boundary is likely to be seen off in a high-speed chase that may end in a fight. The fights can be serious, since the males use their long canine teeth to gash their opponents. The pairs sleep in separate nests and only spend about a fifth of their active time within eye contact of each other. For most of the day they forage or rest alone, but communicate using scent and sound.

Golden-rumped elephant shrews are able to breed throughout the year. A single infant is born fully furred and well developed. It suckles for a couple of weeks, growing rapidly. It then leaves the nest and forages with its mother for five days. Afterward it becomes fully independent, but stays on the parent's home range for up to 20 weeks before it finds its own territory. Meanwhile, the mother is free to have another baby.

Local people sometimes trap golden-rumped elephant shrews for meat, but the activity is not thought to be a major threat. Far more serious is the destruction of their habitat. The shrews live only in small, isolated patches of coastal forest in Kenya north of Mombasa. As towns grow and people need more timber and more land for agriculture, vulnerable pockets of forest are disappearing. If the forests go, so will the elephant shrews, since they cannot survive on open ground.

ANTEATERS, ARMADILLOS, AND PANGOLINS

This assortment of bizarre-looking creatures comes from three different mammalian orders. They all share the habit of eating ants and other small insects such as termites. Consequently, they all have small teeth, or no teeth at all, since ants do not need much chewing. Some of them are called Edentates, a word that means "without teeth." The word was also used as the old group name for the South American anteaters and their relatives (now classified as the order Xenarthra). In fact, some of those Xenarthrans actually eat plants, but they still have reduced, peglike teeth, so they remain classified with the true anteaters. Ant eating has also evolved in another group—the pangolins. Pangolins have no teeth and feed mainly on ants and termites. They are distinguished by having a body covered in horny plates, including the long tail. The remaining anteater is the aardvark of Africa. This piglike creature eats termites and has teeth that are so different from all other mammals that it is classified in an order of its own.

The true anteaters (order Xenarthra) exhibit many characteristics common to most members of the group. They dig into termite nests with their powerful legs and strong claws. Probing with their tubular nose and flicking their sticky tongue in and out, they lick up insects by the hundred.

Pangolins (order Pholidota) have a similar body shape to anteaters, but are covered in tough, overlapping scales like a pine cone. The scales are like sheets of compressed hair, and are similar in texture (and chemical composition) to fingernails. Their name comes from a Malay word that means "rolling over," since they can curl into a tight ball to protect their vulnerable underparts.

Armadillos (order Xenarthra) are also heavily protected. Their common name is from a Spanish word meaning "little armored one." The shell, or carapace, is made of hard bony plates that cover most of the upper body. The plates in turn are covered by thin sheets of horny material to protect the living bone underneath. The carapace often has joints that form bands over the animal's back to allow it to roll up. The number of joints is the basis for their common names. Three-banded armadillos can roll into a ball, while others tend to pull in their limbs when threatened. Armadillos have a relatively varied diet, eating a range of insects, carrion, and even small vertebrates. Their snout is much shorter than in the animals that specialize in probing into insect nests.

The remaining members of the Xenarthra, the sloths, have become extremely specialized herbivores. They

⊖ *Prehistoric edentates: the giant ground sloth* (Megatherium) *(1);* Eomanis waldi, *an armored pangolin (2); the giant shelled* Glyptodon panochthus *(3); the giant anteater* Scelidotherium *(4).*

1

2

3

4

Who's Who among the Anteaters and their Relatives?

ORDER: Xenarthra—New World anteaters, armadillos, and sloths: 29 or 30 species in 4 families
Family: Myrmecophagidae—true anteaters: 4 species in 3 genera, including giant anteater (*Myrmecophaga tridactyla*); silky anteater (*Cyclopes didactylus*); southern tamandua (*Tamandua tetradactyla*)
Family: Megalonychidae—two-toed sloths: 2 species in 1 genus, Hoffmann's two-toed sloth (*Choloepus hoffmanni*); southern two-toed sloth (*C. didactylus*)
Family: Bradypodidae—three-toed sloths: 3 species in 1 genus, including brown-throated three-toed sloth (*Bradypus variegatus*); maned three-toed sloth (*B. torquatus*)
Family: Dasypodidae—armadillos: 20 or 21 species in 8 genera, including nine-banded or common armadillo (*Dasypus novemcinctus*); giant armadillo (*Priodontes maximus*); lesser fairy armadillo (*Chlamyphorus truncatus*); southern naked-tailed armadillo (*Cabassous unicinctus*)

ORDER: Pholidota—pangolins: 7 species in 1 family
Family: Manidae, includes giant pangolin (Manis gigantea); ground pangolin (*M. temminckii*); tree pangolin (*M. tricuspis*)

ORDER: Tubulidentata—aardvark: 1 species in 1 family
Family: Orycteropodidae, African aardvark (*Orycteropus afer*)

⊖ *A ground pangolin advances across the sand in southern Africa. The ground pangolin is a burrowing species; the circular chambers of its burrows are sometimes big enough for a man to stand up in.*

are included here because of similarities in their skeleton shared with anteaters. Indeed, the word Xenarthra means "strange joints," a reference to the distinctive vertebrae found in both sloths and American anteaters. Sloths eat plants that other animals avoid. Their digestion is incredibly slow—food can sit in the huge stomach for more than a month, apparently to help neutralize plant toxins. Despite their ponderous lifestyles, sloths have become successful mammals in the forests of Central and South America. Sloths do not need the probing muzzle of the insectivorous anteaters and instead have a rounded head, flattened face, and small ears hidden by fur. Their hands and feet have long, curved claws for hanging from branches, and the fur often has a green tinge caused by blue-green algae that grow in grooves in the hair shafts. The coloring helps camouflage the animals in the trees.

The aardvark is a completely weird creature, so different from all other mammals that the single species is classified in the order Tubulidentata all to itself. The name originates from the peculiar teeth that are simple stumps made up of hundreds of tubular sections of hard tooth material. No other mammals have teeth like this, and its nearest living relatives seem to be elephants or hyraxes. The aardvark occupies an ecological niche in Africa similar to the true anteaters of the New World. It has evolved many similar features in a process known as convergent evolution. The name aardvark means "earth pig" in Afrikaans, since the animals live in huge burrows and bear a superficial resemblance to pigs.

Origins

These anteating animals had already followed separate evolutionary paths by the early Tertiary epoch (60 million years ago). The small, armorless animals from which the pangolins are assumed to have descended quickly became extinct. However, the xenarthrans (true anteaters, sloths, and armadillos) were far more successful. Isolated in South America during the Tertiary, they shared that continent with few other mammals. In the absence of competition they evolved into many spectacular forms, including giant sloths and heavily armored armadillolike creatures. One of them, *Glyptodon*, had a carapace the size of a small car. At one time there were 10 times as many xenarthran genera as there are today; but as competitors migrated into South America, only those in specialized niches survived.

ⓐ *The southern naked-tailed armadillo has five curved claws on each of its forefeet. Its gait is unusual—it walks on the soles of its hind feet, but on the tips of the claws on its forefeet.*

Specialized Diets, Shared Adaptations

Pangolins, anteaters, and the aardvark have specialized in eating social insects such as ants and termites. The giant pangolin may eat as many as 200,000 termites in a night. A long nose, conical head, and long tongue with sticky saliva are characteristics shared by them all. In pangolins the salivary gland is huge, holding nearly two cupfuls of saliva. The tongue can be extended 16 inches (40 cm) and is so long that the sheath that houses it is attached to the animal's pelvis. Giant anteaters have a tongue that protrudes even farther, up to 25 inches (64 cm).

Anything that feeds on ants and termites needs some protection from their bites, since armadillos will even eat ferocious fire ants. Aardvarks have thick, tough skin, and pangolins even have thickened eyelids. Giant anteaters have thick skin on their muzzle, but even so, will avoid aggressive, large-jawed solider ants if they can. All species have powerful limbs and strong claws. They are used for digging, breaking into ant nests and termite mounds, slashing at attackers, and in the terrestrial species, for climbing. In aardvarks the claws are wide and hooflike.

Burrowing and Tree-Climbing

Many species in this group are tree-dwellers. All living sloths are arboreal. They come to the ground only once a week, to urinate and defecate. Two of the four African species of pangolin spend most of their time in trees, and both have a long, prehensile tail with a sensitive bare patch at the tip to help grip branches. Asian pangolins are usually terrestrial, but are still good climbers.

Three of the four species of true anteater (but not the giant anteater) live in trees. Silky anteaters (and sloths) can hang onto a branch with their back legs and tail and stretch the body out horizontally, supported by extra articulations (called xenarthrales) between the lumbar vertebrae. A unique joint in the sole of the foot also means they can turn their claws back under their foot to improve their grip.

The terrestrial species are all good burrowers, including the aardvark, terrestrial pangolins, and most armadillos. As well as

Teeth—None to a Hundred and Variations Between

True anteaters have no teeth and simply crush insects on their hard palate before swallowing them. Pangolins are also toothless and grind swallowed insects in their specialized horny stomach. Armadillos have rudimentary, peglike teeth. The giant armadillo has 80 to 100 of them, more than any other mammal. Aardvarks have only premolars and molars that grow continuously to compensate for wear. The teeth have a peculiar structure and are covered with a thin layer of bonelike cementum instead of enamel. Sloths have teeth unlike any other tree-dwelling mammal, just 18 simple molars.

digging for food, many excavate tunnels for shelter, sleeping, or rearing young. Armadillo burrows can be up to 6 feet (2 m) underground. Those of the ground pangolin end in a huge chamber, big enough to accommodate a man. Aardvarks are probably the biggest of all burrowing creatures and dig tunnels up to 43 feet (13 m) long. Armadillos dig, too, avoiding predators by rapidly sinking into soft ground when threatened.

Sluggish Energy Savers

Anteaters and sloths both specialize in low-energy food. To minimize the calories they burn, they have a low metabolic rate and a low, variable body temperature of 91 to 95°F (32.7 to 35°C). Like lizards, sloths move in and out of the sun to help regulate their temperature. These low-energy animals generally move slowly and do not travel far. They also breed slowly and produce small litters. Armadillos have a more varied, energy-rich diet; so although they show similar trends in behavior, they are much more active and can scurry around surprisingly fast.

Solitary Lives

Most of these animals live solitary lives, socializing only in the breeding season. Even though they rarely meet, they communicate using scent to convey information about their presence, status, and sexual condition.

All these species have pungent secretions from anal glands that they wipe onto surfaces within their home range. Armadillos and pangolins use feces and urine as scent markers, and the dung sites of sloths probably act similarly. Pangolins spray urine and anal gland secretions in the face of attackers.

⊕ A silky anteater takes a rest suspended from a branch. The tiny mammal is almost entirely arboreal, hardly ever coming to the ground. Its claws can be turned back under the foot to help improve grip.

Common name Giant anteater

Scientific name *Myrmecophaga tridactyla*

Family	Myrmecophagidae
Order	Xenarthra
Size	Length head/body: 39–51 in (100–130 cm); tail length: 25.5–35.5 in (65–90 cm)
	Weight Male 53–86 lb (24–39 kg); female 48–77 lb (22–35 kg)
Key features	Narrow, powerful body; small head with long, tapering snout; coat gray with black stripe from shoulders to chest and neck; hair coarse and stiff; long, bushy tail
Habits	Solitary; generally diurnal; breaks into ant and termite nests
Breeding	One young born in spring after gestation period of 190 days. Weaned at 6 months; sexually mature at 2 years. May live up to 26 years in captivity, unknown in the wild
Voice	Generally silent
Diet	Ants and termites; occasional beetle larvae and fruit
Habitat	Grassland, swamp, and lowland tropical forest
Distribution	Central America from southern Belize through South America to Northern Argentina
Status	Population: unknown, but probably thousands; IUCN Vulnerable; CITES II

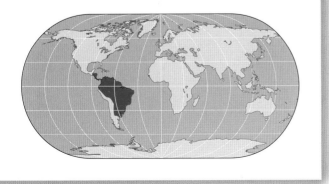

Giant Anteater

Myrmecophaga tridactyla

The giant anteater is the largest of the four species of anteaters and the only fully terrestrial one. Its strange body is perfectly adapted to its needs as a specialized ant- and termite-feeder.

THE GIANT ANTEATER HAS AN instantly recognizable profile, with its small head tapering to a long snout, a chunky body, and long, bushy tail. Most of its physical features relate to a highly specialized mode of feeding—breaking into ant and termite nests and capturing the insects on a long, sticky tongue.

Elongated Profile

The giant anteater's braincase is small and rounded, so the tapering, tubular 12-inch (30-cm) long snout dominates the head. The long snout contains an even longer tongue. The ears and eyes are small, so the elongated profile is not interrupted. The body is narrow but muscular, with the forelimbs being particularly strong. Each ends in large, sharp claws on the second and third fingers (unlike the smaller tree-living anteaters known as tamanduas, which have three long claws). The first and fifth fingers are tiny, so it looks as though the giant anteater has only three digits, hence the scientific name *tri-*, meaning "three," and *dactyla,* meaning "fingers." The fingers are constructed so that the heavy claws can be folded against the palms when not in use.

Giant anteaters have a lumbering walk in which they keep their nose close to the ground. The fingers of the forefeet are flexed and turned inward, so the knuckles and sides of the fist touch the ground. Such an arrangement keeps the claws from being blunted. The hind feet tread in a more usual plantigrade (flat-footed) fashion. Most of the coat is a grizzled gray, with a black stripe bordered with white that runs from the shoulders to the chest and neck. The coat is coarse, with a bristly crest

⊖ A giant anteater inserts its long snout into a hollow log to feed on the insects inside.

along the back, while the body hairs are curiously flat. The tail is over half the length of the body and extremely bushy.

While all the anteaters specialize in eating ants and termites, giant anteaters tend to prefer the larger-bodied, less ferocious species such as carpenter ants. The smaller anteaters focus on smaller prey. Even though some of the termite nests are prominent, forming large mounds that stand out against the horizon, a giant anteater's eyesight is poor, so it finds food by smell. When an anteater encounters a nest, it quickly digs a hole in the side, using its huge, curved claws. As soon as the hole is large enough, it pushes in its thin snout and flicks its long, sticky tongue in and out, catching the worker ants as they run around frantically. The anteater will also eat larvae and cocoons.

Flypaper Tongue

The giant anteater's tongue is an incredibly efficient ant collector. It is covered in sticky saliva and backward-pointing spines. The spines help keep the insects firmly in place as the tongue is taken back into the mouth, rather than being dislodged and lost against the walls of the nest. The anteater can flick its tongue in and out up to 150 times a minute. With a tongue 24 inches (60 cm) long, the animal's ant-trapping capacity is equivalent to laying down 300 feet (90 m) of sticky flypaper every minute.

The giant anteater's whole eating apparatus has been honed to enable it to pull in lots of tiny insects as quickly as possible. Most mammals open their mouth by moving the jaw up and down, allowing them to chew food. Anteaters do not need to open their mouth wide, and in fact they can only open it to a small O-shape, the

69

Anteater Self-Defense—Claws and Forelimbs

Giant anteaters tend to avoid trouble and usually run away from potential danger at an ungainly gallop. If cornered, however, an anteater is more than a match for most predators. Rearing up on its hind legs and using the bushy tail as a prop, it slashes at attackers with its sharp claws. The claws can be up to 4 inches (10 cm) long. If the attacker comes any closer, a brutal bear hug from the anteater's strong forelimbs can be fatal. The animal's forelegs are so powerful because of the strength it builds up by demolishing concrete-hard termite nests.

width of a pencil. Nor do they need to chew, since ants are already small—so they do not have any teeth. Instead, giant anteaters have an unusual anatomical arrangement that enables them to almost hoover up ants. The jawbones are not joined at the tip, and the chewing muscles make the two halves of the jaw roll inward and outward, instead of up and down. The rolling motion helps the tongue flick in and out, and pushes any trapped insects toward the back of the mouth, where they can be swallowed in an almost continuous motion.

Giant anteaters also have an unusual tongue attachment. The tongue is even longer than the head, so it is attached in the throat—part way down the neck—to a structure called the hyoid. In most animals hyoid bones are small or fused together. However, in the giant anteater they are large and well articulated, making a supple structure that enables the tongue to move rapidly. Speed is important because ants and termites are so small and scurry around very fast. The anteater has to eat lots of ants to obtain enough nutrition. It also does not have long at each nest before the soldier ants are mustered to chase away the intruder. Although the tough skin and thick hairs provide some protection against the ants, the soldiers' fierce bites and acidic stings usually force the anteater to retreat. In the few minutes

it spends at each nest an anteater will probably only eat about 150 insects. At such a slow rate it needs to visit about 200 nests per day to obtain enough nutrition.

A tough, muscular stomach grinds up the ants. Unlike in other animals, the giant anteater's stomach does not secrete hydrochloric acid, but instead relies on the ants' own formic acid to create the right chemical conditions needed for digestion.

Giant anteaters are usually active during the day; but in areas where they are disturbed by humans, they can become nocturnal. They are still

⊕ In giant anteaters the largest claws are on digits two and three . If threatened by a jaguar or puma, anteaters will rear up on their hind legs and lash out with their claws.

able to find food at night, relying on their sense of smell rather than eyesight. But a nocturnal lifestyle may make them more vulnerable to their only natural predators, pumas and jaguars. Giant anteaters rest for up to 15 hours a day, using shallow scrapes, hollow logs, or modified burrows of other animals rather than digging their own. In these relatively exposed sleeping spots they disguise themselves by curling up and covering their body with the huge brushlike tail. Giant anteaters are mainly solitary, except for mothers and their offspring. However, although they tend to avoid each other, males may fight. In such encounters the animals will probably just circle each other and then give chase. But if serious fighting ensues, their sharp claws can cause severe injuries.

Termites and Territory

Giant anteaters keep out of each other's way by having well-defined home ranges that are marked with pungent-smelling secretions from the anal gland. Females are less territorial than males, with home ranges that can overlap by as much as 30 percent. Those of males hardly overlap at all. The size of the home range occupied by each animal depends on the density of ant and termite nests.

Each anteater needs to be able to snack on many tens or even hundreds of nests every day, but without doing lasting damage to them. In areas where there are several nests, home ranges may be as small as 0.2 square miles (0.5 sq. km). In poorer-quality habitats that support fewer ants and termites, an anteater may need 50 times as much space.

Giant anteaters mate in the fall (March to May in the Southern Hemisphere) and give birth in spring, usually to a single baby. Females give birth standing on their hind legs, using their tail as a prop. The newborns are well developed and climb on their mother's back soon after birth. Their eyes open after six days, and by about a month they are able to gallop around. However, they generally walk slowly or ride on their mother. The young are miniature versions of the adults, identical in color and markings.

Young giant anteaters are suckled for up to six months, but stay with their mother for up to two years. By that time they have reached sexual maturity. After leaving their mother, they establish a home range of their own and begin the largely solitary, food-focused life of adult giant anteaters.

⊕ *A baby giant anteater rides piggyback on its mother. The stripes of the mother and young usually line up, breaking up the baby's outline and making it difficult for predators to spot.*

Common name Three-toed sloth (brown-throated three-toed sloth)

Scientific name *Bradypus variegatus*

Family Bradypodidae

Order Xenarthra

Size Length head/body: 22–24 in (56–61 cm); tail length: 2.5–3 in (6–7 cm)

Weight 7.7–10 lb (3.5–4.5 kg)

Key features Long, shaggy fur; forelegs noticeably longer than hind legs; general color grayish-fawn, often with green tinge; small eyes; stumpy tail

Habits Hangs from branches, rarely descends to ground; stays in same tree for days at a time; moves only very slowly; active during day and at night

Breeding Single young born each year after gestation period of 5 months. Weaned at about 1 month, but stays with mother for further 4–6 months; sexually mature at about 2 years. May live over 20 years in the wild, not normally kept in captivity

Voice Normally silent

Diet Leaves collected from tree canopy

Habitat Lowland tropical forests

Distribution Honduras south to northern Argentina

Status Population: unknown, but probably declining. Close relative *B. torquatus* is classified Endangered by IUCN

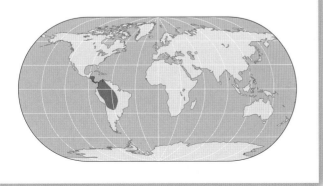

Three-Toed Sloth

Bradypus variegatus

The three-toed sloth economizes on energy expenditure to such an extent that it moves only very slowly and hardly ever goes anywhere.

THE THREE-TOED SLOTH FEEDS exclusively on leaves, particularly from the silk cotton tree (*Cecropia*). It pulls the vegetation toward its mouth using the long front limbs. Three-toed sloths can also move their head through a wide arc, helping them reach food without having to move their body. Such flexibility is made possible by having nine neck vertebrae—more even than a giraffe. Leaves contain little nourishment, and so the sloth needs to eat large quantities. Its full stomach may weigh almost one-third of the whole animal. The leaves have to be digested with the help of microorganisms in the sloth's complex stomach. It can take up to a month before they pass to the animal's intestine.

Nice and Easy

The sloth's diet yields little energy, so being a sloth is all about reducing effort and saving energy. The animals do so by having a low body temperature and by not bothering to maintain it at night or in wet weather. Consequently, their body temperature is unusually variable for a mammal, being between 86 and 93°F (30 to 34°C). They often warm themselves by climbing to part of their tree where they can bask in the sun, retreating to the shade if it gets too hot. Sloths burn up as little energy as possible by having a metabolic rate that is less than half that of other mammals of comparable size. They move around slowly, too, although they are capable of a spurt of speed if needed. They are active intermittently for about 10 hours a day, spending the rest of the time asleep.

An extremely slow, calm way of life is often associated with unsuccessful animals that

green owing to the presence of two species of encrusting algae. The algae grow along the hairs, and their greenish tinge helps camouflage the sloth in the tree canopy. Other creatures live in the fur, including moths, ticks, and beetles. They are probably able to survive because the sloth cannot groom itself effectively. Also, the animal moves so slowly that tenants are not dislodged.

Three-toed sloths have overlapping home ranges, averaging about 15 acres (6 ha) each. However, they rarely travel more than 125 feet (38 m) in a day and often spend many days at a time in the same tree. They come to the ground only once or twice a week to defecate and urinate. They are clumsy on the ground, crawling around awkwardly with their legs splayed in all directions.

The sloth's small eyes and long, stiff fur are not generally considered attractive, and the animal is not collected for the pet trade. Anyway, sloths would be difficult to keep in captivity because of their specialized feeding requirements. They are not normally hunted for food either, and their skins have no commercial value. As a result, sloths have been largely left alone. The main threat to sloth populations is from logging and fragmentation of the forests by the expansion of roads and grazing land. Such activities create open spaces that the sloths are reluctant to cross.

⊕ The three-toed sloth characteristically hangs below the branches along which it moves. It grips with huge, hooked claws, 3 to 4 inches (8 to 10 cm) long, with three on each foot.

evolution has passed by. But the three-toed sloth is actually a highly successful creature. In places it can be one of the most common medium-sized mammals in the forest. In some areas there are more than three sloths per acre (8 per ha). The sloth has achieved success by being specialized for life in the treetops, out of reach of most predators. Its feeding methods also reduce the problem of competing with other animals for food.

Shaggy Appearance

The three-toed sloth spends much time hanging from branches, even sleeping or giving birth suspended from a tree. Because it hangs upside down, its fur slants toward its back rather than the belly—the opposite way from other mammals. The body is covered with fine insulating underfur that is hidden below the long, coarse hairs that give the sloth its shaggy appearance. The long, stiff hairs often turn

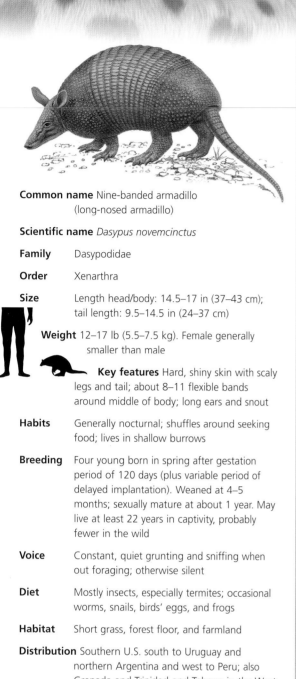

Common name Nine-banded armadillo
(long-nosed armadillo)

Scientific name *Dasypus novemcinctus*

Family Dasypodidae

Order Xenarthra

Size Length head/body: 14.5–17 in (37–43 cm);
tail length: 9.5–14.5 in (24–37 cm)

Weight 12–17 lb (5.5–7.5 kg). Female generally
smaller than male

Key features Hard, shiny skin with scaly
legs and tail; about 8–11 flexible bands
around middle of body; long ears and snout

Habits Generally nocturnal; shuffles around seeking
food; lives in shallow burrows

Breeding Four young born in spring after gestation
period of 120 days (plus variable period of
delayed implantation). Weaned at 4–5
months; sexually mature at about 1 year. May
live at least 22 years in captivity, probably
fewer in the wild

Voice Constant, quiet grunting and sniffing when
out foraging; otherwise silent

Diet Mostly insects, especially termites; occasional
worms, snails, birds' eggs, and frogs

Habitat Short grass, forest floor, and farmland

Distribution Southern U.S. south to Uruguay and
northern Argentina and west to Peru; also
Grenada and Trinidad and Tobago in the West
Indies

Status Population: abundant

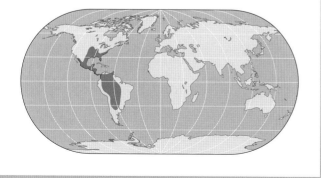

Nine-Banded Armadillo

Dasypus novemcinctus

*The armored armadillo is an unmistakable creature,
and the nine-banded species has been a successful
colonizer of the United States.*

INSTEAD OF HAVING A SOFT, FURRY skin like most
other mammals, the armadillo is encased in a
bony carapace that is covered with shiny plates.
Around the animal's middle is a series of flexible
bands that allow the creature to roll up when
threatened. Usually there are about eight such
bands, but armadillos living in Central America
have nine or more. The tail and legs are scaly,
and there are sparse yellowish hairs here and on
the animal's belly. The armadillo has large,
sensitive ears and a long snout. The powerful
front feet each have four toes, but the hind feet
have five. Despite its heavily armored body, the
armadillo is a strong swimmer and can remain
underwater for long periods. It can also run
surprisingly fast, and the smooth and shiny
body is difficult for predators to grasp.

Traveling North

The main home of armadillos is in South
America. The nine-banded species is widespread
there, being found as far south as Uruguay and
northern Argentina. In the last 200 years it has
also staged a remarkably successful invasion of
North America. From the late 1800s onward the
nine-banded armadillo rapidly expanded its
range in northern Mexico and had reached as
far north as the Rio Grande region of southern
Texas by 1890. Since then it has spread steadily
deeper into the United States, appearing in
Tennessee by the 1970s. It is now found as far
north as Nebraska and southern Missouri.
Meanwhile, in the 1920s armadillos were
released or escaped from captivity in Florida in
several places. The animal has now become well
established there and has spread north and
west to colonize the southern states of the

United States, reaching Georgia and South Carolina by the 1950s. It is now sufficiently numerous in Florida to have become one of the more frequent victims of road traffic accidents.

It is not clear what has brought about the rapid extension of the armadillo's geographical range, but climatic changes might have something to do with it. More significantly perhaps, the persecution and removal of large predators such as cougars leaves the way open for the armadillo to go where it pleases, with the smaller carnivores posing little danger. Another helpful factor might be the steady expansion of ranching. Overgrazing by cattle leaves the grass short and the soil nicely warmed by the sun. Such conditions are ideal for many ground invertebrates, and the short grass enables armadillos to find them easily. Further spread to the north is now probably limited by the cold, especially in winter. In many parts of the western states the summers are also too hot and dry.

⊖ The armadillo is an unusual-looking creature. It has large, rounded ears, a long snout, and is covered in hard, shiny armor plating.

Well Protected

In the warmer parts of its range the nine-banded armadillo prefers to live in shady cover. Elsewhere, it thrives in various habitats from sea level to altitudes of more than 10,000 feet (3,000 m). The armadillo is mainly active in the late evening and at night, although it may sometimes come out during daylight on cloudy days. It shuffles around slowly, nose to the ground as it sniffs for prey. When rooting, the animal grunts almost constantly, ignoring the potential danger of drawing attention to itself. But it is well protected by its thick, bony skin. The animal can also roll up to hide its softer underbelly. Being relatively safe from predators means the armadillo can potter around confidently, even out in the open.

Periodically the armadillo will rear up on its hind legs, supported by the tail, and sniff the air. The animal has a keen sense of smell and pokes its nose into clumps of dry vegetation and leaf litter, seeking out food. It will often pause to dig something up, using the strong claws on its forefeet, and it may also rip apart rotting logs. Insects make up more than three-quarters of the diet, with termites a frequent item on the menu. Even the nests of fire ants may be attacked to get at the ant larvae within. The armadillo's thick, bony skin protects it from painful insect bites. The animal will also eat small worms, mollusks, and occasionally the eggs of ground-nesting birds.

Unimpressive Fighters

The armadillo's home range extends over about 3 to 4 acres (1.5 ha) in good habitat, but in poorer areas it may cover more than 30 acres (12 ha). The animals are tolerant of each other, and their home ranges often overlap. However, at high population densities the animals may become less accommodating, and the males will fight, scratching each other with their front feet. Armadillos are unlikely to cause serious harm and do not bite because their teeth are small and form only simple pegs. The jaws are weak too, since they are meant only for picking up small insects.

Armadillos excavate a burrow by digging with the forefeet and kicking loose dirt out of the tunnel with the hind feet. The burrow is

simple and usually has only one or two entrances. The tunnels extend about 10 feet (3 m), but may be up to 25 feet (7.5 m) long. They are usually shallow, lying just below the surface, but may sometimes go down 12 feet (3.5 m) into the soil. The armadillo builds a large nest in part of its burrow. Nesting material, in the form of leaves, grass, and twigs, is gathered nearby and carried into the burrow in bundles held beneath the body. Grasping the bundle close to its belly, the armadillo shuffles backward into its burrow, often leaving a little trail of debris behind. Each armadillo has several burrows within its home range, and the same one may be used for up to four weeks before the animal moves on.

Armadillos and Leprosy

In the 1960s it was discovered that nine-banded armadillos—unlike most other mammals—could be infected with the leprosy bacillus. For the first time the disfiguring disease could be studied in the laboratory. Leprosy was later found in wild armadillo populations in Texas and Louisiana, and (less often) in Florida. There is probably little risk of humans catching the disease from these wild animals, since leprosy is an uncommon disease, and people living outside the tropics tend to be less susceptible to leprosy.

young are born in March or April, but as early as February in Mexico. Litter sizes are small, normally four identical same-sex quadruplets derived from a single egg. Young armadillos are born fully formed with their eyes open. They weigh 1 to 2 ounces (28 to 56 g) and can walk within a few hours. They will accompany their mother on foraging expeditions within a few weeks and become fully independent at an age of four or five months.

Popular Food Source

Armadillos can become quite numerous in places and may reach densities of 130 per square mile (50 per sq. km) on the coastal prairies of Texas. In parts of South America they are a popular source of food, and catching them remains a threat to populations in many areas. The animals are also threatened by deforestation, agricultural expansion, and other forms of habitat loss. In the United States armadillos sometimes make themselves unpopular by digging in gardens and farmland. They are also accused of causing erosion and undermining buildings by their burrowing activities. However, on the whole armadillos are beneficial animals that destroy many harmful insects and are generally regarded with amusement and tolerance. Their bony skin is made into baskets, which are sold as souvenirs, and the animals are also used in various forms of medical research.

Occasionally, armadillos can be found nesting above the ground in large piles of dry vegetation.

Armadillos normally live alone, but meet to breed once a year in the summer months. (In captivity they may breed throughout the year.) They breed for the first time at about one year. Courtship is often a drawn-out affair, with the males eagerly following females and seeking an opportunity to mate. In North America the mating takes place in July and August, but implantation of the fertilized egg is delayed until November. Farther south mating may occur earlier in the summer, but implantation is then delayed for longer. Elsewhere, development of the embryos may start immediately after mating. Actual fetal development takes about 120 days. In Texas the

⤴ A nine-banded armadillo excavates the earth by digging with its powerful clawed forefeet. Its body is well protected by bony armored skin.

⤵ A mother and infant nine-banded armadillo in a burrow. The armadillo builds a nest from leaves, twigs, and grass in part of its burrow.

Common name Aardvark

Scientific name *Orycteropus afer*

Family	Orycteropodidae
Order	Tubulidentata
Size	Length head/body: 41–51 in (105–130 cm); tail length: 18–25 in (45–63 cm)
	Weight 88–143 lb (40–65 kg)
Key features	Muscular, piglike animal with long nose, long tail, and big ears; fur is coarse and sparse
Habits	Solitary, shy, nocturnal, and rarely seen; digs large burrows
Breeding	Single young born after gestation period of about 7 months. Weaned at 6 months; sexually mature at 2 years. May live up to 18 years in captivity, probably similar in the wild
Voice	Occasional grunts
Diet	Termites, ants, and insect larvae caught on long, sticky tongue
Habitat	Grassland, open woodland, and scrub where ants and termites are abundant throughout year; avoids stony soils and flooded areas
Distribution	Patchily distributed throughout most of sub-Saharan Africa
Status	Population: unknown. Widespread, but exterminated in many areas

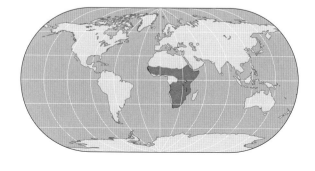

Aardvark *Orycteropus afer*

The unmistakable aardvark is one of the most specialized of all mammals. It is so peculiar that it is classified in a separate order all by itself. It is also the largest animal that feeds exclusively on ants and termites.

AARDVARK MEANS "EARTH PIG" in Afrikaans, and it is a good description of the strange animal. Its snout is long and flat-ended, rather like a pig's, and the legs are relatively short. It has sparse, pale-colored hair that is often stained by soil. Older animals may be almost naked as their hair gets worn away through constant burrowing. However, the similarities end here, since the aardvark has a heavy, tapering tail and large upright ears. While pigs are adaptable creatures that eat almost anything, aardvarks are among the most specialized of all mammals, feeding only on ants, termites, and small insect larvae.

Sniffing Out Supper

Although it occasionally comes out in late afternoon, the aardvark is normally exclusively nocturnal. It is also shy and secretive, so it is rarely seen. However, it is sometimes possible to watch one as it follows a zigzag course, sniffing for food. The animal sweeps its long snout from side to side with the nostrils close to the ground as it searches for insects. A dense mass of hairy bristles acts to filter out soil and dust. When it finds suitable prey, the aardvark pushes its nose firmly against a patch of ground and starts to dig rapidly with its forefeet, sitting back on its haunches. Its short, powerful front limbs have four fingers, each with large claws, which can excavate all but the stoniest ground. The long tongue is flicked out constantly to pick up insects on the sticky saliva secreted by large glands in the mouth. The food is swallowed directly and ground up by the muscular stomach. The teeth are hardly used, but they

 SEE ALSO Aardwolf **2**:110; Pig Family, The **5**:74; Anteater, Giant **9**:68; Numbat **10**:34

Large Warrens

Aardvarks are among the largest burrowing mammals and excavate huge tunnels. The warren has up to 50 yards (43 m) of tunnels, with up to eight entrances. Some burrows go 20 feet (6 m) into the ground. The aardvark is a solitary creature, although its home range may overlap with those of several of its neighbors. Both sexes have large scent glands under the base of the tail. The glands produce a strong-smelling yellow secretion, probably used to advertise an animal's sex and social status.

Females have only one young at intervals of about a year. The baby leaves the burrow when it is only two weeks old to follow its mother on foraging trips. Females are sometimes seen with two young of different ages, suggesting that offspring may stay with their mother beyond the time that the next baby is born.

In winter the aardvark may be active above ground for only five or six hours in a night, but in summer up to 10 hours is possible. An aardvark can travel up to 19 miles (30 km) in a single night, although normal excursions probably cover about 1 to 3 miles (2 to 5 km).

Aardvarks are champion diggers. Despite their large size, they can disappear completely into soft soil within a few minutes. All the excavating of burrows and digging for insects has a significant impact on the local terrain. It can be beneficial, since the abandoned burrows provide shelter for a wide range of smaller animals from snakes to bats. But digging up the land is unpopular in agricultural areas, and in many places aardvarks have been exterminated. Increased cattle farming, on the other hand, actually benefits aardvarks because it creates ideal conditions for large numbers of termites.

The aardvark is widely believed to have magical properties. The animals are therefore often killed for lucky charms made from teeth and other body parts.

An aardvark emerges from its warren. Some tunnels are simple refuges to escape danger or shelter from rain, but the animals will have at least one large warren.

become worn because of the gritty food. The teeth are flat-topped, peglike, and grow continuously. There are no incisors or canines. An aardvark probably eats more than 50,000 insects in one night, including over 20 different species of ants. Aardvarks are the largest animals to feed exclusively on the tiny insects.

BATS

Bats are fascinating creatures, but they are often misunderstood. Considering that one-quarter of all known mammal species are bats, we know surprisingly little about them. Of all the mammalian orders, only rodents have more species. Although they are all built to a similar body plan, bats are highly diverse in terms of their lifestyles, diet, and appearance.

Bats are the only mammals to have mastered powered flight. "Flying" squirrels and lemurs, for example, can only glide, while bats can sustain flight for long distances. Their ability to fly has enabled them to spread throughout the world, living everywhere except the highest mountains, extreme polar regions, and a few isolated islands. Their ability to echolocate (using echoes to detect objects) means they can hunt in complete darkness, catching tiny insects and dodging obstacles at speeds of up to 30 miles per hour (50 km/h).

Bats vary in size from the largest flying foxes, which weigh 2.9 pounds (1.3 kg) and have a wingspan of 5.6 feet (1.7 m), to Kitti's hog-nosed bat, which is 1 to 1.3 inches (2.5 to 3.3 cm) long and weighs only 0.05 to 0.07 ounces (1.5 to 2 g). Many bats have strangely elaborated snouts and ears, particularly the hammerheaded and horseshoe bats. Although they may look ugly, these complex faces are finely honed instruments, with each wrinkle serving to channel sound waves for echolocation.

Origins

Bats are divided into two major groups, the Microchiroptera (small bats, most living species) and Megachiroptera (large fruit bats.) There is some evidence that the two groups evolved independently of each other.

Bat bones are delicate and do not fossilize well, so we know little about their origins. The earliest fossil bat known was found in Wyoming and is 50 million years old. This and other bats dating from the Eocene period share many features with modern microchiropterans. Fossilized details of their inner ear structure suggest they could echolocate, and some even have identifiable traces of

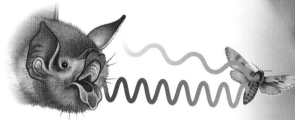

→ *Two typical bat specializations: The enormous ears of the Bechstein's bat help in the hunt for insects. Below: By analyzing ultrasound waves bouncing off a flying insect, a bat can pinpoint it in total darkness.*

insects in their stomachs. The oldest known megachiropteran lived 35 million years ago.

There are various theories as to how and why the first bats evolved wings. The most likely explanation is that they evolved from gliding membranes similar to those of sugar gliders and flying squirrels. However they arose, bats' wings have enabled them to become one of the most successful groups of mammals.

Echolocation

Bats are among the few creatures that can "see" with sound. Other echolocators include dolphins and a few cave-dwelling birds. To create a "sound picture," a bat emits a short burst of noise through its mouth or nostrils, then interprets the echoes that bounce back. An echo from a nearby object will return quickly, while ones from objects farther away will take longer and be fainter. Most echolocation calls are ultrasonic, which means they are above a frequency of 20 kHz and too high-pitched for humans to hear. Unlike the relatively simple "clicks" of dolphins, bats' echolocation calls are longer "tonal" sounds that vary according to species and circumstance.

Because a bat has to listen for the echo, the sound cannot be continuous. Instead, it has to be made in pulses. High-intensity echolocation calls are also incredibly loud, equivalent to a human making a noise like a

pneumatic drill. To avoid deafening themselves, the muscles in the bat's middle ear contract just as the bat is calling. This separates the three middle ear bones (malleus, incus, and stapes) slightly, making the bat momentarily deaf. A split second later they spring back again, ready to capture the echo.

Other Senses

Despite their reputation, bats are not blind. The fruit bats (Megachiroptera) rely on their good eyesight, since they do not echolocate. Even the best echolocators still use their vision to some extent. The hearing ability of bats is

Who's Who among the Bats?

ORDER: Chiroptera, more than 900 species in 2 suborders

SUBORDER: Megachiroptera—flying foxes, fruit bats of the Old World: 164 species in 41 genera and 1 family
Family: Pteropodidae includes straw-colored flying fox (*Eidolon helvum*); hammer-headed bat (*Hypsignathus monstrosus*); Egyptian fruit bat (*Rousettus aegyptiacus*)

SUBORDER: Microchiroptera—about 740 species in 133 genera and 17 families
Family: Rhinopomatidae—mouse-tailed bats: 3 species in 1 genus, including greater mouse-tailed bat (*Rhinopoma microphyllum*)
Family: Craseonycteridae—hog-nosed bat: 1 species in 1 genus (*Craseonycteris thonglongyai*)
Family: Emballonuridae—sheath-tailed bats: 47 species in 12 genera, including greater white-lined bat (*Saccopteryx bilineata*)
Family: Nycteridae—slit-faced bats: 13 species in 1 genus, including large slit-faced bat (*Nycteris grandis*)
Family: Megadermatidae—Old World false vampire bats: 5 species in 4 genera, including greater false vampire bat (*Megaderma lyra*); yellow-winged bat (*Lavia frons*)
Family: Rhinolophidae—horseshoe and Old World leaf-nosed bats: 129 species in 10 genera, including greater horseshoe bat (*Rhinolophus ferrumequinum*); diadem roundleaf bat (*Hipposideros diadema*); short-eared trident bat (*Cleotis percivali*)
Family: Mystacinidae—New Zealand short-tailed bats: 1 species in 1 genus, New Zealand lesser short-tailed bat (*Mystacina tuberculata*)
Family: Noctilionidae—bulldog bats: 2 species in 1 genus, greater bulldog bat (*Noctilio leporinus*); lesser bulldog bat (*N. albiventris*)
Family: Mormoopidae—spectacled bats: 8 species in 2 genera, including Parnell's mustached bat (*Pteronotus parnellii*)
Family: Phyllostomidae—New World leaf-nosed bats: 139 species in 48 genera, including hairy big-eyed bat (*Chiroderma villosum*); greater spear-nosed bat (*Phyllostomus hastatus*); fringe-lipped bat (*Trachops cirrhosus*); Seba's short-tailed bat (*Carollia perspicillata*); tent-making bat (*Uroderma bilobatum*); common vampire bat (*Desmodus rotundus*); lesser long-nosed bat (*Leptonycteris curasoae*)
Family: Natalidae—funnel-eared bats: 5 species in 1 genus, including Cuban funnel-eared bat (*Natalus micropus*)
Family: Furipteridae—thumbless bats: 2 species in 2 genera, smoky bat (*Amorphichilus schnablii*); thumbless bat (*Furipterus horrens*)
Family: Thyropteridae—disk-winged bats: 2 species in 1 genus, Peter's disk-winged bat (*Thyroptera discifera*); Spix's disk-winged bat (*T. tricolor*)
Family: Myzopodidae—Old World sucker-footed bat: 1 species in 1 genus (*Myzopoda aurita*)
Family: Vespertilionidae—vespertilionid bats: 308 species in 34 genera, including large mouse-eared bat (*Myotis myotis*); Daubenton's bat (*M. daubentonii*); little brown bat (*M. lucifugus*); common pipistrelle (*Pipistrellus pipistrellus*); noctule (*Nyctalus noctula*); big brown bat (*Eptesicus fuscus*); bamboo bat (*Tylonycteris pachypus*); red bat (*Lasiurus borealis*); Bechstein's bat (*Myotis bechsteini*)
Family: Antrozoidae—pallid bat: 1 species in 1 genus (*Antrozous pallidus*)
Family: Molossidae—free-tailed bats: 77 species in 12 genera, including Mexican free-tailed bat (*Tadarida brasiliensis*); European free-tailed bat (*T. teniotis*); black mastiff bat (*Molossus ater*); hairless bat (*Cheiromeles torquatus*)

excellent. Old World false vampire bats have the best hearing of any mammal tested. As well as using their hearing for echolocation, some bats hunt by listening. Some can even hear the footsteps of an insect on a leaf. Bats also have a good sense of smell, which some use in courtship, to find food, or to identify their young.

Roosting

Most bats are nocturnal. By flying at night, bats avoid daytime predators such as birds of prey. They can also make use of a huge, otherwise almost untapped prey resource—namely, nocturnal insects. During the day or when hibernating, bats tend to cluster in roost sites, which can contain thousands or even millions of bats. The Mexican free-tailed bat holds the world record for the largest aggregation of vertebrates, with over 20 million individuals in one roost.

Roost sites include caves, rock crevices, hollow trees, houses, and abandoned mines. Some roost in burrows, like the African slit-faced bats that use aardvark holes. Two bat species roost inside bamboo shoots, entering through beetle holes. Some even make their own tents by biting through the supporting veins of large leaves, making them fold over to form a protective canopy.

Hanging Around

Bats are famous for hanging upside down, often resembling tiny fruits or furled umbrellas as they wrap their wings around them like a cloak. Their feet have small claws that can grip bark or rough stone. Once attached, a special arrangement of tendons means that the bat does not have to expend any energy hanging on—its weight makes the feet grip tightly even when the animal is dead. A few species of bat roost in places that are too smooth for claws to get a proper hold. They hang using suckers on their hands and feet or ankles.

Bats also have very flexible necks. When hanging, they can bend their head backward through 180 degrees: Imagine dropping your head back onto your spine to look behind you!

Saving Energy

Bats have a high-energy lifestyle. Being warm-blooded animals, they need a lot of energy to maintain their body temperature. Retaining body heat is particularly difficult for small bats, since they have a high surface-area-to-volume ratio, so they lose heat quickly. Flying and making echolocation calls also uses a lot of energy. Altogether, bats must eat a lot and conserve energy whenever they can.

In temperate climates bats hibernate during the cold season when there is little food available. They shut down their body system so that there is barely any sign of life. Even in warmer climates, during cool periods or when nursing and food is scarce, nocturnal bats go into torpor during their daytime sleep. In hibernation the body temperature drops to just above that of the air around them, which can be close to freezing. The heart rate falls from about 400 beats per minute when active to between just 12 and 25. The energy bats use in this state is less than 1 percent of the amount they would use when active.

Social Life and Breeding

The social life of bats varies from living alone to assembling in huge aggregations. They also have a full range of mating strategies, from monogamy—with pairs forming long-term partnerships—to polygamy, with both males and females having multiple partners. Most bats are polygynous, with one "successful" male mating with many females while other males get no matings at all. DNA analysis of twins has revealed that females can be polyandrous, mating with more than one male.

Females give birth only once a year. In temperate areas they become pregnant within a few days of waking

from hibernation, using sperm that they stored within their reproductive system from matings up to seven months earlier. Sperm storage is unique to bats. In tropical areas, where food is available year-round, females can give birth at different times of the year.

Usually a single baby is born, although some species may occasionally have twins. Red bats can have three or even four babies. The offspring are usually large, up to 40 percent of the mother's weight, which is equivalent to a human baby about eight times larger than normal. The babies also grow fast, and some can fly within two or three weeks of birth. Producing milk requires a great deal of energy, so births are usually timed to match the season of highest food availability. Another advantage is that there is plenty of food available when the young bats start to catch their own.

Surviving

Bats are surprisingly long-lived for their size. Little brown bats can live more than 20 years, while shrews or mice of

Migrating

Although flying is expensive in energy terms, it is an efficient way of traveling long distances. Some bats, such as the Mexican free-tailed bat, migrate up to 1,000 miles (1,600 km) from summer feeding grounds to winter hibernation roosts or to follow seasonal changes in food supply. Their navigation systems are highly developed—they can find roost sites even if released well away from their familiar range. Scientists are still not sure how they manage to find their way home. However, despite their ability to fly, many bats cope with seasonal food shortages by giving up both their mobility and warm-bloodedness to spend several months in hibernation.

similar size will rarely survive 20 months. To reach that age, a bat must avoid many potential causes of mortality.

Some predators take bats, although few do so regularly. Carnivorous mammals, including monkeys, cats, and even other bats sometimes eat them. Certain snakes prey on roosting bats. As they leave their roosts at dusk, bats can fall victim to owls and other birds of prey. Bat hawks from Africa and the East Indies specialize in catching bats. They hunt on the wing and can swallow a bat whole while still aloft, ready to quickly catch the next.

Bats also succumb to a range of diseases, including rabies, and they are hosts to a huge range of parasites, both external and internal. There are tiny mites that live on the wing membranes, nibbling through to feed on the bat's blood. Other mites, fleas, bedbugs, and flies feed on bat blood or other body fluids. Some spend all their time on the bats; others live at the roost sites, only crawling onto the bats when they settle. Most bat parasites are specialists and do not live on other animals.

Diverse Diets

Bats eat the widest range of foods of any mammal group. Invertebrates are the most common food type, especially flies, beetles, moths, bugs, and termites. The American pallid bat and some African slit-faced bats even eat scorpions. Carnivorous bats catch and eat fish, amphibians, reptiles, birds, and mammals (including other bats), and three species drink blood. Around one-third of the world's bats are vegetarian. They eat fruit, nectar, and pollen. In doing so, they pollinate many important trees and shrubs. Most bats specialize in just one type of food, but some, such as the spear-nosed bats, are omnivores. They eat an assortment of insects, vertebrates, and fruit.

The feeding methods that bats use are varied. Although famous for catching insects in midair, some of the slower-flying bats pick them from foliage as they fly past (called "gleaning"). Others hunt from a perch, swooping out to grab a moth, for example, and carrying it back to eat while hanging up. Some use their claws to trawl the surface of rivers and ponds for insects, frogs, or with bulldog bats, even fish. The vampire bats nibble a hole in an animal's skin to lap the flowing blood.

Bats and People

In the western world bats have long suffered from myths and misconceptions associated with witchcraft and evil and immortalized in vampire stories. In Chinese culture, however, bats are a symbol of joy. One frequent story is that bats will get caught in your hair. Their sophisticated echolocation system makes such entrapment highly unlikely, and human hair does not easily entangle animals. Even if a bat does get caught, no harm will result, since most species are small and passive creatures.

Bats do cause a few genuine concerns. They can transmit certain diseases that humans can catch, including rabies. Large roosts in buildings can be smelly, and fruit-eating species can be pests in plantations. On the whole, however, bats do much more good than harm. They consume vast numbers of insect pests. It has been estimated that in Texas alone, large roosts of Mexican

Teeth

Bats have the same types of teeth as other mammals, namely, incisors, canines, premolars, and molars. In most small bats there are 38 in total. Bats that eat tough insects have fewer, more robust teeth; vampire bats have only 20, since they do not need to chew; nectar-drinking bats have a long snout with large canines and small, pointed cheek teeth, while the cheek teeth of fruit-eaters have broad crushing surfaces.

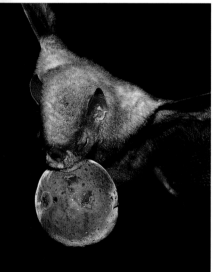

← *Foraging for fruit and flowers: lesser long-nosed bats line up to feed from a cactus flower (far left). These bats cannot hover for long, so they only spend a fraction of a second at a time feeding; a hairy big-eyed bat with a fig (left).*

free-tailed bats are capable of eating over 2,000 pounds (900 kg) of bollworm moths (a serious pest of corn) in one night. Bats are also essential pollinators of many tropical crops such as balsa, mango, durian, and wild banana. In many natural habitats bats are a key part of the ecosystem.

Bat Conservation

Because they often roost in huge groups, bats are vulnerable. They usually have only one baby at a time, so losses are not easily made up, and bat populations across the world are declining. In some places people have traditionally hunted bats for food. Such harvesting can probably be sustained as long as the bat populations are not under any additional threats. Conflicts with plantation owners are more serious. Farmers have poisoned entire roosts of thousands of bats to protect their fruit crops.

As with many other mammals, habitat destruction is a major threat. When land is cleared for farming or building, feeding and roosting sites are destroyed. Even bats that can live in seminatural farmland habitats are suffering as a result of intensification of farming methods. More pesticides are used now than in the past, and "nonproductive" areas such as hedgerows are cleared.

In the face of these threats there is now a growing worldwide recognition of the need to protect bats. Some important roost sites and habitats are being safeguarded, and national and international bat legislation is improving. People are only now beginning to understand and appreciate bats' vital role in ecosystems, their fascinating lifestyles, and incredible diversity.

Bat Families

There are over 900 species of bats grouped into 174 genera and 18 families. There are two suborders—the megachiropterans (large bats) and the microchiropterans (small bats). There is some overlap in size, but they can be best told apart by their features and habits.

The megachiropterans are the fruit bats and flying foxes of the Old World tropics and subtropics. They tend to be large in size and have large eyes, relying on their eyesight to find their way around rather than echolocation. Only one member of the group (the Egyptian fruit bat) can echolocate, using a rather crude mechanism based on clicking its tongue. Most species have a claw on the second digit as well as the thumb,

and the tail is generally small or absent. All are members of the same family—Pteropodidae. There are 164 species in 41 genera. They include the rousettes, hammerheaded bat, and flying foxes in the genera *Pteropus* and *Eidolon*, fruit bats in the genus *Cyanophenus*, and the long-tongued bats in the genus *Macrostylus*.

Most bat species are microchiropterans. They are generally insectivorous and small in size, with the largest, the American false vampire (*Vampyrum spectrum*), weighing 6 ounces (175 g). They can all echolocate.

Microchiropterans are divided into 17 families. Many families are small, containing only one or a few species. They include the mouse-tailed bats (Rhinopomatidae); Kitti's hog-nosed bat (Craseonycteridae); the New Zealand

Wings and Flight

The name of the bat order, Chiroptera, is derived from the Greek *cheiro*, meaning "hand," and *ptera*, meaning "wing." The title aptly describes one of the bat's unique features—its wing is a membrane that stretches from the elongated fingers and hand bones down the animal's side to its feet. The thumb remains free as a claw.

The size and shape of the wing dictate the style of the bat's flight. For example, a small wing compared to body weight allows the bat to fly fast, but with reduced maneuverability. On the other hand, bats with a large wing surface compared to body weight have a slower, but much more controllable flight. Some nectar-feeding bats are even able to hover like hummingbirds. The shape of the wing is another factor that affects maneuverability. Long, thin wings are ideal for fast flying in open areas, but bats that hunt in cluttered woodland need the maneuverability of shorter, broader wings.

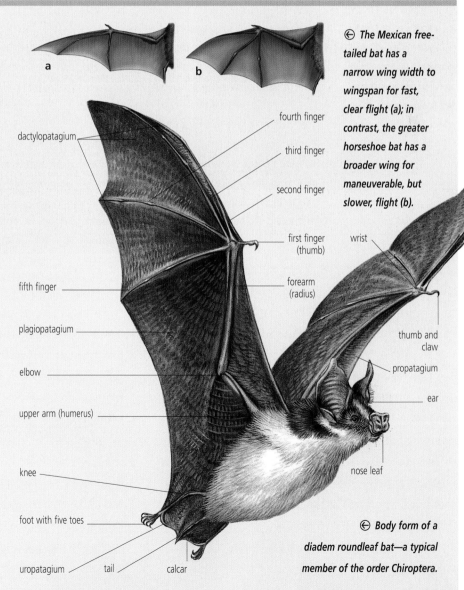

a b

⬅ The Mexican free-tailed bat has a narrow wing width to wingspan for fast, clear flight (a); in contrast, the greater horseshoe bat has a broader wing for maneuverable, but slower, flight (b).

dactylopatagium

fourth finger

third finger

second finger

first finger (thumb)

wrist

forearm (radius)

fifth finger

plagiopatagium

thumb and claw

elbow

propatagium

upper arm (humerus)

ear

knee

nose leaf

foot with five toes

uropatagium   tail   calcar

⬅ Body form of a diadem roundleaf bat—a typical member of the order Chiroptera.

short-tailed bat (Mystacinidae), which is the only mammal native to New Zealand; bulldog bats (Noctilionidae); spectacled bats (Mormoopidae); funnel-eared bats (Natalidae); thumbless bats (Furipteridae); disk-winged bats (Thyropteridae), which have suckers on their wrists and feet; and the Old World sucker-footed bat (Myzopodidae), a rare species from Madagascar.

The largest bat family is the Vespertilionidae, the "ordinary bats," with about 308 species in 34 genera. They have a plain, doglike face and simple ears. Most are insectivorous and have a tail pouch. They include the American little brown bat, Daubenton's bat, and various species of pipistrelles. Some bat families have distinctive, fleshy elaborations of the face. They include the slit-faced bats (Nycteridae), which have a hollow running from their nostrils to their eyes from which complex nose-folds emerge. Horseshoe and Old World leaf-nosed bats

⊕ Caves are a favorite roosting place for many bat species, such as this mixed group of funnel-eared, spear-nosed, and mustached bats in Tamana Cave, Trinidad, West Indies.

(Rhinolophidae) also have a complex, flared nose, and New World leaf-nosed bats (Phyllostomidae) have a fleshy spike on the snout or multiple leaves of skin around the face. This family also has the widest-ranging diet of any bat family, with members that are insectivores, carnivores, herbivores, or a mixture of all three. They include the vampire bats. Old World false vampire bats (Megadermatidae) feed mainly on insects, mammals, and frogs. Their ears are joined at the base. Free-tailed bats (Molossidae) have a protruding tail, narrow wings, and a wrinkled upper lip. Sheath-tailed bats (Emballonuridae) have a tail that emerges from the back of the membrane between the legs.

87

Common name Indian flying fox

Scientific name *Pteropus giganteus*

Family   Pteropodidae

Order   Chiroptera

Size Length head/body: 9–12 in (23–30 cm); forearm length: 6.5–7 in (16.5–18 cm); wingspan: 47–67 in (120–170 cm)

Weight   Male 2–3.5 lb (0.9–1.6 kg); female 1.3–2.5 lb (0.6–1.1 kg)

Key features Large bat with a dark-brown body and black wings; male has light-yellow color on back of neck and shoulders

Habits   Roosts in trees in large, mixed-sex groups; feeds at night on ripe fruit

Breeding   Single young born usually in February after gestation period of 4–5 months. Weaned at 5 months; probably sexually mature at 1–2 years. May live up to 30 years in captivity, about 15 in the wild

Voice   Variety of squawks and loud screams

Diet   Ripe fruit, including mangoes, bananas, papayas, and figs

Habitat   Forests and swamps, always near a large body of water

Distribution Maldives, Pakistan, India, Sri Lanka, and Myanmar (Burma)

Status   Population: unknown, but probably many thousands; CITES II

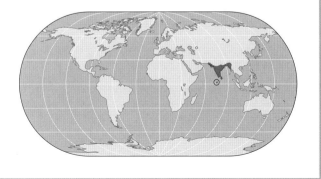

Indian Flying Fox

Pteropus giganteus

Indian flying foxes are among the world's largest bats. They spend their days hanging in large colonies in the tops of trees, then at night fly off to feed on ripe fruit.

LIKE OTHER FRUIT BATS, the Indian flying fox has a long, doglike face, hence the name "flying fox." The long nose and tongue help the bats reach among leaves and clusters of fruits. The bats have large eyes, and their vision is good for finding their way, but they cannot see color, even in daylight. They find the ripe fruit on which they feed mainly by smell. Like most other megachiropterans (large bats), they do not echolocate. Because they do not rely on their hearing as much as microchiropterans, their ears are relatively small and simple. Like other fruit bats, they have two claws on each wing and no tail or tail membrane.

Huge Wingspan

With a wingspan of around 5.5 feet (1.7 m), Indian flying foxes are among the largest bats in the world. They live in large colonies in the tropics and subtropics of India and surrounding regions. A separate population living on the Maldives forms a local subspecies.

    Indian flying foxes usually live in forests or other habitats with fruiting trees nearby, often close to a lake or other large body of water. Some colonies even roost within villages and towns. Large groups leaving their roost together at sunset make an impressive and noisy spectacle. During the day groups of bats roost in large, spreading trees such as banyan, fig, or tamarind trees. There can be up to several thousand in one roost, all hanging by their feet and long legs, looking like umbrellas or some kind of giant fruit. Males and females roost together. In forests they roost in the tallest trees

A flying fox grooms its fur. The flying fox family (Pteropodidae) *is restricted to tropical and subtropical regions of the Old World, where it feeds mainly on fruit and nectar.*

that emerge above the canopy. The height keeps them safe from most nonflying predators and gives them a good vantage point to keep an eye out for danger. The bats use the same roosting site year after year for generations. The bat roosts are not particularly peaceful resting places. There is constant movement as bats fidget and jockey for the best roost position, crawling along branches and flying from tree to tree. There is frequent squabbling, and the bats often fan their wings to keep cool. The appearance of an intruder, especially a snake or other predator, will set off a cacophony of raucous squawking and chattering.

At dusk the bats leave their roosts to feed on fruit trees. Feeding sites can be up to 10 miles (16 km) away. The bats are strong fliers and can easily cover that distance in less than an hour. An Indian flying fox once landed, exhausted but alive, on a boat that was more than 200 miles (320 km) from land. The bat had been blown off course and had been flying continuously for many hours. The bats stay at their feeding sites all night, eating, resting, and digesting their food before flying back to their roost trees about two hours before dawn.

Natural Juicing Machines

Indian flying foxes feed mainly on ripe fruit, preferring that which is soft and rotten. They particularly favor figs, mangoes, and papayas. They tear chunks out of fruit while hovering; otherwise they bite pieces off and carry them to a branch. Here they hang by one foot, holding the fruit with the other foot while they eat. They first chew the fruit, then press the pulp against the ridged roof of their mouth to squeeze out and swallow the juice, before spitting out the seeds and pulp. With bananas and other soft fruit they swallow some of the pulp, too. They also chew eucalyptus and other flowers, and sometimes eat insects.

Their teeth are well suited to a soft diet, with flattened molars, strong canines, and powerful jaws for piercing the tough rinds of fruit. Because their food is easy to digest, their guts are relatively short and simple. On average, food only takes half an hour to pass through their digestive system. The bats also need to drink regularly and do so when flying between feeding and roost sites. They swoop low to reach the surface of large bodies of open water. Some also drink seawater, apparently to obtain mineral salts that they lack in their diet.

The bats are important dispersal agents for fruiting trees because they drop seeds far and wide. They also help pollinate the flowers on which they sometimes feed. An estimated 40 percent of the trees in their rainforest habitats depend on the bats for pollination or dispersal.

Competition for Roosts

In the restless, crowded environment of the roost females choose males to mate with on the basis of good roosting spots. The males compete for the prime roost sites, with the largest and strongest getting the best positions near the tops of the trees. Males are highly possessive of females in their area, but there is no bonding between individual males and females. Females will move around the tree from male to male, sometimes on a daily basis. A male courts a female by shrieking shrilly into her ear until she allows him to mate.

Indian flying foxes breed seasonally, with births timed for the period when most fruit is available. Births occur at various times depending on the region. In parts of India they peak in January, while in Sri Lanka they

Keeping Cool

Fruit bats maintain a fairly constant body temperature of 91 to 98.6°F (33 to 37°C.) They never hibernate or go into torpor; saving energy is not necessary, since fruit is available all year round. In hot weather the bats fan themselves by gently flapping their wings. Instead of sweating, they drool onto their chest fur, which cools them as the liquid evaporates. They also pant. In cool weather they wrap their wings around their body and tuck in their head. Otherwise, they keep active to stay warm.

continue through to June. Very young bats cling to their mother, who carries them when she flies off to feed at night. By about three weeks the babies can hang upside down by themselves. By their sixth or seventh week they are getting too heavy to carry around and are left in the roost tree all night; the mother only returns at dawn to feed them and to rest.

The young bats begin to fly by 11 weeks and start to forage for themselves close to the nursery roost. For a couple of months they eat a mixture of fruit and milk. When young males become independent, they leave the main

Roosts for flying foxes are in the branches of a spreading tree, such as a banyan or tamarind. They can be noisy places, with animals jostling for the best sites and frequently flapping their wings to keep cool.

The flying fox's outstretched wings can reach a massive 5.5 feet (1.7 m) across, making it one of the largest of all bat species.

group and go to a "bachelor tree" nearby. Indian flying fox populations are relatively large, and they are not threatened to the same extent as many other species of fruit bat. However, many populations are declining owing to habitat destruction and hunting.

In India flying foxes are killed because they raid fruit crops. In many areas this is becoming an increasing problem as natural feeding trees are cut down, and bats are forced to feed in plantations. However, the damage they cause is often exaggerated, since the bats prefer to feed on overripe, rotting fruit, which would have had little market value anyway.

Habitat destruction can cause local extermination. For example, entire colonies can be displaced when roost trees are cut down for firewood, timber, or land development. On a larger scale deforestation destroys both the roost sites and feeding trees of huge numbers of bats. In many regions the bats are also hunted for food and traditional medicine. In Pakistan fat from fruit bats is thought to be a cure for rheumatism. According to an Indian folk remedy, a flying fox's wing bone tied to the ankle with a tail hair from a black cow will result in a painless childbirth.

In a few villages in India the resident flying foxes are revered and protected. One village has a large colony of bats in a tree around which the god Muni is believed to reside. Any villager who fails to protect the bats will be punished by the god through misfortune, accident, or even the death of a family member.

Common name Egyptian rousette bat

Scientific name *Rousettus aegyptiacus*

Family   Pteropodidae

Order   Chiroptera

Size   Length head/body: 4–7 in (9.5–18 cm); tail length: 0.5–1 in (1–2 cm); forearm length: 2.5–4 in (6.5–10 cm); wingspan: 16–20 in (41–51 cm)

Weight 3–6 oz (85–170 g)

Key features Smallish fruit bat; male much larger than female; gray-brown color, underparts paler; rounded ears and large eyes

Habits   Roosts communally in caves, tombs, temples, and rock crevices; active during the day and at night; activity peaks at dawn and dusk

Breeding   Usually single offspring or occasionally twins born October–December after gestation period of 4 months. Probably weaned at 2–3 months; sexually mature at about 1 year. May live over 20 years in captivity, probably similar in the wild

Voice   Loud clicking echolocation call, often sufficiently low-pitched (15–150 kHz) to be audible to humans; variety of social calls, including screams and barks

Diet   Fruit juices, flower pollen, and nectar

Habitat   Wherever there is fruit and flowers

Distribution North Africa from Senegal to Egypt south to South Africa; Cyprus, Turkey, and Yemen east to Pakistan

Status   Population: many thousands. Widespread and common

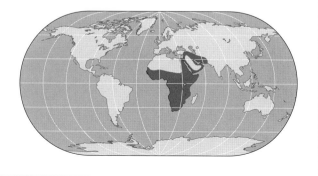

Egyptian Rousette Bat

Rousettus aegyptiacus

Egyptian rousettes are the only fruit bats to roost in caves. They have a basic form of echolocation that allows them to navigate in the dark.

THE EGYPTIAN ROUSETTE IS one of 10 species of *Rousettus*. Although called Egyptian, the bat is found throughout most of Africa into the Arabian Peninsula and east into Pakistan. It is relatively small for a fruit bat and, like other "flying foxes," has a long, doglike muzzle. The body and wings are a drab-brown color, the eyes are large, and the simple ears are constantly twitching. Males have very strong jaw muscles attached to a prominent bony crest on the top of the skull.

Egyptian rousettes roost in groups that can be as small as two or three animals, or form large aggregations of up to 9,000 individuals. Males and females roost together; roosting bats always huddle close, especially mothers with their young. Fighting and bickering between roosting bats are common, accompanied by loud screaming and coughlike barks.

Basic Echolocation

Rousettes are unique among megachiropteran bats in being able to roost in dark caves rather than in open tree canopies. They are also found in ancient tombs and temples, rock crevices, and even cellars and underground parking lots. They are able to roost in dark places because they are possibly the only megachiropterans that can echolocate. They find their way around in the gloom by listening for echoes of their own sounds.

However, they do not seem to rely totally on their echolocation system, since they never

Egyptian rousettes feed in a way similar to the Indian flying fox, preferring overripe fruit and chewing mouthfuls to a pulp before squeezing out the juice and swallowing it. They also feed from flowers, poking in their furry noses to drink the nectar, and picking up pollen in the process. Flying from flower to flower, they act as important pollinators. The Egyptian fruit bat is one of only four species that pollinate the baobab tree. This characteristic tree of the African savanna is economically important for local people, and so many animals depend on it that it is known as the "tree of life," yet it depends on rousette bats for its survival.

The bats breed seasonally, with most births occurring between October and December. About one in four births is to twins, giving them a higher reproduction rate than most other bat species. The mother carries the young when they are small; then as they get bigger, she leaves them in the roost when she goes to feed. The offspring stay in the same colony as their parents for most, if not all, of their lives.

Extermination Programs

In Israel a campaign began in the 1950s to eradicate fruit bats because they were thought to damage commercial fruit crops. Whole roosts were destroyed by fumigating caves with strong pesticide. But as well as killing fruit bats, the spray also killed many other cave-dwellers, including many thousands of insect-eating bats that ate moths whose caterpillars are crop pests. Killing the bats led to an explosion of moth populations, causing serious crop damage. When the fruit bats' feeding behavior was studied, there was no evidence that they caused damage to fruit crops. In fact, they actually provide a "cleaning" service to farmers by eating unharvested, overripe fruit.

Egyptian fruit bat populations recovered from the campaign surprisingly well, partly because they are flexible about where they roost, and also because of their relatively high reproduction rate. Public education programs in Israel are now helping improve the bats' image.

⊕ Egyptian rousette bats huddle together in a cave in northeastern South Africa. Rousettes are unique among fruit bats in their ability to roost in caves.

roost far from the entrance, preferring to stay where there is at least faint light.

Their echolocation system is very basic. They use a different method of generating noise than the expert echolocators—the microchiropterans. The noise is a burst of short clicks made with tongue against the roof of the mouth, not generated by the larynx.

The bats leave their roosts to fly to feeding grounds that can be up to 25 miles (40 km) away. They use different feeding grounds as different trees come into flower and fruit at different times. As with other fruit bats, they are thought to find their food mainly by smell.

Common name
Vampire bat

Scientific name *Desmodus rotundus*

Family   Phyllostomidae

Order   Chiroptera

Size   Length head/body: 3–3.5 in (7–9 cm);
                  forearm length: 2–2.5 in (5–6.3 cm);
                  wingspan: about 20 in (50 cm)

Weight 0.5–1.8 oz (15–50 g)

Key features Dark-gray bat, paler on
underside; snout flattened; vertical groove in
lower lip

Habits   Strictly nocturnal; usually lives in colonies of
                  20–100; roosts in caves, hollow trees, and old
                  mines

Breeding   Single young born once a year after gestation
                  period of about 7 months. Weaned at 10
                  months; sexually mature at 1 year. May live at
                  least 19.5 years in captivity, 15 in the wild

Voice   Ultrasonic squeaks (too high-pitched for
                  humans to hear); also aggressive squeaks if
                  other vampires attempt to feed close by

Diet   Feeds exclusively on blood, normally taken
                  from mammals, including humans

Habitat   Dry and wet areas of tropical and subtropical
                  Central and South America

Distribution From Argentina and central Chile to
                  northern Mexico; also Trinidad

Status   Population unknown, but many thousands.
                  Abundant, but probably declining

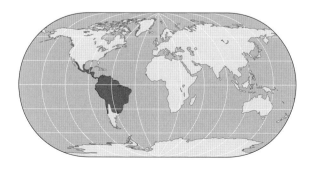

Vampire Bat   *Desmodus rotundus*

One of the world's most specialized and notorious mammals, the vampire bat is actually a highly sociable species and less of a threat to humans than is commonly supposed.

REAL-LIFE VAMPIRE BATS HAVE somehow become confused with the spine-chilling mythical fiends featured in European folklore. As a result, the species is widely known, but not because of its fascinating ecology. The vampire bat is in fact an extremely specialized animal, found only in Central and South America. Here it inhabits a wide variety of country, but especially favors forests and open grazing land.

Blood Specialist

Like its mythical counterpart, the vampire bat does indeed feed on blood and actually eats nothing else. Yet it is a mystery how such a specialized form of feeding ever evolved. Why does blood feeding occur in three species of tropical American vampires, but in none of the hundreds of other bat species that live in the rest of the world? The vampire's normal food is the blood of cattle, but horses, donkeys, and wild mammals such as peccaries and tapirs may be attacked. In coastal areas, where these animals are often scarce, vampires may even turn to sea lions for food.

Because of their specialized diet, vampires would probably be quite rare. However, the import of farm animals to the Americas, especially large cattle and horses, has provided them with more feeding opportunities than they would get from native mammals alone. Occasionally humans are bitten, but that is a rare event. In some areas vampires prey on domestic chickens and turkeys, although feeding on birds is the principal speciality of the other two species of vampire, the white-winged vampire (from Mexico to Argentina) and the hairy-legged vampire (from southern Texas and Mexico to Brazil and Bolivia).

⊕ *A common vampire bat. The truncated muzzle allows the bat to press its mouth close to the flesh of the animal on which it is feeding.*

Nighttime Feasts

Soon after dark a vampire bat will leave its daytime roost and fly straight and silently, close to the ground, using smell and sound to locate a suitable victim. Cattle are most commonly attacked because they are large, abundant, and tend to lie asleep out in the open. The vampire selects a suitable victim and lands nearby. It does not alight on the sleeping animal, since its weight would probably wake it up, and twitching ears or a flicking tail would prevent the vampire from going about its business. The vampire scurries toward its victim like a giant spider, with the body raised up high on its wrists and hind legs. It explores the surface of the animal, using its heat-sensitive muzzle to locate warm areas where the skin is thin and blood vessels come close to the surface. That is why cattle and horses tend to be bitten around the anus and ears, often on the neck, too, while chickens and turkeys are usually bitten around the wattles.

Having found a suitable bite site, the vampire bat licks the skin with its tongue, cuts away any obstructing hair or feathers with its teeth, and then uses its extremely sharp incisor teeth to scoop out a small piece of skin. The teeth are so sharp that this operation is almost painless; but if the victim notices, the bat may have to abandon its feeding attempt. Successful feeding takes practice, and inexperienced young vampires may frequently fail to feed. The bite is not deep, barely more than one-eighth of an inch (2 to 5 mm). The vampire presses the flat end of its snout close to the wound, but it does not actually suck blood. Instead, as the blood flows, the bat laps it up. The tongue forms a tube and is used almost like a drinking straw, slowly pumping up and down along a prominent groove in the lower lip. Blood is drawn up to

Teeth

Owing to its unique diet, the vampire bat has highly specialized dentition. There are only 20 teeth, fewer than in any other bat. Since blood does not require chewing, the teeth are small and have a greatly reduced grinding surface. The incisors and canines are big, triangular, and exceedingly sharp. They are used for cutting out the sliver of skin to initiate the bleeding process.

the mouth, and at the same time, the bat dribbles saliva into the wound. The saliva contains a special anticoagulant ingredient that slows the clotting of the blood, ensuring a continued flow for longer than the bat needs to feed. Bleeding will sometimes continue for up to eight hours, so the victim loses more blood than is actually consumed by the bat. Blood consists mainly of water, which is heavy, and could impede flying after a good meal. The bat will therefore frequently urinate before it has finished feeding to rid its body of excess water. A vampire bat is known to return to the same wound on consecutive nights.

Messy Roosts

Usually vampires roost in caves, but they also use hollow trees, abandoned buildings, and old mines. A vampire roost can be easily recognized. Instead of having piles of the neat droppings that other bats produce, vampire roosts accumulate slimy masses of digested blood on the walls and floor, looking like tar but smelling strongly of ammonia.

Vampires pass the day in these dark and cool places, sleeping and grooming themselves. They are highly sociable and caring toward

others of their species and will often spend long periods grooming each other's fur, just as monkeys and apes do. They will also regurgitate blood from a meal and share it with neighboring bats. Vampires are agile animals and will run around rapidly on vertical or horizontal surfaces. They are shy creatures and scurry away or retreat into protective crevices if they are disturbed in the roost. Normally the bats do not leave the roost until it is completely dark outside, and they are reluctant to emerge on nights when the moon is shining brightly. They are active until about midnight, after which those that have fed successfully may return to the roost, often long before dawn. The bats usually forage within 5 miles (8 km) of their daytime roost, but sometimes travel up to 12 miles (20 km) to feed. One colony of 100 to 150 vampires ranged over nearly 5 square miles (13 sq. km), using 1,200 head of cattle as prey.

Large vampire colonies seem to consist of sets of females with their offspring, each set belonging to a single adult male. Several other males are often close by, awaiting mating opportunities. The principal male defends his position and access to females aggressively and is thought to father about half the offspring in his group of females. He maintains his position as top bat for about two years before being displaced by a younger male. A female vampire, like other bats, normally has only a single youngster each year. It is born after a gestation lasting about seven months. The new-born young is already well developed, with its eyes open. It weighs about one-fifth of an ounce (6 g), nearly a quarter of the mother's own

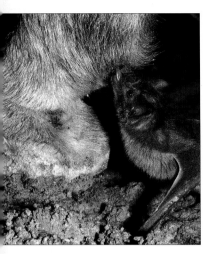

⊕ *In Trinidad a vampire bat takes blood from a resting donkey. Vampire bats feed for up to half an hour. Each bat can drink over half its body weight of blood in a single bout of feeding.*

Food Sharing

Vampires will chase others away from a good feeding place, but are amazingly generous toward their friends and relatives who may have been unsuccessful in their feeding excursions. Young vampires in particular fail to get a full blood meal in about one-third of their attempts, and even the adults are not always successful in getting sufficient food—their victims may sometimes be too vigilant to permit the bats to feed freely. Disrupted feeding attempts can be serious because vampires will starve if they do not feed properly for more than three days in a row. Bats that have failed to feed successfully will return to their roost, where they will be given blood by one of their better-fed neighbors. Usually food sharing involves closely related bats and those that normally roost close together. Sharing food with each other prevents other members of the colony from starving and helps ensure a higher overall survival rate. Such unselfish behavior is extremely rare among animals and totally unexpected in a species with such a gruesome reputation.

weight. It is fed initially on milk, but is also given regurgitated blood from about two months. The young vampire grows slowly and is looked after by its mother for longer than any other bat of comparable size. It can feed itself on blood at four months old, but will not be completely weaned before about 10 months of age. Young males often disperse when they reach sexual maturity, probably driven away from the colony dominated by their father.

Rabies Risk

Vampire bats can be a serious problem, but not necessarily as a direct consequence of the blood they remove. The wounds they create often become septic, causing pain and even death to many animals. They also attract flies to lay their eggs, which then develop into larvae in the skin. Vampire bites result in extensive blood loss due to the anticoagulants produced by the bats and subsequent failure of the wound to heal. But the main problem posed by the vampire is transmission of the rabies virus. The bats pass the disease to any mammal they bite. Tens of

thousands of cattle die from bat-borne rabies each year, representing a loss of nearly $50 million annually. Occasionally humans become infected and die from this particularly horrific disease. The bats die too, and vampire bat populations suffer severe losses as a result.

Attempts to eradicate rabies have often focused on removing the bats by dynamiting roosts or netting the animals as they come to feed. A more subtle form of attack is to smear a mixture of syrup and strychnine poison around vampire bites on a cow, so that a bat returning to a previously successful feeding site will get the sticky poison on its fur. When it returns to the roost, it will be groomed by other bats who will then be poisoned. In some small recompense for the problems it causes, the vampire's saliva may turn out to be valuable. A drug company has taken out a patent for producing the protein that prevents blood from clotting. Blood clots are the main cause of heart attacks and strokes in humans, so the vampire's anticoagulant protein (christened "Draculin") could help rescue the bat's dire public image.

⊕ Sometimes vampires roost alone or in small groups, but normally they live in colonies of 20 to 100 bats. Occasional roosts may contain more than 2,000 vampires, and at least 20 other bat species are known to live with vampires at times.

False Vampire Bat

Megaderma lyra

One of the few truly carnivorous bats, false vampires will eat any small creature from rodents and fish to insects. They hunt at night, using echolocation, vision, and their excellent hearing.

MEGADERMA LYRA IS OFTEN known as the greater false vampire bat and is among the largest of the microchiropteran bats. It lives in southern and Southeast Asia and is one of only five species in the Old World false vampire bat family (Megadermatidae). These bats are carnivorous, eating a diverse range of prey, which may sometimes include other bats.

Misleading Name

The name "vampire" is misleading, since none of the bats draw blood from prey as true vampires do. The confusion arose back in the 16th century, when reports of bats that drank blood led overimaginative biologists to call almost any fierce-looking bat with sharp canines a "vampire." The characteristic teeth of false vampires include no upper incisors, and the large canines have secondary points (cusps).

With their huge ears and strange, fleshy nose-leaf, false vampire bats have a distinctive face. False vampires' eyes are large, which is unusual among microchiropteran bats. They therefore have good vision even in low light levels. They also have excellent hearing, with their huge ears joined at the base by a band of skin across the forehead. The arrangement presumably helps ensure that as much sound information as possible is captured. It may also help support the large ears in flight. The echolocation calls are emitted through the nose, as with horseshoe bats. The tall, protruding nose-leaf forms a fleshy spike on the muzzle and helps channel the sounds rather like a

---

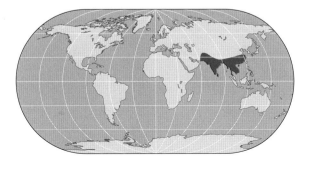

Common name False vampire bat
(greater false vampire, Indian false vampire)

Scientific name *Megaderma lyra*

Family Megadermatidae

Order Chiroptera

Size Length head/body: 3–4 in (7.5–10 cm); forearm length: 2.5–3 in (6.5–7 cm); wingspan: about 30 in (70 cm)
Weight 1.4–2.1 oz (40–60 g)

Key features Large ears joined over forehead, each with divided tragus; large, erect nose-leaf forming spike on snout; fur grayish-brown above, whitish-gray below

Habits Nocturnal; hunts small animals, flying low around trees and bushes; roosts in small groups, usually of fewer than 30

Breeding Normally only 1 offspring born per year after gestation period of 150–160 days. Weaned at 2–3 months; males sexually mature at 15 months, females at 19 months. Not normally kept in captivity, probably lives at least 10 years in the wild

Voice Social and faint echolocation calls

Diet Carnivorous: preys on rodents, birds, frogs, lizards, invertebrates, and other bats

Habitat Variety of habitats with broad-leaved trees; roosts in caves, well shafts, crevices, large buildings, and tree holes

Distribution Afghanistan to southern China south to Sri Lanka and Malay Peninsula

Status Population: total figure unknown, but likely to be many thousands

megaphone. The echolocation system is so sensitive that the bats can differentiate between objects with different textures—useful for telling the difference between a mouse-sized stone and something furry.

The false vampire hunts after dark, skimming low through trees and undergrowth. The bats hunt mainly by listening. Their hearing is especially sensitive in the frequency range 10 to 20 kHz, enabling them to capture the sounds made by creatures rustling in the undergrowth. When there is enough light, they also use vision to detect moving prey. The bat homes in on its victim and pounces, swiftly killing the animal with a quick bite to the back of the neck. Small prey may then be eaten on the wing. Larger animals are carried back to a feeding roost to be eaten at leisure, while the bat hangs by its feet. The roosts often contain an untidy assortment of scattered animal remains, where indigestible parts of prey are bitten off and dropped to the ground.

⬱ *A false vampire bat pounces on a mouse. While they will sometimes drink their victim's blood before eating its flesh, the bats never feed on blood alone.*

Well-Suited Wings

The wings of false vampire bats are also well suited to their needs. Searching for prey in a habitat cluttered by low branches demands slow and maneuverable flight, with the ability to make tight turns. Yet it is hard to fly slowly without stalling. The bats have the short, broad wings that are perfect for this type of flight. Their wings are large for their body weight, which means that they can easily take off from the ground carrying the extra load of a mouse.

False vampires roost in caves, rock crevices, hollow trees, and buildings such as temples. There are usually up to 30 animals in a roost, but groups are sometimes much larger. Males and females roost together until it is time for females to give birth.

Most bat caves around the world will have more than one species of bat in residence. However, in those caves used by false vampires they are usually the only species present. This is perhaps not surprising, considering that other bat species are often on their menu!

Cannibalism has been reported in captive false vampire bats, when a juvenile from the previous year killed a new baby by biting it. How often such behavior might occur in the wild is not known.

99

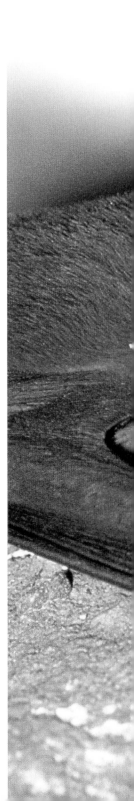

Mexican Free-Tailed Bat

Tadarida brasiliensis

Mexican free-tailed bats can roost in huge crowds numbering over 20 million animals. Their prodigious appetite for migrating moths helps minimize pest damage to crops in southwestern America.

Common name
Mexican free-tailed bat (guano bat, Brazilian free-tailed bat)

Scientific name *Tadarida brasiliensis*

Family   Molossidae

Order   Chiroptera

Size   Length head/body: 3.5–4 in (9–10 cm); tail length: 1–1.5 in (2.5–4 cm); forearm length: 1.5–2 in (4–5 cm); wingspan: 12–14 in (30–35 cm)

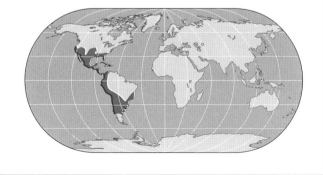

Weight 0.4–0.5 oz (11–14 g)

Key features Medium-sized bat with tail that projects well over tail membrane; ears broad; velvety reddish to black fur; wings long and narrow

Habits   Roosts in groups of up to 20 million individuals; flies high, hunting insects at night

Breeding   Single baby born in June after gestation period of about 90 days. Weaned at 6 weeks; sexually mature at about 1 year. Not kept in captivity, may live at least 18 years in the wild

Voice   Ultrasonic echolocation calls at 40–62 kHz; variety of social calls, including squeals, chirps, and buzzing audible to humans

Diet   Small insects such as mosquitoes, flies, beetles, and moths

Habitat   Wide variety of habitats from desert to pine and broad-leaved forest; roosts in caves, old mines, hollow trees, and buildings

Distribution U.S. to Chile, Argentina, and southern Brazil; Greater and Lesser Antilles

Status   Population: many millions; IUCN Lower Risk: near threatened. Believed to be fewer now than in recent past

MEXICAN FREE-TAILS ARE medium-sized bats with short, velvety fur that can be reddish, dark brown, or almost black. Some individuals have white patches, which can be anywhere on the body. An almost mouselike tail gives the species its common name. Over half the length of the tail extends beyond the tail membrane that stretches between the legs. The ears are broad and black; and unlike most bats in the Molossidae family, they are not joined on top of the head. However, their upper lips have vertical wrinkles common to all bats in the family. The feet have distinct white bristles, used for grooming, on the sides of the toes.

Insect-Eaters

Mexican free-tailed bats are insectivorous; and like most chiropterans, they use echolocation to find and catch insects on the wing. Bats can eat their own weight in insects each night, with the appetite of nursing mothers being particularly demanding. A large bat colony might eat several hundred pounds (about 100 kg) of insects in a single night.

Although the first specimen to be described scientifically was from Brazil (hence the species name of *brasiliensis*), Mexican free-tailed bats are most common in Texas and Mexico. Their wide distribution stretches across the southern states of North America down through Central America, the Antilles, and most of western South America to central Chile and east to the coastal provinces of Brazil.

Mexican free-tails roost in caves and under bridges. They may sometimes use old mines, well shafts, and hollow trees. Because they frequently occur in buildings they are often called "house bats." They usually roost near lakes and ponds where they can get drinking water, but mainly because of the insects that live around them. Although most of these roost sites will contain relatively small numbers of bats, some roosts are huge. There are caves in Texas where over 20 million bats congregate to have their young—that is more than the number of people in our largest cities. These bats form the largest known colonies of vertebrates anywhere in the world. At some famous caves, such as the Carlsbad Cavern in New Mexico, the dramatic sight of millions of

⊙ *The tail of the Mexican free-tailed bat is thicker than in other bats. It does not lie in a broad tail membrane, but instead hangs free.*

⊙ *Mexican free-tails are insectivorous. They are known to feed on corn earworm moths, whose caterpillars are a major crop pest.*

bats emerging like smoke from the cave entrance at sunset draws hundreds of spectators every night.

As well as the tourists, the bats also attract predators such as owls, hawks, and snakes, which wait at the cave mouth and snatch bats as they fly past. But with such huge numbers of bats, the predators can only catch a tiny fraction of the population.

Such huge numbers of bats create enormous mounds of waste. The levels of ammonia in the roost caves make the air stink. Concentrations can be so high that it is difficult to breathe and can even be lethal. The bats survive partly by producing large quantities of mucus in their airways. The stinking piles of guano (excrement) below the roosts are used as fertilizer, and sodium nitrate extracted from guano was once used to produce gunpowder.

The Mexican free-tailed bat clearly demonstrates one of the dilemmas of many bat species, especially those that feed on insects. The energy costs of flying and rearing fast-growing young are high. Furthermore, because of their relatively small size bats lose heat quickly, so they use a lot of energy in keeping warm. To compensate for their high energy needs, bats need to eat a lot; but in seasonal climates the numbers of flying insects fluctuate widely over the year. As the weather gets cooler, the insects disappear just when the bats' energy needs are increasing. Bats have two options: to sit out the cold period in torpor, using as few energy reserves as possible, or to fly to warmer, more productive climates.

In Mexican free-tails migration patterns vary depending on where the populations are based. Those in the northernmost part of their range in northern California do not migrate, perhaps because they would have to fly too far to reach warmth. During wintry periods the bats become semitorpid in cold roosts. However, unlike bats that go into true hibernation, their body temperature does not drop to match that of the surroundings. Instead, the bats cool to a few degrees below normal, saving substantial amounts of energy. Populations in Arizona do not migrate either, but spend winter resting in relatively warm roosts in chimneys, caves, and tunnels. Those in other southwestern states, such as Texas, migrate to Mexico. Migrating bats can travel distances of over 620 miles (1,000 km) in a couple of weeks.

A Bat Calendar

The populations that have been studied most closely are those migratory bats that fly south in winter to follow the warmth and insects. In spring they leave Mexico to fly to Texas. When they arrive, they mate. Males and females then separate into bachelor and nursery colonies. Little is known about mating behavior in the wild, but in captivity males claim territories and are aggressive toward intruding males. They mark their territory by rubbing their chests and scented throat glands on the roost surfaces. They "sing" to the females, who do the rounds, visiting different males' territories for mating.

Females give birth around June to a single naked pup. Most births in a roost fall within a 10-day period, so all the young are of a similar age. When the mothers fly off to feed, they leave their babies hanging huddled together in a "nursery patch" on one part of the roost. The

mothers return once during the night to feed their young. When a mother arrives back, she is greeted by a barrage of youngsters all trying to steal a feed. Each female finds her own baby, first by using high-pitched "peep" contact calls, then by sniffing it to confirm its identity by smell. Sometimes a mother will feed a youngster that is not her own, but 85 percent of the time she manages to find and feed her own offspring among the thousands of others.

The appetite of the young bat is enormous. It can consume its own weight of milk every day, which means that the mother has to produce up to a quarter of her body weight in milk every 24 hours. In the warm environment of the nursery roost, kept even hotter by all the tiny bodies, babies grow quickly. Within a month most babies are furred and ready to fly. Males are sexually mature at 18 to 22 months, but females can produce their first youngster at one year old.

Farmers' Friends

A cloud of bats emerging from the mouth of a cave will climb high into the air until they are almost out of sight. Why they fly so high was once a mystery, but solving it has given a reason for farmers to respect these bats.

Radar studies of bats began at an airport, when the bats' movements were mapped to avoid collisions with planes. They have revealed amazing facts about the bats' flight patterns. The bats can fly at least as high as 10,000 feet (3,000 m), with groups showing foraging behavior at 600 to 3,200 feet (200 to 1,000 m). Microphones tied to weather balloons have recorded the feeding buzzes of free-tailed bats (the intense burst of echolocation used to pinpoint an insect just before it is captured) nearly half a mile high.

Although it seems improbable that bats can catch any insects a mile or more above the surface of the earth, they are actually tapping into the migration routes of one of the United States' most serious agricultural pests—the corn earworm moth. These insects gradually spread northward every spring from their winter

Swift Fliers

Free-tailed bats fly very fast and hunt insects in open spaces, particularly above water. They usually fly high, generally above 50 feet (15 m), unless they are swooping low over water to drink. Their efficient flight enables them to cover long distances on migrations. Their long, narrow wings and characteristic flight patterns resemble those of swifts. They are the high-speed bats, contrasting with the smaller, fluttery types found in woodlands and confined spaces.

strongholds in Mexico. Their caterpillars (also known as cotton bollworms) do much damage to crops. The adult moths fly hundreds of feet high into the air to catch the prevailing winds that carry them north in their seasonal migration. This way clouds of moths can travel over 100 miles (160 km) in one night. By intercepting the swarms, the bats eat moths that would otherwise cause damage as far north as Canada. A single colony of 20 million bats could eat nearly 15,000 tons (13,000 tonnes) of insects over one summer.

Insecticide Menace

Many bat colonies in the southern United States have shown a marked decline in numbers over recent years. The drop in numbers has been blamed partly on the use of the insecticide DDT. The bats eat contaminated insects, and the poison accumulates in the bats' bodies. Although DDT is now banned in the United States, if it is used on any part of the bat migration routes, the problem will not disappear. DDT also causes breeding failure, so the effect on the bat population can be serious.

Free-tails have one of the highest rabies infection rates among bats, so it is advisable to avoid handling them. However, the risk of being bitten by an infected bat is quite small.

⊖ *Mexican free-tailed bats emerge from Bracken Cave, Texas. In some places the spectacle of millions of bats appearing like a smokescreen draws crowds of tourists.*

Little Brown Bat

Myotis lucifugus

Little brown bats are common in urban and rural areas across America. In winter they may migrate considerable distances to find suitable caves for hibernation.

Common name
Little brown bat

Scientific name *Myotis lucifugus*

Family Vespertilionidae

Order Chiroptera

Size Length head/body: 3–4 in (8–10 cm); forearm length: about 1.5 in (3.5–4 cm); wingspan: 9–11 in (22–27 cm)

Weight 0.25–0.45 oz (7–13 g)

Key features Small, fluttery bat with glossy fur of shades of brown; underside paler; small, black ears with short, rounded tragus; long hairs on toes

Habits Hunts insects over water; females gather in summer nursery roosts, often in buildings; sexes hibernate together in caves over winter

Breeding Single young born May–July after gestation period of 60 days. Weaned at 3 weeks; sexually mature in first year in southern parts of range, second year farther north. May live several years in captivity (not usually kept for long periods), 30 in the wild

Voice Short pulse echolocation calls 38–78 kHz, peaking at about 40 kHz, too high-pitched for humans to hear

Diet Insects caught on wing, especially mosquitoes, caddis flies, mayflies, and midges

Habitat Urban and forested areas; summer roosts in buildings or under bridges, usually near water; hibernation roosts in caves or mines

Distribution Alaska to Labrador and Newfoundland (Canada) south to Distrito Federal (Mexico)

Status Population: probably several million. Not seriously threatened

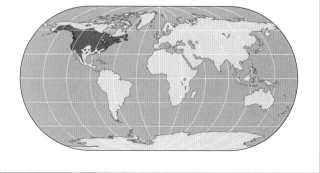

THE LITTLE BROWN BAT IS one of America's most common bats. It has been well studied because of its abundance and wide distribution. Its habit of roosting in houses makes it easy to examine.

Little brown bats are insectivorous. The bats hunt in flight, frequently foraging over water for insects such as mosquitoes, caddis flies, mayflies, and midges. They can catch an insect with the tip of the wing, transfer it onto the tail membrane, then curl their tail forward to scoop it into the mouth—all while flying in the dark at over 20 miles per hour (30 km/h).

Like other insectivorous bats that live in temperate regions of the world, the little brown bat's lifestyle is dictated by the seasons. It spends spring, summer, and fall rearing offspring and feeding, so that by winter it has enough fat reserves to survive winter hibernation. Females have to eat twice as much as males to cover the energy they expend on producing and nursing their young.

Second Homes

During the spring, summer, and fall bats use two types of roost—day roosts and night roosts. They rest in the day roosts, which can be in buildings, trees, under rocks, in piles of wood, and occasionally in caves. In the evening the bats gather in night roosts just before flying off to feed. The purpose of such nightly gatherings is not clear, but clustering together may help the bats raise their body temperature for the evening's flying. It also allows for social interactions and recognition of other members of the colony.

A little brown bat hunts for insect prey. Once detected—by echolocation—the insects are snatched with the teeth in flight or scooped up with the wing tip or tail membrane.

travel up to 300 miles (500 km) to find a suitable place. A single cave in Vermont, for example, draws in bats from all over New England. The bats hibernate in clusters. Their body temperature drops to almost that of their surroundings and slows their metabolic process to practically a standstill. At 35°F (1.6°C) the bat's oxygen consumption is 140 times lower than that of an active bat, and it burns up only 4 milligrams of fat per day. However, even small rises in the temperature of the roost dramatically increase the bats' metabolic rate. They also need to wake up periodically to drink and may move to another hibernation place.

Hibernation ends when nighttime temperatures regularly get above 50°F (10°C), when insects start to fly again in large numbers. In the southern parts of their range the bats can be active as early as February, but in northern Ontario they may not be until April.

Sperm Storage

Bats mate in the fall. Males hang in caves and make echolocation calls, and the females fly around choosing a mate. Both males and females mate with more than one partner. The females store sperm over winter in their reproductive tract, and eggs are only released and fertilized in spring. During birth the female turns around to hang from her thumbs (wing claws). She curls her body around so that as the baby is born, it drops into her tail membrane.

Mothers leave their babies clustered in nursery colonies when they fly off to feed. The young fly at 18 days, when their wings are almost adult size.

Female little brown bats gather in nursery colonies of 50 to 5,000 individuals. The roost sites are usually in the attics of buildings. The females use the same sites year after year. If roosts are sealed, they find it difficult to locate new ones, and many probably die. While the females are gathered in their summer roosts, the males disappear, probably hiding in tree holes and other small crevices during the day.

Toward fall the males rejoin the females, and together they group in swarms to inspect hibernation sites. This happens in August in south Ontario and later in the year farther south. Hibernation sites are almost always underground in caves, mines, or even old wells. The sites need to be cold, but above freezing, ideally at 35.6°F (2°C), and with high humidity. Because their needs are so specific, good hibernation sites are rare, and bats may have to

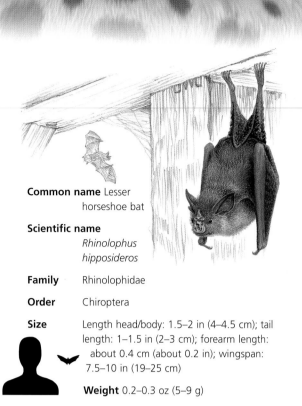

Common name Lesser
horseshoe bat

Scientific name
*Rhinolophus
hipposideros*

Family   Rhinolophidae

Order   Chiroptera

Size   Length head/body: 1.5–2 in (4–4.5 cm); tail
length: 1–1.5 in (2–3 cm); forearm length:
about 0.4 cm (about 0.2 in); wingspan:
7.5–10 in (19–25 cm)

Weight 0.2–0.3 oz (5–9 g)

Key features Small, delicate bat with fine, fluffy gray fur;
horseshoe-shaped nose-leaf

Habits   Nocturnal; flies fast with shallow wing beats;
hibernates alone, but summer roosts often
colonial

Breeding   Single baby born mostly mid-June–early July
after gestation period of about 4 months.
Weaned at 6–7 weeks; sexually mature at 1
year. May live at least 21 years in the wild,
soon dies in captivity

Voice   Quiet chirping noises using very high
frequencies of 108–110 kHz

Diet   Small moths, mosquitoes, flies, and beetles;
mostly taken on the wing but some from the
ground

Habitat   Prefers wooded areas on limestone;
hibernates in caves; often uses warm roof
spaces as nursery roosts in northern parts

Distribution Southern Europe from Ireland east to
Kyrgyzstan and Kashmir

Status   Population: unknown; IUCN Vulnerable.
Threatened with extinction throughout
northern European part of its range

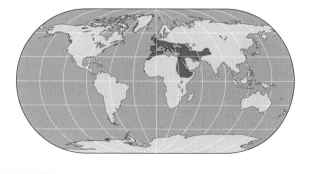

Lesser Horses[ ]
Bat
Rhinol[

*The diminutive lesser horseshoe bat lo[
black fruit when in hibernation, hangir[
with its wings wrapped around itself.*

LIKE OTHER HORSESHOE BATS, the lesser horseshoe
bat has a distinct horseshoe-shaped fleshy ring
around the nostrils and a pointed fleshy prong
above them. The structure is important for
echolocation, since the ultrasonic sound pulses
are emitted through the nostrils and focused
into a narrow beam by the nose-leaf. The ears
have no tragus, and they waggle constantly in
order to interpret any returning echoes.

Delicately Built

Lesser horseshoe bats are delicately built
creatures, but they seem able to tolerate a wide
variety of environmental conditions. However,
their preferred habitat seems to be open
woodland, especially where there are caves
nearby. Such conditions are often found in
limestone country, but the bats will also live
among the lower foothills of mountain ranges,
using rock crevices as roosts.

In northern latitudes the lesser horseshoe
bat's summer roosts and nursery colonies are in
sheltered buildings and sun-warmed roof
spaces. In the southern parts of its range the
summer roosts can be in caves or mine tunnels.
The bats emerge around sunset and are active
throughout the night. They have faster wing
beats than any other European horseshoe bat,
but fly almost silently, picking prey off leaves
and stones. They occasionally drop to the
ground to seize spiders and tiny beetles. They
also hunt flying insects.

At the end of summer the bats migrate up
to 100 miles (150 km) to their winter quarters.
They seek out cool places, with stable
temperatures of 43 to 48°F (6 to 9°C), such as
caves, mines, and cellars. Such places must be
humid, too, since horseshoe bats hibernate with

their wings wrapped around them like little furled umbrellas. In that position they expose a large area of skin surface to the air and so would lose a lot of precious body water by evaporation if they tried to hibernate in a drier place. Often, groups of lesser horseshoe bats will choose the same place to hibernate. However, each bat hangs up without touching its neighbors and usually finds a spot at least 20 inches (50 cm) from another. Many other bat species cluster together for the winter.

When horseshoe bats hang by their tiny hind feet, the leg tendons are stretched, causing the toes to grip automatically. As a result, the bat will not fall even when it is profoundly asleep.

Delayed Fertilization

Mating takes place in the fall, with the male wrapping the female in his wings. The female stores sperm in her reproductive tract until she ovulates. Fertilization usually occurs in March and April. At the end of winter the bats begin to assemble in their summer roosts. Initially both sexes may live together, but the adult males usually depart before the young are born.

At birth the baby lesser horseshoe bat is covered in fine hair, except on the belly, and is almost completely helpless. Its eyes open after three days. At the height of summer the nursery colonies are often quite noisy places, with the bats chirping and chittering constantly. The groups disperse between August and October as the bats prepare for hibernation.

The need for special hibernation places, like limestone caves, means that horseshoe bats are vulnerable to the removal of such sites when they are quarried away. Loss of habitat and contamination of farmland insects by pesticides have added to the problems. The species is threatened across the whole of its northern European range. In the last 50 years it has become extinct in northern England and other parts of northern Europe. Farther south, where the climate is warmer and agriculture less intensive, the bats seem more secure.

⊕ *A lesser horseshoe bat roosting in Germany. When roosting, the bat's toes grip automatically, so the animal will not fall even when in a deep sleep.*

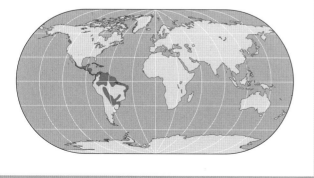

Common name Fisherman bat (bulldog bat)

Scientific name *Noctilio leporinus*

Family Noctilionidae

Order Chiroptera

Size Length head/body: 4–5 in (10–13 cm); forearm length: 3–4 in (8–10 cm); wingspan: 11–20 in (28–51 cm)

Weight 2.1–3.1 oz (60–88 g)

Key features Large bat with heavy doglike muzzle; nostrils slightly tubular and downward pointing with "hare-lip" fold of skin hanging below; large ears; tragus with serrated edge; upperparts bright reddish-orange in males, gray or dull brown in females

Habits Hunts at night over water, catching surface-swimming fish and insects; roosts in groups of 30 to several hundred; active year-round

Breeding Single young born after gestation period of about 4 months. Weaned at 3–4 months; sexually mature at about 1 year. May live 11.5 years in captivity, probably more in the wild

Voice High-pitched chirping echolocation calls; lower-frequency communication calls, including warning honk

Diet Mainly fish, but also crustaceans and insects such as winged ants, crickets, and stinkbugs

Habitat Near rivers, lakes, lagoons, or other water; roosts in caves, rock clefts, and fissures

Distribution Southern Mexico to Guianas, Peru, southern Brazil, northern Argentina, Trinidad, Greater and Lesser Antilles, and southern Bahamas

Status Population: probably low thousands

Fisherman Bat

Noctilio leporinus

As its name suggests, the fisherman bat catches fish. It uses echolocation to detect ripples from small fish swimming near the water's surface, then hooks them out with its large, long-clawed feet.

THE FISHERMAN BAT IS A specialized animal. Only two or three other types of bat are known to eat fish at all, and none use fish as their main food like the fisherman bat. Fish-eating, or piscivorous, bats probably evolved from bats that caught insects as they floated or swam on the surface of the water. A closely related species, the lesser bulldog bat (*Noctilio albiventris*), often feeds using that method. The fisherman bat's major modifications for fish-catching are its legs and feet. The legs are long, and the feet are up to four times larger than those of related nonfishing bats. The huge feet have long, strong claws that are used as gaffs to hook out the bat's prey. As the bat trawls its feet through the water, its tail membrane is held clear by cartilaginous spikes called calcars that project from the ankles.

Greasy Fur

The bat's fur is short and greasy, so it does not become waterlogged when the animal gets splashed by its prey. Fisherman bats can even fall into the water and take off again successfully. The wings are long and narrow, allowing for powerful, efficient flight over open water. The wing loading (body-weight-to-wing-area ratio) is low, so the bat can carry heavy loads in the form of fish. The bat can even swim, using its wings as oars. The fisherman bat's face has distinctive bulldoglike jowls that expand into pouches for carrying food.

Fisherman bats hunt over freshwater ponds, rivers, lakes, saltwater lagoons, and even at the edge of the ocean surf. They usually take small surface-swimming fish such as minnows. They also eat insects and small crustaceans. In Puerto Rico there is a group that catches fiddler crabs.

within 8 to 20 inches (20 to 50 cm) of the water's surface. At the same time, it uses chirping echolocation calls to detect disturbances in the water. When the bat spots a ripple or protrusion above the water's surface that may be the fin or back of a small fish, it swoops low, flying parallel to the water about 1.5 to 4 inches (4 to 10 cm) above it. When its echolocation calls pinpoint the fish, the bat grabs it with its sharp talons. The bat's echolocation system is extremely precise. In laboratory experiments a bat detected objects as thin as a human hair sticking up just 0.08 inches (0.2 cm) from the water.

Fish-Hook Feet

In the second type of search pattern the bat trawls its feet randomly through the water for up to 30 feet (10 m) trying to hook any fish that happen to be in its path. Bats tend to use this search strategy if there are lots of fish around. As soon as a fish is hooked, the bat quickly lifts it to its mouth and chews it while still flying. Needle-sharp teeth grip the slippery fish tightly. Small fish are eaten in flight, but larger ones are carried to a roost where they can be eaten while the bat is hanging up.

Fisherman bats are sociable, often hunting in groups of up to 15 animals. They usually roost in groups of around 30 individuals, although huge roosts of hundreds have been found. Roost clusters tend to be "bachelor" groups of nonbreeding males or harem groups with many females to each male. The females in a group roost in the same place and with the same individuals for many years. Roosts have a strong, penetrating musky odor. Male fisherman bats have scent glands in an unusual fold of skin near the scrotum, and female bats have glands under their armpits. Females rub their heads in their neighbors' armpits, covering themselves in scent.

⬆ A fisherman bat flies over water searching for a meal. The fisherman is the only bat species that preys on fish as its main source of food, but it also eats insects and crabs.

Fisherman bats generally feed at dusk, dawn, and during the night. They have been seen in the late afternoon, flying over water where pelicans are swimming, presumably feeding on small fish that the pelicans disturb. Some bats feeding in coastal waters time their hunting to coincide with high tide, when large fish and sharks drive the smaller fish into the shallows, where the bats can easily catch them.

The bats have two types of search pattern. In one—a focused search—they only dip their feet in the water having located potential prey. First, the bat zigzags relatively high, flying to

Common name
Long-eared bat (whispering bat)

Scientific name *Plecotus auritus*

Family   Vespertilionidae

Order   Chiroptera

Size   Length head/body: 1.5–2 in (4–5 cm); tail length: 1.5–2 in (4–5 cm); forearm length: 1–1.5 in (3–4 cm); wingspan: 9–11 in (24–28 cm)

      Weight 0.2–0.4 oz (6–12 g)

Key features Medium-sized bat; ears as long as body; fur brown, long, soft, and wispy

Habits   Active at night; one of most frequent species in house roofs, bedrooms, and bat boxes (artificial roosts); hibernates in cracks in walls of caves, mines, cellars, and old buildings

Breeding   Single young (twins rare) born from mid-June after gestation period of about 3 months. Weaned at 4–6 weeks; sexually mature in second year. May live 22 years in the wild, does not survive long in captivity

Voice   Occasional squeak; echolocation calls so quiet that even electronic bat detectors cannot hear them from more than a few feet away

Diet   Moths, spiders, and caterpillars

Habitat   Woodlands, parks, and gardens; often associated with houses, especially in north

Distribution Most of western Europe; scattered localities across Central Asia to China; Sakhalin Island (Russia) and Japan

Status   Population: unknown, but probably about 1–2 million. One of the most common European bats

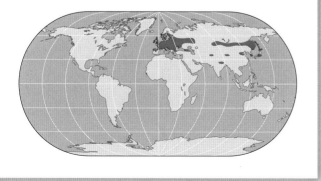

Long-Eared Bat
Plecotus auritus

The long-eared bat probably has the biggest ears in relation to its size of any mammal and an extremely quiet voice. It is often found in houses, where it causes more alarm than is appropriate for its gentle temperament.

WITH EARS AS LONG AS ITS BODY, there is no mistaking the long-eared bat! But why are the ears so large, and how does the bat cope with them, especially in flight? During movement on the ground or when scuttling in the roost, the bat keeps its big ears furled out of harm's way. There is a system of folds along the back edge of each ear that allows it to collapse and lie over the bat's shoulders. During flight tiny muscles, aided by blood pressure, erect the ears so that they are fully extended and point firmly forward. Tiny stiffening rods of cartilage help prevent the ears becoming distorted by the flow of air in flight.

Big Ears
The bat actually flies with its ears pointing out in front, which must make flight more difficult. Needless to say, flying costs the long-eared bat 21 times as much energy as it spends when resting. But it flies slower than other bats can manage; and unlike most other bat species, long-eared bats can even hover. This enables the long-eared bat to pick caterpillars and spiders off twigs or from the surface of leaves.

Bats detect their prey by echolocation; and since a flying insect is clearly distinct from the surrounding air, it is easy to pick out by its echo. But a caterpillar on a leaf is hard to detect by echoes alone. So, by having enormous and highly sensitive ears, the long-eared bat can manage with a very quiet echolocation system specially tuned to the job of identifying its prey on surfaces in the dark. Long-eareds are often called whispering bats because their voice is so faint that even sensitive electronic bat detectors cannot pick them up clearly.

Unprotesting

Long-eared bats are often found in the attics of houses, and they are probably the commonest bats to enter bedrooms. A bat inside the house often causes panic. However, long-eared bats are gentle creatures and do not bite or even squeak in protest when handled gently.

House attics provide warm places where the females can give birth. Each year the mothers gather in April to await the birth of their babies, often with males present (unlike in most other bats). A house roof can get very warm and may exceed 100°F (40°C). A warm roost is particularly important to the babies, which have no fur for the first two or three weeks of life. In the cooler parts of Europe living in a warm roof can make the difference between the babies surviving or dying of cold.

Long-eared bats are usually found in and around woodland. Here they live in tree holes and are one of the species most likely to colonize special bat roosting boxes. Long-eared bats prefer closed habitats among trees and houses. If they need to travel from one area to another, they tend to follow lines of trees or other prominent landscape features.

Occasionally, long-eared bats have been found on ships and oil rigs far out at sea, but they were probably animals that had been blown off course by strong winds. Normally, long-eared bats do not travel more than a mile or two from home (3 to 5 km). Few—and then only males—ever go to live in another roost, so almost all the animals in each colony are closely related. DNA analysis reveals that most are fathered by the same few males. Long-eared bats live together in small groups during the summer. In winter they hibernate alone, although others of the same group may be nearby. During normal sleep and in hibernation, when there is a danger of the ears drying out or getting frostbitten, the bat folds them down and tucks them away safely under its wings.

Most colonies consist of 10 to 20 bats, and only rarely are there more than 40. Female long-eareds can identify their own baby from its calls and scent from among the cluster of young despite the darkness.

↑ A long-eared bat in flight. The bat's huge, highly sensitive ears allow it to detect the echoes from a caterpillar on a leaf—prey that would elude most other bat species.

111

List of Genera

The following lists all genera of insectivores and bats:

Order Macroscelidea
Elephant shrews

FAMILY MACROSCELIDIDAE

Elephantulus Long-eared elephant shrews
Macroscelides Short-eared or round-eared elephant-shrew
Petrodromus Four-toed elephant shrew
Rhynchocyon Checkered elephant shrews

Order Insectivora
Insectivores

FAMILY TENRECIDAE
Tenrecs

SUBFAMILY GEOGALINAE
Geogale Large-eared tenrec

SUBFAMILY ORYZORICTINAE
Limnogale Aquatic tenrec
Microgale Shrew tenrecs
Oryzorictes Rice tenrecs

SUBFAMILY POTAMOGALINAE
Micropotamogale Dwarf otter shrews
Potamogale Giant otter shrew

SUBFAMILY TENRECINAE
Echinops Lesser hedgehog tenrec
Hemicentetes Streaked tenrec
Setifer Greater hedgehog tenrec
Tenrec Tailless or common tenrec

FAMILY SOLENODONTIDAE
Solenodons

Solenodon Solenodons

FAMILY ERINACEIDAE
Hedgehogs and moonrats

SUBFAMILY ERINACEINAE
Atelerix African hedgehogs
Erinaceus Eurasian hedgehogs
Hemiechinus Desert hedgehogs
Mesechinus Steppe hedgehogs

SUBFAMILY HYLOMYINAE
Echinosorex Greater moonrat
Hylomys Asian gymnures
Podogymnura Philippine gymnures

FAMILY SORICIDAE
Shrews

SUBFAMILY CROCIDURINAE
White-toothed shrews
Congosorex Poll's shrew
Crocidura White-toothed shrews
Diplomesodon Piebald shrew
Feroculus Kelaart's long-clawed shrew
Myosorex Mouse shrews
Paracrocidura African shrews
Ruwenzorisorex Ruwenzori shrew
Scutisorex Armored or hero shrew
Solisorex Pearson's long-clawed shrew
Suncus Pygmy and dwarf shrews
Surdisorex Kenyan shrews
Sylvisorex Forest musk shrews

SUBFAMILY SORICINAE
Red-toothed shrews
Anourosorex Mole-shrew or Sichuan burrowing shrew
Blarina American short-tailed shrews

Blarinella Asiatic short-tailed shrews
Chimarrogale Oriental water shrews
Cryptotis Small-eared shrews
Megasorex Mexican shrew
Nectogale Elegant water shrew
Neomys Old World water shrews
Notiosorex Desert shrew
Sorex Holarctic shrews
Soriculus Asiatic shrews

FAMILY CHRYSOCHLORIDAE
Golden moles

Amblysomus South African golden moles
Calcochloris Yellow golden mole
Carpitalpa Arend's golden mole
Chlorotalpa African golden moles
Chrysochloris Cape golden moles
Chrysospalax Large golden moles
Cryptochloris Secretive golden moles
Eremitalpa Grant's golden mole
Neamblysomus Gunning's golden mole

FAMILY TALPIDAE
Desmans, moles, and shrew moles

SUBFAMILY DESMANINAE
Desmana Russian desman
Galemys Pyrenean desman

SUBFAMILY TALPINAE
Condylura Star-nosed mole
Euroscaptor Oriental moles
Mogera East Asian moles
Nesoscaptor Ryukyu or senkaku mole
Neurotrichus American shrew mole
Parascalops Hairy-tailed mole
Parascaptor White-tailed mole
Scalopus Eastern mole
Scapanulus Gansu mole
Scapanus Western American moles
Scaptochirus Short-faced mole
Scaptonyx Long-tailed mole
Talpa Old World moles
Urotrichus Japanese shrew moles

SUBFAMILY UROPSILINAE
Uropsilus Asiatic shrew moles

Order Chiroptera
Bats

Suborder Megachiroptera
Fruit-eating bats

FAMILY PTEROPODIDAE
Old World fruit bats and flying foxes

SUBFAMILY PTEROPODINAE
Acerodon Island fruit bats
Aethalops Pygmy fruit bat
Alionycteris Mindanao pygmy fruit bat
Aproteles Bulmer's fruit bat
Balionycteris Spotted-winged fruit bat
Boneia Manada fruit bat
Casinycteris Short-palated fruit bat
Chironax Black-capped fruit bat
Cynopterus Short-nosed fruit bats
Dobsonia Naked-backed fruit bats
Dyacopterus Dyak fruit bat
Eidolon Eidolon fruit bats
Epomophorus Epauletted fruit bats
Epomops African epauletted bats
Haplonycteris Philippine or Fischer's pygmy fruit bat
Harpyionycteris Harpy fruit bats
Hypsignathus Hammer-headed fruit bat
Latidens Salim Ali's fruit bat
Megaerops Tailless fruit bats

Micropteropus Dwarf epauletted fruit bats
Myonycteris Little collared fruit bats
Nanonycteris Veldkamp's bat or little flying cow
Neopteryx Small-toothed fruit bat
Nyctimene Tube-nosed fruit bats
Otopteropus Luzon fruit bat
Paranyctimene Unstriped tube-nosed bat
Penthetor Lucas' short-nosed fruit bat
Plerotes Anchieta's fruit bat
Ptenochirus Musky fruit bats
Pteralopex Monkey-faced bats
Pteropus Flying foxes
Rousettus Rousette fruit bats
Scotonycteris West African fruit bats
Sphaerias Blanford's fruit bat
Styloctenium Stripe-faced fruit bat
Thoopterus Swift fruit bat

SUBFAMILY MACROGLOSSINAE
Eonycteris Dawn bats
Macroglossus Long-tongued fruit bats
Megaloglossus Woermann's bat or African long-tongued fruit bat
Melonycteris Black-bellied fruit bats
Notopteris Long-tailed fruit bat
Syconycteris Blossom bats

Suborder Microchiroptera
Insect-eating bats

FAMILY RHINOPOMATIDAE
Mouse-tailed bats

Rhinopoma Mouse-tailed bats

FAMILY CRASEONYCTERIDAE

Craseonycteris Kitti's hog-nosed bat

FAMILY EMBALLONURIDAE
Sheath-tailed bats

Balantiopteryx Least sac-winged bats
Centronycteris Shaggy bat
Coleura Peters' sheath-tailed bats
Cormura Chestnut sac-winged bat
Cyttarops Short-eared bat
Diclidurus Ghost or white bats
Emballonura Old World sheath-tailed bats
Mosia Dark sheath-tailed bats
Peropteryx Doglike bats
Rhynchonycteris Proboscis or sharp-nosed bat
Saccolaimus Pouched bats
Saccopteryx Sac-winged bats
Taphozous Tomb bats

FAMILY NYCTERIDAE
Slit-faced bats

Nycteris Slit-faced bats

FAMILY MEGADERMATIDAE
Old World false vampire bats

Cardioderma Heart-nosed bat
Lavia African yellow-winged bat
Macroderma Australian false vampire bat
Megaderma False vampire bats

FAMILY RHINOLOPHIDAE
Horseshoe bats

SUBFAMILY RHINOLOPHINAE
Rhinolophus Horseshoe bats

SUBFAMILY HIPPOSIDERINAE
Anthops Flower-faced bat
Asellia Trident leaf-nosed bats
Aselliscus Tate's trident-nosed bats

Cloeotis Percival's trident bat
Coelops Tailless leaf-nosed bats
Hipposideros Roundleaf bats
Paracoelops Vietnam leaf-nosed bat
Rhinonicteris Orange leaf-nosed bat
Triaenops Triple nose-leaf bats

FAMILY NOCTILIONIDAE
Bulldog bats

Noctilio Bulldog bats

FAMILY MORMOOPIDAE
Spectacled bats

Mormoops Ghost-faced bats
Pteronotus Moustached bats

FAMILY PHYLLOSTOMIDAE
New World leaf-nosed bats

SUBFAMILY PHYLLOSTOMINAE
Chrotopterus Big-eared woolly bat
Lonchorhina Sword-nosed bats
Macrophyllum Long-legged bat
Macrotus Leaf-nosed bats
Micronycteris Little big-eared bats
Mimon Hairy-nosed bats
Phylloderma Pale-faced bat
Phyllostomus Spear-nosed bats
Tonatia Round-eared bats
Trachops Fringe-lipped bat
Vampyrum Spectral bat (Linnaeus's false vampire bat)

SUBFAMILY LONCHOPHYLLINAE
Lionycteris Chestnut long-tongued bat
Lonchophylla Nectar bats
Platalina Long-snouted bat

SUBFAMILY BRACHYPHYLLINAE
Brachyphylla West Indian fruit-eating bats

SUBFAMILY PHYLLONYCTERINAE
Erophylla Buffy flower bat
Phyllonycteris Smooth-toothed flower bats

SUBFAMILY GLOSSOPHAGINAE
Anoura Tailless bats
Choeroniscus Long-tailed bats
Choeronycteris Mexican long-tongued bat
Glossophaga Long-tongued bats
Hylonycteris Underwood's long-tongued bat
Leptonycteris Long-nosed bats
Lichonycteris Dark long-tongued bat
Monophyllus Single leaf bats
Musonycteris Banana bat or Colima long-nosed bat
Scleronycteris Ega long-tongued bat

SUBFAMILY CAROLLIINAE
Carollia Short-tailed bats
Rhinophylla Little fruit bats

SUBFAMILY STENODERMATINAE
Ametrida Little white-shouldered bat
Ardops Tree bat
Ariteus Jamaican fig-eating bat
Artibeus Fruit-eating bats
Centurio Wrinkle-faced bat
Chiroderma Big-eyed bats
Ectophylla White bat
Mesophylla MacConnell's bat
Phyllops Cuban fig-eating bat
Platyrrhinus Broad-nosed bats
Pygoderma Ipanema bat
Sphaeronycteris Visored bat
Stenoderma Red fruit bat
Sturnira Yellow-shouldered bats
Uroderma Tent-making bats
Vampyressa Yellow-eared bats
Vampyrodes Great stripe-faced bat

SUBFAMILY DESMODONTINAE
Desmodus Common vampire bat
Diaemus White-winged vampire bat
Diphylla Hairy-legged vampire bat

FAMILY NATALIDAE
Funnel-eared bats

Natalus Funnel-eared bats

FAMILY FURIPTERIDAE
Thumbless bats

Amorphochilus Smoky bat
Furipterus Thumbless bat

FAMILY THYROPTERIDAE
Disk-winged bats

Thyroptera Disk-winged bat

FAMILY MYZOPODIDAE

Myzopoda Sucker-footed bat

FAMILY VESPERTILIONIDAE
Vespertilionid bats

SUBFAMILY KERIVOULINAE
Kerivoula Woolly bats

SUBFAMILY VESPERTILIONINAE
Antrozous Pallid bats
Barbastella Barbastelles
Chalinolobus Wattled bats
Eptesicus Serotine bats
Euderma Spotted or pinto bat
Eudiscopus Disc-footed bat
Glischropus Thick-thumbed bats
Hesperoptenus False serotine bats
Histiotus Big-eared brown bats
Ia Great evening bat
Idionycteris Allen's big-eared bat
Laephotis African long-eared bats
Lasionycteris Silver-haired bat
Lasiurus Hairy-tailed bats
Mimetillus Moloney's flat-headed bat
Myotis Little brown bats
Nyctalus Noctule bats
Nycticeius Broad-nosed bats
Nyctophilus Long-eared bats
Otonycteris Desert bat (Hemprich's long-eared bat)
Pharotis New Guinea big-eared bat
Philetor Rohu's bat
Pipistrellus Pipistrelle bats
Plecotus Big-eared bats
Rhogeessa Little yellow bats
Scotoecus House bats
Scotomanes Harlequin bats
Scotophilus Yellow bats
Tylonycteris Bamboo bats
Vespertilio Particolored bats

SUBFAMILY MURININAE
Harpiocephalus Hairy-winged bat
Murina Tube-nosed insectivorous bats

SUBFAMILY MINIOPTERINAE
Miniopterus Bent-winged bats

SUBFAMILY TOMOPEATINAE
Tomopeas Blunt-eared bat

FAMILY MYSTACINIDAE
New Zealand Short-tailed bats

Mystacina New Zealand short-tailed bat

FAMILY MOLOSSIDAE
Free-tailed bats

Chaerephon Lesser free-tailed bats

Cheiromeles Hairless bat
Eumops Bonneted bats
Molossops Dog-faced bats
Molossus Mastiff bats
Mops Greater free-tailed bats
Mormopterus Little mastiff bats
Myopterus African free-tailed bats
Nyctinomops New World free-tailed bats
Otomops Big-eared free-tailed bats
Promops Crested mastiff bats
Tadarida Free-tailed bats

Order Xenarthra
Edentates

FAMILY MYRMECOPHAGIDAE
True American anteaters

Cyclopes Silky anteater
Myrmecophaga Giant anteater
Tamandua Tamanduas

FAMILY BRADYPODIDAE
Three-toed sloths

Bradypus Three-toed sloths

FAMILY MEGALONYCHIDAE
Two-toed tree sloths

Choloepus Two-toed sloths

FAMILY DASYPODIDAE
Armadillos

SUBFAMILY CHLAMYPHORINAE
Chlamyphorus Fairy armadillos

SUBFAMILY DASYPODINAE
Cabassous Naked-tailed armadillos
Chaetophractus Hairy armadillos
Dasypus Long-nosed armadillos
Euphractus Yellow armadillo
Priodontes Giant armadillo
Tolypeutes Three-banded armadillos
Zaedyus Pichi

Order Scandentia
Tree shrews

FAMILY TUPAIIDAE

SUBFAMILY TUPAIINAE
Tupaia Tree shrews
Anathana Indian tree shrew
Urogale Philippine tree shrew
Dendrogale Smooth-tailed tree shrews
Lyonogale Terrestrial tree shrews

SUBFAMILY PTILOCERCINAE
Ptilocercus Pen-tailed tree shrew

Glossary

Words in SMALL CAPITALS refer to other entries in the glossary.

Adaptation features of an animal that adjust it to its environment; may be produced by evolution—e.g., camouflage coloration

Adaptive radiation when a group of closely related animals (e.g., members of a FAMILY) have evolved differences from each other so that they can survive in different NICHES

Adult a fully grown animal that has reached breeding age

Amphibian any cold-blooded VERTEBRATE of the class Amphibia, typically living on land but breeding in the water, e.g., frogs, toads, newts, salamanders

Anal gland (anal sac) a gland opening by a short duct either just inside the anus or on either side of it

Arboreal living among the branches of trees

Arthropod animals with a jointed outer skeleton, e.g., crabs and insects

Biodiversity a variety of SPECIES and the variation within them

Biomass the total weight of living material

Breeding season the entire cycle of reproductive activity from courtship, pair formation (and often establishment of TERRITORY), through nesting to independence of young

Browsing feeding on leaves of trees and shrubs

Cache a hidden supply of food; also (verb) to hide food for future use

Calcar cartilaginous prong from the heel supporting the rear edge of a bat's tail membrane

Canine (tooth) a sharp stabbing tooth usually longer than rest

Canopy continuous (closed) or broken (open) layer in forests produced by the intermingling of branches of trees

Capillaries tiny blood vessels that convey blood through organs from arteries to veins

Carnassial (teeth) opposing pair of teeth especially adapted to shear with a cutting (scissorlike) edge; in living mammals the arrangement is unique to Carnivora, and the teeth involved are the fourth upper PREMOLAR and first lower MOLAR

Carnivore meat-eating animal

Carrion dead animal matter used as a food source by scavengers

Cecum a blind sac in the digestive tract opening out from the junction between the small and large intestines. In herbivorous mammals it is often very large; it is the site of bacterial action on CELLULOSE. The end of the cecum is the appendix; in SPECIES with a reduced cecum the appendix may retain an antibacterial function

Cheek pouch a pocket in or alongside the mouth used for the temporary storage of food

Cheek teeth teeth lying behind the CANINES in mammals, consisting of PREMOLARS and MOLARS

Chromosomes strings of genetic material (DNA) within the cell nucleus; responsible for transmitting features from one generation to the next and for controlling cell growth and function

CITES Convention on International Trade in Endangered Species. An agreement between nations that restricts international trade to permitted levels through a system of licensing and administrative controls. Rare animals and plants are assigned to categories: (for instance Appendix 1, 2). See Volume 1 page 17

Congenital condition animal is born with

Coniferous forest evergreen forests found in northern regions and mountainous areas dominated by pines, spruces, and cedars

Crustaceans INVERTEBRATE animals with a hard outer skeleton and jointed limbs, e.g., crabs, lobsters (and also planktonic creatures resembling shrimp and water fleas)

Crepuscular active in twilight

Cursorial adapted for running

Deciduous forest dominated by trees that lose their leaves in winter (or the dry season)

Deforestation the process of cutting down and removing trees for timber or to create open space for activities such as growing crops and grazing animals

Delayed implantation when the development of a fertilized egg is suspended for a variable period before it implants into the wall of the UTERUS and completes normal pregnancy. Births are thus delayed until a favorable time of year

Dental formula a convention for summarizing the dental arrangement, in which the numbers of all types of tooth in each half of the upper and lower jaw are given. The numbers are always presented in the order: INCISOR (I), CANINE (C), PREMOLAR (P), MOLAR (M). The final figure is the total number of teeth to be found in the skull. A typical example for Carnivora would be I3/3, C1/1, P4/4, M3/3 = 44

Dentition an animal's set of teeth

Desert area of low rainfall dominated by specially adapted plants such as cacti

Digit a finger or toe

Digitigrade method of walking on the toes without the heel touching the ground. See PLANTIGRADE

Dispersal the scattering of young animals going to live away from where they were born and brought up

Display any relatively conspicuous pattern of behavior that conveys specific information to others, usually to members of the same SPECIES; can involve visual or vocal elements, as in threat, courtship, or greeting displays

Diurnal active during the day

DNA (deoxyribonucleic acid) the substance that makes up the main part of the chromosomes of all living things; contains the genetic code that is handed down from generation to generation

DNA analysis "genetic fingerprinting," a technique that allows scientists to see who is related to whom, for example, which male was the father of particular offspring

Dormancy a state in which—as a result of hormone action—growth is suspended and metabolic activity reduced to a minimum

Dorsal relating to the back or spinal part of the body; usually the upper surface

Droppings see FECES and SCATS

Echolocation using echoes to detect objects by bouncing sounds off them (used by whales and bats mainly)

Ecosystem a whole system in which plants, animals, and their environment interact

Edentate toothless, but is also used as group name for anteaters, sloths, and armadillos

Endemic found only in one small geographical area and nowhere else

Estivation inactivity or greatly decreased activity during hot or dry weather

Estrus the period when eggs are released from the female's ovaries, and she becomes available for successful mating. Estrous females are often referred to as "in heat" or as "RECEPTIVE" to males

Exoskeleton system of boxes and tubes around the outside of INVERTEBRATE animals (e.g., crabs and insects) supporting their weight. Bones form an endoskeleton inside VERTEBRATE animals such as mammals

Extinction process of dying out in which every last individual dies, and the SPECIES is lost forever

Family technical term for a group of closely related SPECIES that often also look quite similar. Zoological family names always end in "idae." See Volume 1 page 11. Also used as the word for a social group within a species consisting of parents and their offspring

Feces remains of digested food expelled from the body as pellets. Often accompanied by SCENT secretions

Feral domestic animals that have gone wild and live independently of people

Flystrike where CARRION-feeding flies have laid their eggs on an animal

Fossorial adapted for digging and living in burrows or underground tunnels

Frugivore an animal that eats fruit as main part of the diet

Fur mass of hairs forming a continuous coat characteristic of mammals

Fused joined together

Gene the basic unit of heredity enabling one generation to pass on characteristics to its offspring

Generalist an animal that is capable of a wide range of activities, not specialized

Genus a group of closely related SPECIES. The plural is genera. See Volume 1 page 11

Gestation the period of pregnancy between fertilization of the egg and birth of the baby

Gregarious living together in loose groups or herds

Guano word describing accumulated FECES/dung, especially at roosting site of bats

Harem a group of females living in the same TERRITORY and consorting with a single male

Herbivore an animal that feeds exclusively on plants (grazers and browsers are herbivores)

Heterodont DENTITION specialized into CANINES, INCISORS, and PREMOLARS, each type of tooth having a different function. See HOMODONT

Hibernation becoming inactive in winter, with lowered body temperature to save energy. Hibernation takes place in a special nest or DEN called a hibernaculum

Homeothermy maintenance of a high and constant body temperature by means of internal processes; also called "warm-blooded"

Home range the area that an animal uses in the course of its normal periods of activity. See TERRITORY

Homodont DENTITION in which the teeth are all similar in appearance and function

Hybrid offspring of two closely related SPECIES that can interbreed, but the hybrid is sterile

Inbreeding breeding among closely related animals (e.g., cousins) leading to weakened genetic composition and reduced survival rates

Incisor (teeth) simple pointed teeth at the front of the jaws used for nipping and snipping

Indigenous living naturally in a region; NATIVE (i.e., not an introduced SPECIES)

Insectivore animals that feed on insects and similar small prey. Also used as a group name for animals such as hedgehogs, shrews, and moles

Interbreeding breeding between animals of different SPECIES or varieties within a single FAMILY or strain; interbreeding can cause dilution of the gene pool

Interspecific between SPECIES

Intraspecific between individuals of the same SPECIES

Invertebrates animals that have no backbone (or other true bones) inside their body, e.g., mollusks, insects, jellyfish, and crabs

IUCN International Union for the Conservation of Nature, responsible for assigning animals and plants to internationally agreed categories of rarity. See table below

Juvenile a young animal that has not reached breeding age

Keratin tough fibrous material that forms hairs, feathers, and protective plates on the skin of VERTEBRATE animals

Lactation process of producing milk in MAMMARY GLANDS for offspring

Larvae immature forms of certain animals. Caterpillars are larvae of moths and butterflies, for example

Larynx voice box where sounds are created

Latrine place where FECES are left regularly, often with SCENT added

Leptospirosis disease caused by leptospiral bacteria in the kidneys and transmitted via urine

Lumbar vertebrae section of the backbone that lies in front of the hips, but behind the rib cage

Mamba (black) a poisonous African snake

Mammary glands characteristic of mammals, glands for production of milk

Metabolic rate rate at which chemical activities occur within animals, including the exchange of gasses in respiration and the liberation of energy from food

Metabolism the chemical activities within animals that turn food into energy

Migration movement from one place to another and back again, usually seasonal

Millipede long, thin arthropod with two pairs of legs per segment and seemingly hundreds of legs

Molars large crushing teeth at the back of the mouth

Molt the process in which mammals shed hair, usually seasonal

Monogamous animals that have only one mate at a time

Montane in a mountain environment

Mutation random changes in genetic material

Native belonging to that area or country, not introduced by human assistance

IUCN CATEGORIES

EX **Extinct**, when there is no reasonable doubt that the last individual of a species has died.

EW **Extinct in the Wild**, when a species is known only to survive in captivity or as a naturalized population well outside the past range.

CR **Critically Endangered**, when a species is facing an extremely high risk of extinction in the wild in the immediate future.

EN **Endangered**, when a species faces a very high risk of extinction in the wild in the near future.

VU **Vulnerable**, when a species faces a high risk of extinction in the wild in the medium-term future.

LR **Lower Risk**, when a species has been evaluated and does not satisfy the criteria for CR, EN, or VU.

DD **Data Deficient**, when there is not enough information about a species to assess the risk of extinction.

NE **Not Evaluated**, species that have not been assessed by the IUCN criteria.

Natural selection when animals and plants are challenged by natural processes (including predation and bad weather) to ensure survival of the fittest

New World the Americas; OLD WORLD refers to the non-American continents (not usually Australia)

Niche part of a habitat occupied by an ORGANISM, defined in terms of all aspects of its lifestyle

Nocturnal active at night

Nomadic animals that have no fixed home, but wander continuously

Noseleaf fleshy structures around the face of bats; help focus ULTRASOUNDS used for ECHOLOCATION

Old World non-American continents. See NEW WORLD

Olfaction sense of smell

Omnivore an animal that eats almost anything, meat or vegetable

Opportunistic taking advantage of every varied opportunity that arises; flexible behavior

Opposable fingers or toes that can be brought to bear against others on the same hand or foot in order to grip objects

Order a subdivision of a class of animals consisting of a series of related animal FAMILIES. See Volume 1 page 11

Organism any member of the animal or plant kingdom; a body that has life

Ovulation release of egg from the female's ovary prior to its fertilization

Pair bond behavior that keeps a male and a female together beyond the time it takes to mate; marriage is a "pair bond"

Palate hard roof of the mouth

Parasite an animal or plant that lives on or within the body of another

Parturition process of giving birth

Pelage the furry coat of a mammal

Pheromone SCENT produced by animals to enable others to find and recognize them

Physiology the processes and workings within plants and animal bodies, e.g., digestion. Maintaining a warm-blooded state is a part of mammal physiology

Placenta the structure that links an embryo to its mother during pregnancy, allowing exchange of chemicals between them

Plantigrade walking on the soles of the feet with the heels of the feet touching the ground. See DIGITIGRADE

Polygamous when animals have more than one mate in a single mating season. MONOGAMOUS animals have only a single mate

Polygynous when a male mates with several females in one BREEDING SEASON

Population a distinct group of animals of the same SPECIES, or all the animals of that species

Posterior the hind end or behind another structure

Predator an animal that kills live prey for food

Prehensile grasping tail or fingers

Premolars teeth found in front of the MOLARS, but behind the CANINES

Primate a group of mammals that includes monkeys, apes, and ourselves

Promiscuous mating often with many mates, not just one

Protein chemicals made up of amino acids. Essential in the diet of animals

Quadruped an animal that walks on all fours (a BIPED walks on two legs)

Range the total geographical area over which a SPECIES is distributed

Receptive when a female is ready to mate (in ESTRUS)

Reproduction the process of breeding, creating new offspring for the next generation

Retina light-sensitive layer at the back of the eye

Retractile capable of being withdrawn, as in claws of typical cats, which can be folded back into the paws to protect them from damage when walking

Riparian living beside rivers and lakes

Roadkill animals killed by road traffic

Roost place that a bat or a bird regularly uses for sleeping

Savanna tropical grasslands with scattered trees and low rainfall, usually in warm areas

Scats fecal pellets, especially of CARNIVORES. SCENT is often deposited with the pellets as territorial markers

Scent chemicals produced by animals to leave smell messages for others to find and interpret

Scrub vegetation dominated by shrubs—woody plants usually with more than one stem

Secondary forest trees that have been planted or grown up on cleared ground

Social behavior interactions between individuals within the same SPECIES, e.g., courtship

Sonar underwater ECHOLOCATION, finding objects by reflected sound. Sometimes used instead of echolocation

Species a group of animals that look similar and can breed to produce fertile offspring

Steppe open grassland in parts of the world where the climate is too harsh for trees to grow

Sub-Saharan all parts of Africa lying south of the Sahara Desert

Subspecies a locally distinct group of animals that differ slightly from normal appearance of SPECIES; often called a race

Symbiosis where two or more SPECIES live together for their mutual benefit more successfully than either could live on its own

Taxonomy the branch of biology concerned with classifying ORGANISMS into groups according to similarities in their structure, origins, or behavior.

The categories, in order of increasing broadness, are: SPECIES, GENUS, FAMILY, ORDER, class, and phylum. See Volume 1 page 11

Termites ("white ants") insects that live in huge colonies and build massive nests in trees or as mounds and pillars on ground

Terrestrial living on land

Territory defended space

Testes ("testicles") pair of organs within the scrotum where male sperm are produced

Thermoregulation the maintenance of a relatively constant body temperature either by adjustments to METABOLISM or by moving between sunshine and shade

Torpor deep sleep accompanied by lowered body temperature and reduced METABOLIC RATE

Tragus fleshy lobe at the base of a mammal's ear, important for identifying bat SPECIES

Translocation transferring members of a SPECIES from one location to another

Underfur fine hairs forming a dense, woolly mass close to the skin and underneath the outer coat of stiff hairs in mammals

Uterus womb in which embryos of mammals develop

Ultrasounds sounds that are too high-pitched for humans to hear

Ventral the belly or underneath of an animal (opposite of DORSAL)

Vertebrate animal with a backbone (e.g., fish, mammals, reptiles), usually with a skeleton made of bones, but sometimes softer cartilage

Vibrissae sensory whiskers, usually on snout, but can be on areas such as elbows, tail, oreyebrows

Viviparous animals that give birth to active young rather than laying eggs

Vocalization making of sounds such as barking and croaking

Zoologist person who studies animals

Further Reading

General

Cranbrook, G., **The Mammals of Southeast Asia**, Oxford University Press, New York, NY, 1991

Eisenberg, J. F., and Redford, K. H., **The Mammals of the Neotropics**, University of Chicago Press, Chicago, IL, 1999

Estes, R. D., **The Behavioral Guide to African Mammals**, University of California Press, Berkley, CA, 1991

Garbutt, N., **The Mammals of Madagascar**, Pica Press, Sussex, U.K., 1999

King, C. M., **The Handbook of New Zealand Mammals**, Oxford University Press, Oxford, U.K., 1995

Kingdon, J., **The Kingdon Field Guide to African Mammals**, Academic Press, San Diego, CA, 1997

MacDonald, D., **Collins Field Guide to the Mammals of Britain and Europe**, Harper Collins, New York, NY, 1993

MacDonald, D., **The Encyclopedia of Mammals**, Barnes and Noble, New York, NY, 2001

Nowak, R. M., Walker's **Mammals of the World**, The John Hopkins University Press, Baltimore, MD, 1999

Skinner, J. D., and Smithers, R. H. N., **The Mammals of the Southern African Subregion**, University of Pretoria, Pretoria, South Africa, 1990

Strahan, R., **The Mammals of Australia**, Reed New Holland, Australia, 1998

Whitaker, J. O., **National Audubon Society Field Guide to North American Mammals**, Alfred A. Knopf, New York, NY, 1996

Wilson, D. E., **The Smithsonian Book of North American Mammals**, Smithsonian Institution Press, Washington, DC, 1999

Wilson, D. E., and Reeder, D. M., **Mammal Species of the World. A Taxonomic and Geographic Reference**, Smithsonian Institution Press, Washington, DC, 1999

Young, J. Z., **The Life of Mammals: Their Anatomy and Physiology**, Oxford University Press, Oxford, U.K., 1975

Specific to this volume

Altringham, J. D., **Bats: Biology and Behavior**, Oxford University Press, New York, NY, 1996

Fenton, M. B., **Bats**: Facts on File, New York, NY, 1992

Hill, J. E., and Smith, J. D., **Bats: A Natural History**, British Museum (natural history), London, U.K., 1984

Kunz, T. H., and Racey, P. A., **Bat Biology and Conservation**, Smithsonian Institution Press, Washington, DC, 1998

Neuweiler, G., **The Biology of Bats**, Oxford University Press, New York, NY, 2000

Nowak, R. M, Walker's **Bats of the World**, John Hopkins University Press, Baltimore, MD, 1995

Useful Websites

General

http://animaldiversity.ummz.umich.edu/
University of Michigan Museum of Zoology animal diversity websites. Search for pictures and information about animals by class, family, and common name. Includes glossary

http://www.cites.org/
IUCN and CITES listings. Search for animals by scientific name, order, family, genus, species or common name. Location by country and explanation of reasons for listings

http://endangered.fws.gov
Information about threatened animals and plants from the U.S. Fish and Wildlife Service, the organization in charge of 94 million acres (38 million ha) of American wildlife refuges

http://www.iucn.org
Details of species and their status; listings by the International Union for the Conservation of Nature, also lists IUCN publications

http://www.nccnsw.org.au
Website for threatened Australian species

http://www.ewt.org.za
Website for threatened South African wildlife

http://www.panda.org
World Wide Fund for Nature (WWF), newsroom, press releases, government reports, campaigns

http://www.aza.org
American Zoo and Aquarium Association

http://www.ultimateungulate.com
Guide to world's hoofed mammals

http://www.wcs.org
Website of the Wildlife Conservation Society

http://www.nwf.org www.nwf.org
Website of the National Wildlife Federation

http://www.nmnh.si.edu/msw/
Mammals list on Smithsonian Museum site

http://www.press.jhu.edu/books/walkers_mammals_of_the_world/prep.html
Text of basic book listing species, illustrating almost every genus

Specific to this volume

http://www.batcon.org
Bat Conservation International

http://www.bats.org.uk
Bat Conservation Trust

http://www.cccoe.k12.ca.us/bats/welcome.html
Resources about bats for teachers and students

http://www.lads.com/BasicallyBats/
Rehabilitation of sick and injured bats

http://www.desertusa.com/jan97/du_bats.html
Desert bats (U.S.)

hedgehogclub.com/
International nonprofit organization dedicated to the care of pet African hedgehogs

http://www.software-technics.co.uk/bhps/
British Hedgehog Preservation Society

members.vienna.at/shrew/
A site promoting the investigation of shrew biology

http://www.maiaw.com/anteater/
Giant anteater information, pictures, links

http://www.msu.edu/~nixonjos/armadillo/
Armadillos: photos, facts, biology, and life history for all 20 species

http://www.tpwd.state.tx.us/nature/wild/mammals/dillo.htm
Nine-banded armadillo

http://www.panasia.org.sg/nepalnet/ecology/pangolin.htm
Pangolin or scaly ant eater

Set Index

A **bold** number shows the volume and is followed by the relevant page numbers (e.g., **1**: 52, 74).

Common names in **bold** (e.g., **aardwolf**) mean that the animal has an illustrated main entry in the set. Underlined page numbers (e.g., **9**: 78–79) refer to the main entry for that animal.

Italic page numbers (e.g., **2**: *103*) point to illustrations of animals in parts of the set other than the main entry.

Page numbers in parentheses—e.g., **1**: (24)—locate information in At-a-Glance boxes.

Animals that get main entries in the set are indexed under their common names, alternative common names, and scientific names.

A

aardvark 1: *10*; **5**: (10), (12); **9**: 64, 65, (66), 67, 78–79
  African **9**: 65
aardwolf 2: 102, *103*, 110–111
Abrocoma bennetti **8**: 30
Abrocomidae **8**: 31
acacia **6**: 87
Acinonyx
  A. jubatus **2**: 10, 26–29
  A. rex **2**: 29
Aconaemys fuscus **8**: 30
acouchi **7**: *12*
  red **8**: 30
Acrobates pygmaeus **10**: 74, 84–85
Acrobatidae **10**: (76)
addax **6**: 62
Addax nasomaculatus **6**: 62
Aepyceros melampus **6**: 62, 86–87
Aepyprymnus rufescens **10**: 48
Aeromys tephromelas **7**: 34, 36
Africa, national parks/reserves **2**: 16, 31; **5**: 34
Afrotheres **5**: (10)
Afrotheria **9**: 10
agouti 7: 8, *10*, *12*, 14; **8**: 28
  black **8**: 8–9
  Central American **8**: 30
  common 8: 42–43
  spotted (common) **8**: 42–43
Agouti
  A. paca **8**: 30
  A. taczanowskii **8**: 30
Agoutidae **7**: *12*
agriculture **1**: 46; **2**: 21, 28, 44, 69, 77, 79
Ailuridae **2**: (99)
Ailurinae **1**: 20
Ailuropoda melanoleuca **2**: 82, 98–101
Ailurops ursinus **10**: 74
Ailurus fulgens **1**: 20, 30–31; **2**: (99)
alarm calls **4**: 46, 57, 89, 100; **6**: 79; **7**: 53, 111; **8**: 51, 55, 99
  see also communication
albino **8**: (84)
Alcelaphus
  A. buselaphus **6**: 62
  A. lichtensteinii **6**: 62
Alces
  A. alces **6**: 10, 14–19
  A. alces alces **6**: 15
  A. alces americanus **6**: 15
  A. alces andersoni **6**: 15
  A. alces gigas **6**: 15
  A. alces shirasi **6**: 15
Allenopithecus nigroviridis **4**: 40
Allocebus trichotis **4**: 96
Alopex lagopus see *Vulpes lagopus*
Alouatta
  A. fusca **4**: 72, 74–75
  A. palliata **4**: 72
  A. seniculus **4**: 72
alpaca **5**: 92, 93, 105, (106)
ambergris **3**: 89
Amblonyx cinereus **1**: 32, 70–71
American Sign Language **4**: 13, (16), 27
Ammodorcas clarkei **6**: 62
Ammotragus lervia **6**: 62
angwantibo **4**: 106, *106*
animal farming **2**: (97)
anoa, lowland **6**: 62
Anomaluridae **7**: *12*, (19)
anteater 1: 9, 14; **9**: 64–67
  banded *see* numbat
  giant 9: *64*, 65, 68–71
  marsupial *see* numbat
  short-nosed spiny *see* echidna, short-beaked
  silky **9**: 65, 66
Antechinomys laniger **10**: 27
antechinus 10: 11, 25, 20, (25), 27
  agile **10**: 41
  brown 10: 27, 40–41
  dusky **10**: 27
  sandstone **10**: 27
Antechinus
  A. stuartii **10**: 27, 40–41
  A. swainsonii **10**: 27
antelope 5: *10*, *11*, 12, 13; **6**: 60–63
  American pronghorn **2**: 26; **6**: 63
  four-horned **6**: 60, 62
  pronghorn 6: *60*, 62, (63), 110–111
  pygmy **6**: 60, 62
  roan **6**: 62
  royal **6**: *60*, 62
  sable **6**: 62
  Tibetan **6**: 62
Antidorcas marsupialis **6**: 62, 96–97
Antilocapra americana **6**: 62, 110–111
Antilocapridae **6**: 63, 110
Antilope cervicapra **6**: 62
antlers **6**: 9, 12, (15), 24–25, 34, 38, 40, *60*
ants **9**: 64, 66, 69, 76
Aonyx
  A. capensis **1**: 32
  A. cinereus see *Amblonyx cinereus*
  A. congicus **1**: 32
Aotus
  A. nigriceps **4**: 72
  A. trivirgatus **4**: 72, 84–85
ape
  ape family 4: 12–13
  Barbary *see* macaque, Barbary
  red *see* orangutan
Aplodontia rufa **7**: 28
Aplodontidae **7**: *12*, 28, 29
Apodemus sylvaticus **7**: 78–79
Appaloosa **5**: 59
archaeocetes **3**: 56

Archaeonycteris **1**: *8*
Arctictis binturong **1**: 88
Arctocebus **4**: 106
  A. aureus **4**: 106
  A. calabarensis **4**: 106
Arctocephalus
  A. gazella **3**: 9
  A. pusillus **3**: 9, 16–17
Arctogalidia trivirgata **1**: 88
Arctonyx collaris **1**: 32
Argentinosaurus huinculensis **3**: 98
Arjin Shan Lop Nur Nature Reserve **5**: (102)
armadillo 9: 64–67
  common **9**: 65
  giant **9**: 65
  lesser fairy **9**: 65
  long-nosed (nine-banded) **9**: 65, 74–77
  nine-banded **9**: 65, 74–77
  southern naked-tailed **9**: 65, 66
  three-banded **9**: 64
artiodactyl **1**: *8*; **8**: 102
Artiodactyla **1**: *10*; **5**: (10), 12, 66; **6**: 52
Arvicola terrestris **7**: 98–99
Aspilia **4**: (29)
ass 5: 42, (44)
  African **5**: 42
  Asian wild 5: 56–57
  Asiatic **5**: 42
  domestic **5**: 57
Atelerix
  A. albiventris **9**: 12, 20–21
  A. algirus **9**: 12, *13*
  A. frontalis **9**: 21
Ateles
  A. belzebuth **4**: 72
  A. geoffroyi **4**: 72, 76–77
Atherurus
  A. africanus **8**: 12
  A. macrourus **8**: 12
Atilax paludinosus **1**: 98
aurochs **6**: 63
Australia, mammals introduced into **2**: 80; **5**: (97); **8**: 72
Avahi
  A. laniger **4**: 96
  A. occidentalis **4**: 96
Axis
  A. axis **6**: 10
  A. porcinus **6**: 10
aye-aye 4: 96, 97, 102–103

B

babirusa 5: 74, 75, 86–87
baboon 4: *8*, 40, 42, 42–43
  Chacma **4**: 56–57
  gelada 4: 40, 42, 43, 62–63
  hamadryas 4: 40, 43, 58–59
  long-tailed *see* mangabey
  olive **4**: *10–11*
  sacred (hamadryas) **4**: 40, 43, 58–59
  savanna 4: 40, 42–43, 54–57
  yellow (savanna) **4**: 40, 42–43, 54–57
Babyrusa babyrussa **5**: 74, 86–87
badger 1: 34
  American 1: 32, 76–77; **2**: (60)
  European 1: 32, 34, *35*, 78–81
  hog **1**: 32
  honey 1: 32, 82–83
  Indian ferret **1**: 32
  Palawan stink **1**: 32
Balaena mysticetus **3**: 55, 110–111
Balaenoptera
  B. acutorostrata **3**: 55, 106–107

B. bonaerensis **3**: 107
B. musculus **3**: 55, 98–101
bamboo **2**: 98–99, 100; **4**: 97
bandicoot 10: (10), 24, 25,27
  eastern barred **10**: 8–9
  giant **10**: 27
  golden **10**: 27
  large short-nosed (northern) **10**: 46–47
  long-nosed **10**: 27
  mouse **10**: 27
  northern 10: 46–47
  northern brown (northern) **10**: 27, 46–47
  pig-footed **10**: 27
  rabbit-eared *see* bilby
  Raffray's **10**: 27
  rufous spiny **10**: 27
  Seram Island **10**: 27
  striped **10**: 27
  western barred **10**: 27
banteng **6**: 62
bark stripping **8**: 24
barnacles **3**: *57*, 92, 102, 108
Bassaricyon
  B. alleni **1**: 20
  B. gabbii **1**: 20
Bassariscus
  B. astutus **1**: 20
  B. sumichrasti **1**: 20
bat 1: *8*, *10*, 14; **7**: *12*, (37); **9**: 80–87
  African slit-faced **9**: 82, 84
  American false vampire **9**: 86
  American little brown **9**: 87
  American pallid **9**: 84
  bat families **9**: 86–87
  Bechstein's **9**: 80–81
  Brazilian (Mexican) free-tailed **9**: 82, (83), 84–85, *86*, 100–103
  bulldog (fisherman) **9**: 87, 108–109
  Daubenton's **9**: 87
  diadem roundleaf **9**: 86
  disk-winged **9**: 87
  Egyptian fruit **9**: 86
  Egyptian rousette 9: 92–93
  false vampire 9: 82, 98–99
  fisherman 9: 108–109
  free-tailed **9**: 87
  fruit **9**: 58, 80, 81, 86
  funnel-eared **9**: 87, *87*
  greater false vampire (false vampire) **9**: 82, 98–99
  greater horseshoe **9**: 86
  guano (Mexican free-tailed) **9**: (82), 84–85, *86*, 100–103
  hairy big-eyed **9**: 85
  hairy-legged vampire **9**: 94
  hammerheaded **9**: 80, 86
  horseshoe **9**: 80, 87
  house (Mexican free-tailed) **9**: 82, (83), 84–85, *86*, 100–103
  Indian greater false vampire (false vampire) **9**: 82, 98–99
  Kitti's hog-nosed **1**: *11*, (11); **9**: 38, 80, 86
  lesser bulldog **9**: 108
  lesser horseshoe 9: 106–107
  lesser long-nosed **9**: 84–85
  little brown 9: 83, 104–105
  long-eared 9: 110–111
  long-tongued **9**: 86
  Mexican free-tailed 9: 82, (83), 84–85, *86*, 100–103

mouse-tailed **9**: 86
mustached **9**: *87*
New World leaf-nosed **9**: 87
New Zealand short-tailed **9**: 86–87
Old World false vampire **9**: 82, 87
Old World leaf-nosed **9**: 87
Old World sucker-footed **9**: 87
rousette **9**: 86
sheath-tailed **9**: 87
slit-faced **9**: 87
spear-nosed **9**: 84, *87*
spectacled **9**: 87
thumbless **9**: 87
vampire 9: 84, (85), 94–97
whispering (long-eared) **9**: 110–111
white-winged vampire **9**: 94
see also flying fox; pipistrelle
Bathyergidae **7**: *12*; **8**: 9
Bathyergus
  B. janetta **8**: 56
  B. suillus **8**: 56
Bdeogale
  B. crassicauda **1**: 98
  B. jacksoni **1**: 98
bear 2: 9; **5**: 9
  American black 2: 82, 90–93
  Andean **2**: 82, *83*
  Asian black **2**: 82, *83*
  bear family 2: 82–83
  big brown (brown) **2**: 82, *83*, 92, 94–97
  brown 2: 82, *83*, 92, 94–97
  dancing **2**: (97)
  "dawn bear" **2**: 82
  grizzly 2: 82, *83*, 92, 94–97
  koala *see* koala
  Malaysian sun **2**: 82
  native Australian *see* koala
  panda *see* panda, giant
  polar 2: 9, 82, 84–89; **3**: 83
  skunk *see* wolverine
  sloth **2**: 82, *83*
  spectacled **2**: 82, *83*
  sun **2**: 82, *83*
Beatragus hunteri **6**: 62
beaver 7: 8, 9, *10*, 11, *12*, 13
  American 7: 28, 29, 30–33
  beaver family 7: 28–29
  Canadian (American) **7**: 28, 29, 30–33
  Eurasian **7**: 28, 29
  mountain **7**: *12*, 14, 28, (29)
  mountain beaver family 7: 28–29
  swamp *see* coypu
beetles, dung **2**: 76–77
beira **6**: 60, 62
beluga 3: 55, 80–83
bettong
  burrowing **10**: 48, *51*
  Tasmanian **10**: *8*
Bettongia lesueur **10**: 48
bilby 10: 44–45
  greater **10**: 27, 44, *45*
  lesser **10**: 27, 44
binturong **1**: 88, 89, 90, 91
biomedical research *see* medical research
bipedalism **4**: 10
bison
  American 6: 60, 62, 64–69
  European **6**: 62, (66), *67*
  wood **6**: 68
Bison
  B. bison **6**: 62, 64–69
  B. bison athabascae **6**: 68
  B. bonasus **6**: 62, 66
blackbuck **6**: *61*, 62
Blarina brevicauda **9**: 28, 30–33
Blastocerus dichotomus **6**: 10

blubber **3**: 34, 58, 72, 84, 85, 89, 91, (101)
bluebuck **6**: 63
boar, wild 5: 74, 76–79
boat traffic **3**: 50, 51, 65, 79, 103
bobcat 2: 10, 38–39, 40
body temperature **1**: 9–12
control of **5**: (17); **9**: 24, 67, 72, 82, (90); **10**: 69
desert animals **5**: 95–96
see also hibernation; torpor
bonobo 4: 12, 34–35
bontebok **6**: 62
Borhyaenidae **10**: 26, 36
Bos
B. frontalis **6**: 62
B. grunniens **6**: 74–75
B. javanicus **6**: 62
Boselaphus tragocamelus **6**: 62
boto *see* dolphin, Amazon
Bovidae **6**: 9, 60–63
bovine tuberculosis **1**: 81
brachiation **4**: 38, 72
Brachylagus idahoensis **8**: 64, (93)
Brachyteles arachnoides **4**: 72
Bradypus
B. torquatus **9**: 65
B. variegatus **9**: 65, 72–73
branding, freeze branding **8**: (84)
Brazil, forestation in **4**: 90–91
breaching **3**: 96, 96–97, 103, 104, 109
breeding
K strategists **7**: 14; **8**: 21
R strategists **7**: 14
selective **5**: (43), 74; **6**: 63
synchronized **3**: 20–21; **6**: 83, 88; **7**: 57; **8**: 79; **10**: 41
see also captive breeding; reproduction; inbreeding; interbreeding
breeding mound **7**: 18
brocket, red **6**: 10, 11, 13
bromeliads **4**: (90)
browsing **5**: 12, 13, 38; **6**: 9
brumby *see* mustang
Bubalus
B. depressicornis **6**: 62
B. mindorensis **6**: 62
Bubastis **2**: (12)
bubble netting **3**: 104
bubonic plague **7**: 14, 76–77
Bubulcus ibis **6**: (73)
Budorcas taxicolor **6**: 62, 108
buffalo 1: 15
African 6: 60, 62, 70–73
see also bison, American
Bunolagus monticularis **8**: 64
Buphagus africanus **6**: (73)
Burramys parvus **10**: 74
burrows **7**: 26–27; **9**: 44–45, 67; **10**: 99
ground destabilization **7**: 49, 50, 59; **8**: 29, 57, 66–67; **9**: 77; **10**: 99
see also tunnels
bush baby 4: 106–107
Demidoff's 4: 106, 110–111
bushbuck **6**: 62
bushmeat trade **4**: 27, 32, 40, 53, 61, 85; **5**: 87; **6**: 59, 66, 72
bushpig **5**: 74, 75

C

Cabassous unicinctus **9**: 65
Cacajao **4**: 72
C. calvus **4**: 72, 80–81
C. melanocephalus **4**: 72
cacomistle **1**: 20, 21
Caenolestes **10**: 14
C. caniventer **10**: 14
C. fuliginosus **10**: 14

Caenolestidae **10**: 16
Callicebus
C. moloch **4**: 72
C. personatus **4**: 72
C. torquatus **4**: 72
Callimico goeldii **4**: 86
Callithrix
C. argentata see *Mico argentata*
C. geoffroyi **4**: 86
C. humilis see *Mico humilis*
C. jacchus **4**: 86, 92–93
C. pygmaea see *Cebuella pygmaea*
Callorhinus ursinus **3**: 9, 14–15
Callosciurus
C. nigrovittatus **7**: 36
C. notatusisi **7**: 36
C. prevosti **7**: 36
Caloprymnus campestris **10**: 48
Caluromys
C. derbianus **10**: 14
C. philander **10**: 14
Caluromysiops irrupta **10**: 14
camel 5: 8, 9, 12
Arabian (dromedary) **5**: 92, 93, 94–99, 102
Bactrian 5: 92, 93, (98), 100–103
camel family 5: 92–93
domestication **5**: (98)
dromedary 5: 92, 93, 94–99, 102
one-humped (dromedary) **5**: 92, 93, 94–99, 102
two-humped (Bactrian) **5**: 92, 93, (98), 100–103
camelids **5**: 92–93
Camelus
C. bactrianus **5**: 92, 100–103
C. dromedarius **5**: 92, 94–99
C. ferus (bactrianus) **5**: 92, 100–103
Canidae **1**: 20
Canis
C. dingo **2**: 50, 80–81
C. familiaris **2**: 50, (53)
C. latrans **2**: 50, 58–61
C. lupus **2**: 50, 54–57
C. lupus dingo (C. dingo) **2**: 50, 80–81
C. mesomelas **2**: 50, 62–63
C. simensis **2**: 50
Caperea marginata **3**: 55
Capra
C. aegagrus **6**: 62
C. ibex **6**: 62, 106–107
C. ibex caucasica **6**: 106
C. ibex cylindricornis **6**: 106
C. ibex ibex **6**: 106
C. ibex nubiana **6**: 106
C. ibex sibirica **6**: 106
C. ibex walie **6**: 106
Capreolus capreolus **6**: 10, 38–39
Capricornis
C. crispus **6**: 62
C. sumatraensis **6**: 62, 108
Caprolagus hispidus **8**: 64
Capromyidae **7**: 12; **8**: 31
Capromys pilorides **8**: 30, 52–53
captive breeding **1**: 45, 47, 54, (55), (59), 71; **2**: (23), (29), 59, 100; **4**: (17), 87, 90–91, 98, 101; **5**: 26, 65; **6**: 91; **7**: 15
captivity **1**: 22, 29, 65; **3**: 59, 65, 71, 74; **4**: 27, 78; **6**: 42–43, 58, 66, 91; **9**: 21; **10**: 83
capuchin **4**: 10, 72, 83
brown **4**: 72, 73

weeper **4**: 72
white-faced **4**: 72
capybara 7: 8, *12*, 28; **8**: 8, 9, 10, 28, 48–51
capybara farms **8**: (50)
caracal **2**: 10, *11*
caravaning **9**: 39
caribou 6: 10, *12*, 20–25
Carnivora **1**: 10, 18; **2**: 8
carnivores 1: *10*
large 2: 8–9
small 1: 18–19
teeth **1**: 15
Carterodon sulcidens **8**: 30
Castor **7**: 28
C. canadensis **7**: 28, 30–33
C. fiber **7**: 28
castoreum **7**: (31)
Castoridae **7**: *12*, 28
cat 2: 9
African wildcat **2**: *12*
Asiatic golden **2**: 10, *13*
blackfooted **2**: 10, *13*
cat family 2: 10–13
domestic **2**: 9, 10, (12), 49
European wildcat **2**: *12*
jungle **2**: 10, *13*
leopard **2**: 10, *13*
miner's *see* raccoon, ringtail
saber-toothed **2**: 10
sand **2**: 10, *13*
tiger **2**: 10, *12*
wildcat 2: 10, 13, 48–49
Catagonus wagneri **5**: 88
catamount *see* puma
catarrhines **4**: 11
catatonia **10**: (20)
cattle 1: 15; **5**: 9, *11*, 12; **6**: 60–63; **8**: 62
humped zebu **6**: 63
humpless **6**: 63
cattle rearing **4**: 79
Cavia
C. aperaea **8**: 39
C. porcellus **8**: 30, 38–41
C. tschudii **8**: 39
Caviidae **7**: *12*
Caviomorpha **7**: (8); **8**: 28, 31
cavy 7: 11, *12*, (14)
Brazilian **8**: 39, *41*
cavies and relatives 8: 28–31
common yellow-toothed **8**: 28, 30
domestic *see* guinea pig
Patagonian *see* mara
Peruvian **8**: 39
rock **8**: 30
southern mountain **8**: 10–11, 30
cavylike rodents 8: 8–11
Cebidae **4**: 72, 84
Cebuella pygmaea **4**: 86
Cebus **4**: 72
C. apella **4**: 72
C. capucinus **4**: 72
C. olivaceus **4**: 72
cellulose **4**: 41, 75; **5**: 11–12, 70; **6**: 8; **7**: 103; **8**: 49
Cephalophus **6**: 62, 80
C. dorsalis **6**: 62
C. monticola **6**: 62
Ceratotherium simum **5**: 28, 30–35
Cercartetus **10**: 74
C. concinnus **10**: 74
C. nanus **10**: 74
Cercocebus
C. galeritus **4**: 40
C. torquatus **4**: 40
Cercopithecidae **4**: 40
cercopithecines **4**: 40, 40–41, 42, 43
Cercopithecus
C. aethiops **4**: 44–47
C. cephus **4**: 40
C. neglectus **4**: 40
Cervidae **6**: 9, 10, 12

Cervus
C. canadensis **6**: 10, 26–29
C. canadensis manitobensis **6**: 27
C. canadensis nannodes **6**: 27
C. canadensis nelsoni **6**: 26
C. canadensis roosevelti **6**: 27
C. elaphus **6**: 10, 26, 30–33
Cetacea **1**: *10*; **5**: (10)
cetaceans **3**: 54–59
Chaeropus ecaudatus **10**: 27
Chaetodipus penicillatus **7**: 22–23
Chaetomys subspinosus **8**: 30
Chaga's disease **8**: 27
chain chorusing **5**: 71
chamois **6**: 62
European **6**: 108
Pyrenean **6**: 62
charms **3**: 61; **8**: 67; **9**: 79
cheetah 2: 9, 10, 26–29
king **2**: 29
Cheirogaleus
C. major **4**: 96
C. medius **4**: 96
chemical poisoning *see* pollution
chevrotain **5**: 8; **6**: 10
greater Malay *see* deer, greater mouse
Indian spotted **6**: 10
water **6**: 10
chewing the cud **6**: 8
chimpanzee 4: *11*, 12, 13, 28–33; **5**: 9
common **4**: 12
pygmy *see* bonobo
China, Imperial Hunting Park **6**: 44, 45
chinchilla 7: *12*; **8**: 10, 28, 36–37
fur **8**: (10)
short-tailed **8**: 37
Chinchilla lanigera **8**: 30, 36–37
chinchilla rat **8**: 31
Chilean **8**: 30, *31*
common **8**: 30
Chinchillidae **7**: *12*
chipmunk 7: 15, 18
eastern 7: 34, 48–49
Siberian **7**: 48
Chironectes minimus **10**: 14
Chiroptera **1**: *10*; **9**: (86)
Chiroptes
C. albinasus **4**: 72
C. satanas **4**: 72
chiru **6**: 62
chital **6**: 10, *13*, 45
Chlamydia psittaci **10**: 95
Chlamyphorus truncatus **9**: 65
Chlorocebus aethiops **4**: 40
Choloepus
C. didactylus **9**: 65
C. hoffmanni **9**: 65
chozchori **8**: 29
Chrotogale owstoni **1**: 88
Chrysochloridae **9**: 9
Chrysocyon brachyurus **2**: 50
Chrysospalax trevelyani **9**: 40
chulengo **5**: 109
Citellus tridecemlineatus see *Spermophilus tridecemlineatus*
CITES *see* Convention on International Trade in Endangered Species of Wild Fauna and Flora
civet 1: 98
African **1**: 88
African palm **1**: 88
banded palm **1**: 88, 90, *90*, 91
civet family 1: 88–91

common palm 1: 88, 90, *90*, 94–95
golden palm **1**: 88
Hose's palm **1**: 88
Indian **1**: 90
Jerdon's palm **1**: 88
large Indian **1**: 88
large spotted **1**: 88
Lowe's otter **1**: 88
Malayan **1**: 88, *90*
masked palm **1**: 88
Oriental **1**: 88, *90*
otter **1**: 88, 91
Owston's banded **1**: 88, 91
palm **1**: 90, 91
small Indian **1**: 88
small-toothed palm **1**: 88
Sulawesi palm **1**: 88
civet oil **1**: (91)
Civettictis civetta **1**: 88
Cladonia rangiferina **6**: 23
Clethrionomys gapperi **7**: 94–95
clompers **5**: 58
Clyomis laticeps **8**: 30
coalitions **2**: 28
coati 1: 19, *20*, 21
mountain **1**: 20
ringtailed 1: 28–29
white-nosed **1**: 20, 29
coatimundi *see* coati, ringtailed
Coelodonta **5**: *28*
coendou *see* porcupine, tree
Coendou **8**: 12
C. mexicanus **8**: 12, 26–27
C. prehensilis **8**: 12
colobines **4**: 40, 41–42
colobus 4: 10, 40, 40–42, 68–69, 69, 75
Angola (black-and-white) **4**: 40, 68–69
black **4**: 42
black-and-white 4: 40, 68–69
red **4**: 41–42, 68
satanic black **4**: 40
western red **4**: 40
white-epauleted black (black-and-white) **4**: 40, 68–69
Colobus **4**: 40
C. angolensis **4**: 40, 68–69
C. satanus **4**: 40
colugo 1: *10*; **7**: (37); **8**: 108–111
Malayan **8**: 109, *109*, 110, 110–111
Philippine **8**: 108–109, 109, 110
commensal animals **7**: 14
communication **1**: (23); **3**: (83); **4**: (56), 74, 79, 85, 99–100; **5**: 13, 15, 19, (24), 44, (49), 79; **7**: 53, 101; **8**: 16, 42, 51; **9**: 61; **10**: 80
alarm calls **4**: 46, 57, 89, 100; **6**: 79; **7**: 53, 111; **8**: 51, 55, 99
American Sign Language **4**: 13, (16), 27
see also songs
Condylura cristata **9**: 40, 48–51
Conepatus
C. chinga **1**: 32
C. mesoleucus **1**: 32
coney *see* pika, American
Connochaetes
C. gnou **6**: 62, 82
C. taurinus **6**: 62, 82–85
conservation **1**: 47, (59), 75; **2**: 33, 55, (88), 100; **3**: 15, 19; **4**: 35; **5**: 26, 39, 63; **6**: 25, 64; **7**: 45, 77; **9**: 85; **10**: (77), (95), (101)
see also protection

Convention on International Trade in Endangered Species of Wild Fauna and Flora (CITES) **1:** 17
convergent evolution **9:** 10, 40; **10:** 36, (52)
coon hunting **1:** 26
coonskins **1:** (23)
coppicing **7:** 106
coprophagy **8:** 51, 62
coruro **2:** 29, 30
cotton bollworms **9:** 103
cottontail 8: 62
   desert **8:** 64, 67, (93)
   Dice's **8:** (93)
   eastern 8: 64, 90–93
   Mexican Guerrero **8:** (93)
   New England **8:** (93)
   Omilteneor **8:** (93)
   swamp **8:** (93)
cougar *see* puma
coyote 1: 77; **2:** 50, 58–61
coypu 7: *12*; **8:** 9, 11, 31, 44–47
   South American **8:** (46)
Craseonycteridae **9:** 86
Craseonycteris thonglongyai **9:** 38
cria **5:** 107
Crocuta crocuta **2:** 102, 108–109
crop raiding **5:** 23–24, 41, 72, 91; **6:** 13, 78, 81; **7:** 100, 105; **8:** 18–19; **9:** 85, 91
Crossarchus
   C. alexandri **1:** 98
   C. ansorgei **1:** 98
Cryptomys
   C. damarensis **8:** 56
   C. hottentotus **8:** 56
   C. mechowi **8:** 56
Cryptoprocta ferox **1:** 88, 96–97
Cryptotis parva **9:** 28
Ctenodactylidae **7:** *12*, 108
Ctenodactylus
   C. gundi **7:** 108, 110–111
   C. vali **7:** 108
Ctenomyidae **7:** *12*; **8:** 9
Ctenomys
   C. frater **8:** 30
   C. validus **8:** 30
culls **3:** 15, 43, 45, 67; **6:** 32, 66; **8:** 81; **10:** (95)
Cuon alpinus **2:** 50
cursorial animals **2:** 50
cuscus 10: 76, (77)
   admiralty **10:** 74
   bear **10:** 74
   common spotted (spotted) **10:** *12–13*, 82–83
   ground **10:** 74
   mountain **10:** 74
   peleng **10:** 74
   small Sulawesi **10:** 74
   spotted 10: *12–13*, 82–83
   waigeou **10:** 74
cuy *see* guinea pig
Cyanophenus **9:** 86
Cyclopes didactylus **9:** 65
Cynictis penicillata **1:** 98
Cynocephalidae **8:** 108
Cynocephalus
   C. variegatus **8:** 109
   C. volans **8:** 109
Cynogale
   C. bennettii **1:** 88
   C. lowei **1:** 88
Cynomys ludovicianus **7:** 34, 56–59

D

Dactylomys dactylinus **8:** 30
Dactylopsila
   D. tatei **10:** 74
   D. trivirgata **10:** 74
Dama dama **6:** 10, 40–43
Damaliscus
   D. lunatus **6:** 62, 88–89

D. lunatus jimela **6:** 88
D. lunatus korrigum **6:** 88
D. lunatus lunatus **6:** 88
D. lunatus tiang **6:** 88
D. lunatus topi **6:** 88
D. pygargus **6:** 62
dassie, rock *see* hyrax, rock
Dasycercus cristicauda **10:** 27
Dasykaluta rosamondae **10:** 27
Dasyprocta punctata **8:** 30, 42–43
Dasyproctidae **7:** *12*
Dasypus novemcinctus **9:** 65, 74–77
dasyure
   broad-striped **10:** 27
   narrow-striped **10:** *25*, 27
   red-bellied **10:** 27
   short-furred **10:** *25*, 27
Dasyuridae **10:** 24, 36
Dasyuromorphia **10:** 24
Dasyurus
   D. albopunctatus **10:** 27
   D. hallucatus **10:** 27, 32–33
Daubentonia madagascariensis **4:** 96, 102–103
DDT **9:** 103
deer 5: 8, 9, 10, 12
   barking *see* muntjac
   black musk **6:** 10
   black-tailed (mule) **6:** 10, 34–37
   Chinese water **6:** 10
   deer and relatives 6: 10–13
   dwarf musk **6:** 10
   fallow 6: 10, 12, 13, 40–43
   greater mouse 6: 10, 48–49
   Himalayan musk 6: 10, 50–51
   hog **6:** 10
   lesser mouse **6:** 10, 48
   marsh **6:** 10, *12*
   mouse *see* chevrotain
   mule 6: 10, 34–37
   muntjac *see* muntjac
   musk **6:** 10
   pampas **6:** 10, *12*
   Père David's 6: 10, 13, 44–45
   red 6: 10, 12, 13, 30–33
   roe 6: 10, 12, 38–39, *60*
   Siberian musk **6:** 10
   sika **6:** 12
   spotted **6:** 10, *13*
   tufted **6:** 10
   white-tailed **6:** 10, *13*, 18, (36)
   see also brocket
deer parks **6:** 13, *42–43*, 47
deforestation **1:** 21, 31, 48, 51, 71; **2:** 58–59; **3:** 61; **4:** (17), 27, 32, 37, 61, 69, 73, 75, 81, 90; **5:** 20; **6:** 49, 51; **9:** 23, 91
   see also habitat destruction
degu **8:** 29, *31*
   Bridge's **8:** 30
   mountain **8:** 30
dehydration **5:** 95–96
Delphinapterus leucas **3:** 55, 80–83
Delphinus
   D. capensis **3:** 69
   D. delphis **3:** 55, 68–69
Dendrohyrax **8:** 102
   D. arboreus **8:** 103
   D. dorsalis **8:** 103
   D. validus **8:** 103
Dendrolagus
   D. bennettianus **10:** 48
   D. goodfellowi **10:** 48, 66–67
Dermoptera **1:** *10*; **8:** 108
desman 9: 9, 11, 40–43
   Pyrenean 9: *11*, 40, 52–53
   Russian **9:** 40, 42, 43, *53*

Desmana moschata **9:** 40
Desmodus rotundus **9:** 94–97
devil, Tasmanian 10: (24), 27, 28–31
dhole **2:** 50, *51*
dialects of whale pods **3:** 63
diapause, embryonic **10:** 12–13, 57, 63, 69, 71, 73, 85
diastema **7:** 10, *11*; **8:** 60
   see also reproduction
dibatag **6:** *61*, 62
dibbler **10:** 27
Dicerorhinus sumatrensis **5:** 28
Diceros bicornis **5:** 28, 36–39
dicoumarol **7:** 75
Didelphidae **10:** 14, 16
   common *see* opossum, Virginia
Didelphis
   D. albiventris **10:** 14
   D. virginiana **10:** 14, 18–23
dik-dik
   Kirk's **6:** 60, 62
   Salt's **6:** 62
dimorphism, sexual **3:** 87
dingo 2: 50, 80–81; **10:** (30), 37
Dinomyidae **7:** *12*
Dinomys branickii **8:** 30
dinosaur **3:** 98
Diplogale hosei **1:** 88
Diplomesodon pulchellum **9:** 28
Diplomys labilis **8:** 30
Dipodidae **7:** *12*
Dipodomys ordii **7:** 24–25
Diprotodontia **10:** 25, 75, (94)
diseases **1:** 26, 87
   rodent-borne **7:** 14
distemper **3:** 41
   canine **2:** 79
Distoechurus pennatus **10:** 74
dog 1: 15; **5:** 9
   African hunting (African wild) **2:** 9, 50, 53, 78–79
   African wild 2: 9, 50, 53, 78–79
   bush **2:** 50, 53
   dog family 2: 50–53
   domestic **2:** 9, 50, (53)
   painted hunting (African wild) **2:** 9, 50, 53, 78–79
   raccoon **2:** 50
   see also prairie dog
Dolichotis patagonum **8:** 30, 32–35
Dologale dybowskii **1:** 98
dolphin 1: *10*; **3:** 54–59; **5:** (10)
   Amazon 3: 55, 60–61
   bottlenose 3: 55, 66, 72–75
   clymene **3:** 76
   common 3: 55, 68–69, 71
   dusky **3:** 71
   Fraser's **3:** 71
   Ganges **3:** 55, (61)
   hourglass **3:** 71
   Indus **3:** 55, (61)
   La Plata **3:** 55, (61)
   long-beaked (spinner) **3:** 55, 76–77
   long-beaked common **3:** 69
   Pacific white-sided 3: 55, 70–71
   pink (Amazon) **3:** 55, 60–61
   Risso's **3:** 71
   river **3:** (61)
   rollover (spinner) **3:** 55, 76–77
   short-beaked common **3:** 69
   short-snouted spinner **3:** 76
   spinner 3: 55, 76–77
   spotted **3:** 56–57, 77
   white-beaked **3:** 71
   white-sided **3:** 71
   Yangtze river **3:** 55, (61)

dolphinaria **3:** 71, 74
domestication **2:** 53; **5:** (43), (45), (98), 105–106, 107; **6:** 25, 63; **8:** 38–39, 40, (72)
   see also cat, domestic; dog, domestic
donkey
   domestic **5:** (45)
   wild **5:** 44–45
Dorcatragus megalotis **6:** 62
dorcopsis
   gray **10:** 48
   white-striped **10:** 48
Dorcopsis
   D. hageni **10:** 48
   D. luctuosa **10:** 48
Dorcopsulus
   D. macleayi **10:** 48
   D. vanheurni **10:** 48
dormouse 7: 11, *12*, 13, 15, 17, 19
   African **7:** 103
   Asiatic garden **7:** 102
   Chinese **7:** 102
   Chinese pygmy **7:** 103
   common (hazel) **7:** 102, 103, 106–107
   desert **7:** 102, 103
   dormouse family 7: 102–103
   edible 7: (14), 102, 104–105
   fat (edible) **7:** (14), 102, 104–105
   forest **7:** 102
   garden **7:** 102, *102–103*
   hazel 7: 102, 103, 106–107
   Japanese **7:** 102, *102*
   masked mouse-tailed **7:** 102
   Oriental **7:** 103
   Roach's mouse-tailed **7:** 102
   Setzer's mouse-tailed **7:** 102
   spectacled **7:** 102
   spiny **7:** 103
   woolly **7:** 102
douroucouli *see* monkey, Northern night
Draculin **9:** 97
drill **4:** 40, 42
dromedary *see* camel, dromedary
Dromiciops gliroides **10:** 14
drought **4:** 63; **5:** 34, 94
drug testing **4:** 13, 93
Dryomys
   D. laniger **7:** 102
   D. nitedula **7:** 102
   D. sichuanensis **7:** 102
dugong 1: *10*; **3:** 46–47, 52–53; **5:** (12)
Dugong dugon **3:** 47, 52–53
duiker
   bay **6:** 62
   blue **6:** 62
   bush (common) **6:** 62, 80–81
   common 6: 62, 80–81
   forest **6:** 80
dunnart 10: 27
   common 10: 38–39
   fat-tailed **10:** *25*, 27
   Gilbert's **10:** 38
   Kangaroo Island **10:** 38
   little long-tailed **10:** 38
   red-cheeked **10:** 27
Duplicidentata **8:** 61
Dusicyon australis **2:** 50

E

echidna 1: 14; **8:** 12; **10:** *105*
   long-nosed **10:** 105, 110
   short-beaked 10: 105, 110–111
Echimyidae **7:** *12*; **8:** 31
Echimys pictus **8:** 30

Echinoprocta rufescens **8:** 12
Echinops telfairi **9:** 24
Echinosorex gymnura **9:** 12, 22–23
echolocation **9:** 8, 28, 32, 37, 80–81, 92–93, 99, 106, 109, 110–111
echymipera, Clara's **10:** 27
Echymipera
   E. clara **10:** 27
   E. rufescens **10:** 27
ecotones **6:** 86
Edentates **9:** 64, *64*
egg-laying mammals 10: 104–105
egret **6:** (73)
Eidolon **9:** 86
Eimer's organs **9:** 45, (50)
Eira barbara **1:** 32
eland 5: *13*
   common **6:** *60*, 62, 76
   giant 6: 62, 76–77
   Lord Derby's (giant) **6:** 62, 76–77
Elaphodus cephalophus **6:** 10
Elaphurus davidianus **6:** 10, 44–45
electrocution **4:** 67
elephant 1: *10*, *10*; **5:** 8, (10), 11, (12)
   African 5: 14, 15, 16–21, 26
   Asian 5: 14, 15, 16, 22–27
   circus elephants **5:** *24*, (24)
   elephant family 5: 14–15
   family units **5:** *15*
   forest **5:** 14, *14–15*
   savanna **5:** 14, 15
   elephant shrew 1: *10*; **9:** 10, 58–59
   black and rufous **9:** 59, *59*
   checkered **9:** *58–59*, 59
   four-toed **9:** 59, *59*
   golden-rumped 9: 59, 62–63
   North African **9:** 59, *59*
   short-eared **9:** 59, *59*
Elephantulus rozeti **9:** 59
Elephas maximus **5:** 14, 22–27
Eliomys
   E. melanurus **7:** 102
   E. quercinus **7:** 102
elk 6: 10, 26–29
   eastern **6:** 26
   Irish **6:** 10
   Manitoba **6:** 27
   Merriman **6:** 26
   North American **6:** 12
   Rocky Mountain **6:** 26–27
   Roosevelt's **6:** 27
   Siberian **6:** 15
   Tule **6:** 27
   see also moose
El Niño **3:** 22
Emballonuridae **9:** 87
embryonic diapause **10:** 12– 13, 57, 63, 69, 71, 73, 85
Enhydra lutris **1:** 32, 72–75
Eohippus **5:** 42
Eomanis waldi **9:** 64
Equidae **5:** 42
Equus
   E. asinus **5:** 42, 57
   E. burchelli **5:** 42, 46–51
   E. caballus **5:** 42, 58–61
   E. caballus przewalskii (*E. przewalskii*) **5:** 42, 54–55
   E. grevyi **5:** 42, 52–53
   E. hemionus **5:** 42, 56–57
   E. przewalskii **5:** 42, 54–55
   E. quagga **5:** 48
   E. zebra **5:** 42
Eremitalpa granti **9:** 40, 56–57
Erethizon dorsatum **8:** 12, 20–25

Erethizontidae **7:** *12*; **8:** 12
Erinaceidae **9:** 9, 11
Erinaceus
  E. concolor **9:** 12
  E. europaeus **9:** 12, <u>14–19</u>
ermine **1:** 112
  see also stoat
Erythrocebus patas **4:** 40
Eschrichtiidae **3:** 92
Eschrichtius robustus **3:** 55,
  <u>92–97</u>
estivation **7:** 19; **9:** 13, 21
Ethiopia, geladas in **4:** 63
Eubalaena
  E. australis **3:** <u>108–109</u>
  E. glacialis **3:** 55
eucalyptus **10:** 95–96, 96
Eulemur **4:** 96
  E. coronatus **4:** 96
  E. macaco **4:** 96
  E. mongoz **4:** 96
Eumetopias jubatus **3:** 9,
  <u>18–19</u>
Euoticus
  E. elegantulus **4:** 106
  E. pallidus **4:** 106
Eupleres goudotii **1:** 88
Euroscaptor parvidens **9:** 40
Eurotamandua **1:** *9*
Euryzygomatomys spinosus
  8: 30
Eutheria **10:** (10)
evolution
  convergent **9:** 10, 40;
    10: 36, (52)
  of mammals **1:** *10*
  of rodents **7:** *12*
extermination **6:** 64–66

F

facial expression **4:** (56), 100
falanouc **1:** 88, *91*
fanaloka **1:** 88
  Madagascan **1:** 91, *91*
farmland, expanding **1:** 15–16
Felis **2:** 10
  F. bengalensis **2:** 10
  F. caracal **2:** 10
  F. catus **2:** 10
  F. chaus **2:** 10
  F. concolor **2:** 10, <u>42–43</u>
  F. lynx **2:** 10, <u>40–41</u>
  F. lynx canadensis **2:** 40, 41
  F. lynx lynx **2:** 40, 41
  F. lynx pardinus **2:** 40, 41
  F. margarita **2:** 10
  F. nigripes **2:** 10
  F. pardalis **2:** 10, <u>44–45</u>
  F. rufus **2:** 10, <u>38–39</u>
  F. serval **2:** 10, <u>46–47</u>
  F. silvestris **2:** 10, <u>48–49</u>
  F. temmincki **2:** 10
  F. tigrinus **2:** 10
  F. yaguarondi **2:** 10
Felovia vae **7:** 108
Fennecus zerda see *Vulpes*
  zerda
fermentation **5:** 11
ferret 1: 45
  black-footed 1: 32, *34*, 35,
    <u>46–47</u>
fertilization *see* implantation/
  fertilization; reproduction
fisher **1:** <u>50–51</u>; **8:** 20
fish farms **3:** 65
fishing **3:** 12, 15, 19, 37, 43,
  105
  cooperative, by dolphins
    3: (74)
fishing nets **3:** 22, 30, 50, *59*,
  69, 71, 77, 79, 105
fleas **9:** (18)
flehmen **5:** (11), 62, 65
flood water **4:** 80
flying fox 9: 80, 86
  Indian 9: <u>88–91</u>
food poisoning **7:** 74
food sharing **9:** (96)
forestry operations **5:** 26

forests
  in Brazil **4:** 90–91
  elephants in **5:** 22
  gallery forests **4:** 101
  gorillas in **4:** 26
  see also deforestation
fossa 1: 88, 90, *91*, <u>96–97</u>;
  4: 100
Fossa fossa **1:** 88
fossorial animals **7:** 18, 65
Fouchia **5:** 28
fovea **4:** 107
fox
  Arctic 2: 50, <u>70–73</u>, 87;
    7: (14)
  bat-eared 2: 50, <u>76–77</u>
  Blanford's **2:** 50, 53
  blue Arctic **2:** 71, (72)
  Cape **2:** 50, 53
  corsac **2:** 50, *53*
  "cross fox" **2:** 64, *65*
  fennec 2: 50, 52, <u>74–75</u>
  gray **2:** 50, *52*
  Indian **2:** 50, *53*
  island gray **2:** 50
  kit (swift) **2:** 50, *52*, <u>68–69</u>
  red 1: 9; **2:** 50, (59), <u>64–67</u>,
    70
  Rüppell's **2:** 50, *53*
  Samson **2:** 64
  swift 2: 50, *52*, <u>68–69</u>
  white Arctic **2:** 71, 72
freeze branding **8:** (84)
Funambulus pennantii **7:** 34
fur farming **1:** 22, 35, 54, 55;
  2: (72); **8:** 46–47
fur trade **1:** 22, (23), 51, 54,
  64, 68–69, 87, 93; **2:**
  12–13, 35, 41, 44, 69,
  (72), 75; **3:** 12, 16; **4:** 40,
  85; **7:** 33, 41, 97; **8:** (10),
  36, 37, 46, 61, 90; **9:** 43;
  10: 22, 65, (80)
Furipteridae **9:** 87
Furipterus **9:** 87
see also skin trade

G

galago
  Demidoff's dwarf *see* bush
    baby, Demidoff's
  Gabon **4:** 106
  Garnett's **4:** 106
  northern needle-clawed
    4: 106
  Senegal **4:** 106
  Somali **4:** 106
  southern needle-clawed
    4: 106
  thick-tailed **4:** 106, *107*
  Thomas's **4:** 106
  Zanzibar **4:** 106
Galago
  G. gabonensis **4:** 106
  G. gallarum **4:** 106
  G. senegalensis **4:** 106
Galagoides
  G. demidoff **4:** 106,
    <u>110–111</u>
  G. thomasi **4:** 106
  G. zanzibaricus **4:** 106
Galea musteloides **8:** 30
Galemys pyrenaicus **9:** 40,
  <u>52–53</u>
Galeopithecidae **8:** 108
Galictis
  G. cuja **1:** 32
  G. vittata **1:** 32
Galidia elegans **1:** 98
Galidictis
  G. fasciata **1:** 98
  G. grandidieri **1:** 98
gallery forests **4:** 101
Garamba National Park **5:** 34
gaur **6:** 62
Gazella
  G. dama **6:** 62
  G. leptoceros **6:** 62
  G. subguttarosa **6:** 62
  G. thomsoni **6:** <u>94–95</u>

gazelle 5: 47
  dama **6:** *61*, 62
  goitered **6:** *61*, 62
  slender-horned **6:** *61*, 62
  Thomson's 6: <u>94–95</u>, 97,
    110
  Tibetan **6:** *61*, 62
gelada baboon 4: 40, 42, 43,
  <u>62–63</u>
gemsbok **6:** 62
genet 1: 18, 98
  aquatic **1:** 88, 91
  common 1: 88, <u>92–93</u>
  European (common) **1:** 88,
    <u>92–93</u>
  genet family 1: <u>88–91</u>
  large-spotted **1:** 88
  small-spotted (common)
    1: 88, <u>92–93</u>
Genetta
  G. genetta **1:** 88, <u>92–93</u>
  G. tigrina **1:** 88
Geocapromys browni **8:** 30
Geogale aurita **9:** 24
Geomyidae **7:** *12*
Georychus capensis **8:** 56
gerbil **7:** 13, 15
  bushveld **7:** *13*
  Mongolian 7: <u>88–89</u>
gerenuk 6: 62, <u>98–99</u>
gibbon 4: *8*, 10, 12
  common (lar) **4:** 36,
    <u>38–39</u>
  crested **4:** 37
  crested black **4:** 36
  gibbon family 4: <u>36–37</u>
  kloss **4:** 36, 37, *37*
  lar 4: 36, <u>38–39</u>
  moloch **4:** 36, 37
  Müller's **4:** 36, *37*
  white-handed (lar) **4:** 36,
    <u>38–39</u>
Gibraltar, apes in **4:** 50
Gigantopithecus **4:** 12
Giraffa
  G. camelopardalis **6:** 52,
    <u>54–57</u>
  G. camelopardalis
    angolensis **6:** 52
  G. camelopardalis
    antiquorum **6:** 52
  G. camelopardalis
    camelopardalis **6:** 52
  G. camelopardalis
    capensis **6:** 52
  G. camelopardalis peralta
    6: 52
  G. camelopardalis
    reticulata **6:** 52, 54
  G. camelopardalis
    rothschildi **6:** 52, 54
  G. camelopardalis
    thornicrofti **6:** 52
  G. camelopardalis
    tippelskirchi **6:** 52, 54
giraffe 5: 11, 12; **6:** <u>54–57</u>,
  60
  giraffe family 6: <u>52–53</u>
  kordofan **6:** 52
  Masai **6:** 52, 54
  nubian **6:** 52
  reticulated **6:** 52, *53*, 54
  Rothschild's **6:** 52, 54, *56*
  southern African **6:** 52
  Thornicroft's **6:** 52, 53
  West African **6:** 52
giraffe-gazelle *see* gerenuk
Giraffidae **6:** 52–53
Gir Forest Reserve **2:** (15)
Glaucomys
  G. sabrinus **7:** 61
  G. volans **7:** 34, <u>60–61</u>
gleaning **9:** 84
glider
  feathertail (pygmy) **10:** 74,
    77, <u>84–85</u>
  greater **10:** 74
  mahogany **10:** 74, (77)
  pygmy 10: 74, 77, <u>84–85</u>

sugar 10: 74, 76, (76),
  <u>86–87</u>, 88
gliding marsupials **10:** (76)
Glironia venusta **10:** 14
Glirulus japonicus **7:** 102
glis *see* dormouse, edible
Glis glis **7:** 102, <u>104–105</u>
Globicephala melas **3:** 55,
  <u>66–67</u>
glutton *see* wolverine
Glyptodon **9:** 66
  G. panochthus **9:** *64*
gnawing **7:** 10, 16–17, 64
gnu
  white-tailed **6:** 82
  see also wildebeest, blue
goat 6: <u>60–63</u>
  domestic **6:** 63
  mountain 6: 62, <u>108–109</u>
  wild **6:** 62
Gondwanaland **9:** 10; **10:** (11),
  108
gopher 7: 17, 18
  horned **7:** 12
  northern pocket 7: <u>26–27</u>
  pocket **7:** *12*, 18
  western pocket (northern
    pocket) **7:** <u>26–27</u>
goral **6:** 62, 108
gorilla 4: *8*, 10, 12, 13
  Cross River **4:** 12, (21), 26
  eastern **4:** 12, (21)
  eastern lowland **4:** 12, *13*,
    (21)
  mountain 4: 12, <u>20–25</u>
  silverback **4:** *13*, 22, *22–23*
  western **4:** 12, (21)
  western lowland 4: 8, 12,
    (21), <u>26–27</u>
Gorilla
  G. beringei **4:** 12, (21)
  G. beringei beringei **4:** 12,
    <u>20–25</u>
  G. beringei diehli **4:** 12, (21)
  G. gorilla **4:** 12, (21)
  G. gorilla diehli **4:** 12, (21), 26
  G. gorilla gorilla **4:** 12,
    (21), <u>26–27</u>
Gracilinanus
  G. agilis **10:** 14
  G. dryas **10:** 14
Graphiurus ocularis **7:** 102
grass *see* sea grass
grazing **5:** 12, 13, 30, 31;
  6: 67, 89
Great Gobi Strictly Protected
  Area **5:** 103
grison **1:** 32
  little **1:** 32, *34*
ground destabilization **7:** 49,
  50, 59; **8:** 29, 57, 66–67;
  9: 77; **10:** 99
groundhog *see* woodchuck
guanaco 5: 92, <u>108–109</u>
  wild **5:** 93
guenon **4:** *8*, 10, 40, 42, 43,
  44
guiara **8:** 30
guinea pig 8: 10, 30, <u>38–41</u>
  black **8:** 41
  domestic **8:** 38–39, *39*, 40
  wild **8:** 28, 39–40
Gulo gulo **1:** 32, <u>56–57</u>
gundi 7: *12*, 13
  desert **7:** 108, 109
  felou **7:** 108, 109, *109*
  gundi family 7: <u>108–109</u>
  Lataste's **7:** *109*
  mzab **7:** 108, 109, *109*
  North African 7: 108,
    <u>110–111</u>
  Saharan **7:** 108
  Speke's **7:** 108, 109, *109*
Gymnobelideus leadbeateri
  10: 74, <u>88–89</u>
gymnure **9:** 12, 13
  Hainan **9:** 12, 13
  short-tailed **9:** 12, *12*
  shrew **9:** 12, *12*

H

habitat destruction **1:** 62, 64;
  2: 35, 44, 79; **3:** 83; **4:** 24,
  35, 87, 96, 101; **5:** 26, 63,
  65, 91; **6:** 20, 47, 49, 51,
  59, (66); **7:** 25, 63, 107;
  9: 33, 62, 63, 85, 91;
  10: 27, (77), (95)
  see also deforestation
habitat preservation **4:** 51
habituation **4:** (23)
Halichoerus grypus **3:** <u>42–43</u>
hammer stones **1:** (74);
  4: 31–32, (31)
hamster 7: 11, 15, 18, 19
  golden 7: <u>84–85</u>
  Syrian (golden) **7:** <u>84–85</u>
Hapalemur
  H. aureus **4:** 96
  H. griseus **4:** 96
  H. simus **4:** 96
haplorhines *see* primates,
  higher
hare 8: 61
  Arctic 8: 74, <u>82–85</u>
  brown 8: 62, <u>86–89</u>
  calling *see* pika, American
  Cape **8:** 80
  European **8:** 64
  greater red rockhare **8:** *63*,
    64
  Greenland (Arctic) **8:** 74,
    <u>82–85</u>
  hare family 8: <u>64–67</u>
  hispid **8:** *63*, 64, 66
  Jameson's red rockhare
    8: 64
  mouse *see* pika, American
  Patagonian *see* mara
  polar (Arctic) **8:** 74, <u>82–85</u>
  Smith's red rockhare **8:** 64
  snowshoe 8: 62, 64,
    <u>74–79</u>
hare hunting **8:** (89)
hartebeest **6:** 62
  Lichtenstein's **6:** 62
harvesting **3:** 28; **6:** 18
  controlled **3:** 12, 16
  sustainable **3:** 15
Hawaiian Islands National
  Wildlife Refuge **3:** 31
hawks, bat **9:** 84
hedgehog 1: 9, 10, 14; **8:** 12;
  9: 8, 9, 11
  African **9:** 12, 13
  African pygmy 9: 12,
    <u>20–21</u>
  Asian **9:** 12
  collared **9:** 12
  Daurian **9:** 12
  desert **9:** 12, *13*
  dwarf (African pygmy)
    9: 12, <u>20–21</u>
  eastern European **9:** 12
  four-toed (African pygmy)
    9: 12, <u>20–21</u>
  hairy **9:** 12, 22
  hedgehog family 9: <u>12–13</u>
  Hugh's **9:** 12, 13
  long-eared **9:** 12, *12–13*
  Madagascan **9:** 25
  North African **9:** 12, *13*
  western European
    9: 12, <u>14–19</u>
  white-bellied (African
    pygmy) **9:** 12, <u>20–21</u>
Helarctos malayanus **2:** 82
Heliophobius **7:** 9
  H. argenteocinereus **8:** 56
Helogale parvula **1:** 98,
  <u>106–107</u>
Hemibelideus lemuroides
  10: 74
Hemicentetes semispinosus
  9: 24
Hemiechinus
  H. aethiopicus **9:** 12
  H. auritus **9:** 12, *12–13*
  H. collaris **9:** 12

Hemigalus derbyanus **1:** 88
Hemitragus jemlahicus **6:** 62
herding, predator avoidance
  5: 10
Herpestes
  H. edwardsii **1:** 108–109
  H. ichneumon **1:** 98
  H. naso **1:** 98
Herpestidae **1:** 88
Heterocephalus glaber
  8: 56, 58–59
Heterohyrax **8:** 102
  H. antineae **8:** 103
  H. brucei **8:** 103
  H. chapini **8:** 103
Heteromyidae **7:** 12
Hexaprotodon liberiensis **5:** 66
hibernation **2:** 87–88, 93, 97,
  100; **7:** 19, 51, 54–55,
  107; **9:** 13, 18, 27, 82,
  104, 105, 111; **10:** 111
Himalaya Mountains **1:** 30
hippo *see* hippopotamus
Hippocamelus
  H. antisensis **6:** 10
  H. bisulcus **6:** 10
hippopotamus 5: *8, 9, 10;*
  8: 48
  common 5: 66, *66, 67,*
    68–73
  hippopotamus family
    5: *66–67*
  pygmy **5:** 66, 66–67, *67*
Hippopotamus amphibius
  5: 66, *68–73*
hippotigres **5:** 52
Hippotragus
  H. equinus **6:** 62
  H. leucophaeus **6:** 63
  H. niger **6:** 62
hirola **6:** 62
hog
  giant forest 5: 74, 75,
    84–85
  pygmy **5:** 74
  red river **5:** 74
  see also warthog
homeothermy **1:** 9–10, 14
Hominidae **4:** 10
Homo sapiens **1:** 14; **4:** 12
honeybees **7:** 13
honey guide, African **1:** 83
hoofed mammals 5: *8–13*
Hoplomys gymnurus **8:** 30
hornbill **1:** 107
horns **3:** 29, 31, 36–37, (37),
  40, 41; **6:** 9, 56, 60, 111
horse 1: 15; **5:** *8, 9, 10, 11,*
  11, 12, 62
  ancestral **1:** *8*
  Camargue **5:** 60–61
  dawn **5:** 42
  domestic **5:** (43)
  draft **5:** (43), 58
  feral *see* mustang
  horse family 5: 42–45
  Mongolian wild 5: 42,
    45, 54–55
  Przewalski's (Mongolian
    wild) **5:** 42, 45, 54–55
  racehorses **5:** (43)
  wild (Mongolian wild) **5:**
    42, 45, 54–55
  wild (mustang) *see* mustang
hot springs **4:** 48
huemul
  Chilean **6:** 10
  Peruvian **6:** 10, *12–13*
human **4:** 10–11, 12
hunting partnerships **2:** (60)
hutia 7: *12;* **8:** 11, 31, *31*
  Brown's **8:** 30
  Cuban 8: 30, 52–53
  Desmarest's Cuban (Cuban)
    8: 30, 52–53
  eared **8:** 30
  Hispanolan **8:** 30
  prehensile-tailed **8:** 30
  West Indian **8:** 11

Hyaena
  H. brunnea **2:** 102
  H. hyaena **2:** 102, 104–107
hybridization **2:** 59
Hydrochaeridae **7:** *12*
Hydrochaeris hydrochaeris
  8: 30, 48–51
Hydrodamalis gigas **3:** 47
Hydromys chrysogaster **7:** 9
Hydropotes inermis **6:** 10
Hydrurga leptonyx **3:** 9,
  38–39
Hyemoschus aquaticus **6:** 10
hyena
  brown **2:** 102, 103, *103*
  hyena family 2: 102–103
  spotted 2: 102, *102–103,*
    103, 108–109
  striped 2: 102, 103,
    104–107
Hylobates
  H. concolor **4:** 36
  H. klossii **4:** 36
  H. lar **4:** 36, 38–39
  H. moloch **4:** 36
  H. muelleri **4:** 36
  H. syndactylus **4:** 36
Hylochoerus meinertzhageni
  5: 74, 84–85
Hylomys
  H. hainanensis **9:** 12, *13*
  H. sinensis **9:** 12, *12*
  H. suillus **9:** 12, *12*
Hylopetes
  H. lepidus **7:** 36
  H. spadiceus **7:** 34, 36
Hyperoodon ampullatus
  3: 55, 90–91
Hypsiprymnodon moschatus
  10: 48, 72
Hypsiprymnodontidae **10:** 48
Hyracoidea **1:** *10;* **5:** (12), 14
Hyracotherium **5:** 42
hyrax 1: *10;* **5:** (10), (12), 14;
  8: 68, 102–105
  Ahaggar **8:** 103
  Bruce's yellow-spotted
    8: 103, 104–105
  Cape rock (rock) **8:** 103,
    104–105, 105, 106–107
  eastern tree **8:** 103
  Matadi **8:** 103
  rock 8: 105, 106–107
  southern tree **8:** *102–103,*
    103
  tree **8:** 104
  western tree **8:** 103
  yellow-spotted **8:** 105
Hystricidae **7:** *12;* **8:** 12
Hystricognathi **7:** (8), *12;*
  8: 8–11, 28, 55
Hystrix
  H. africaeaustralis **8:** 12
  H. brachyura **8:** 12
  H. cristata **8:** 12, 16–19

I

ibex 6: 62, 106–107
  alpine **6:** 106, 107
  nubian **6:** 106
  Siberian **6:** 106, 107
  walia **6:** 106, 106–107
Ichneumia albicauda **1:** 98
Ictonyx striatus **1:** 32
impala 6: 62, 86–87, 97
implantation/fertilization,
  delayed **1:** 42, 49, 57, 81;
  2: 82, (86), 93; **3:** 34; **6:**
  39; **8:** 109; **9:** 61, 77, 83,
  105, 107
  see also reproduction
imprinting **6:** 83
inbreeding **1:** (59); **2:** 29, 33,
  109; **4:** 22, 81, 90, 93; **7:**
  13, 66, 70; **8:** 57, 59;
  10: 101
indri **4:** 96, 97
Indricotherium **5:** 8, 28
Indri indri **4:** 96

infanticide **1:** (13); **2:** 24;
  4: (10)
Inia geoffrensis **3:** 55, 60–61
insectivores 1: *8, 10;* **9:** 8–11
interbreeding **2:** 59; **6:** 75,
  107; **10:** 41
International Union for the
  Conservation of Nature
  (IUCN) **1:** 16
introductions **1:** 18, 22, 43
Iomys horsfieldi **7:** 36
Isoodon
  I. auratus **10:** 27
  I. macrourus **10:** 27, 46–47
Isothrix pagurus **8:** 30
IUCN *see* International Union
  for the Conservation of
  Nature
ivory **3:** 26; **5:** 14, 20, 26, 72
  see also tusks
ivory poaching **5:** 20

J

jaca *see* guinea pig
jackal, black-backed 1: 83;
  2: 50, 62–63
jackrabbit
  antelope **8:** *62,* 64, 66, *66*
  black-tailed **8:** 64, 80–81
Jacobson's organ **2:** 12;
  5: (11), 65
jaguar 2: 10, 36–37
  black **2:** 37
jaguarundi **2:** 10, *12*
javelina *see* peccary, collared
jerboa **7:** *12,* 17
jird *see* gerbil

K

kaluta, little red **10:** *25,* 27
kangaroo 8: 62; **10:** 8, (10),
  48–53
  Bennett's tree **10:** 48
  eastern gray (gray) **10:** 48,
    53, 60–63
  Goodfellow's tree 10:
    48, 6–67
  gray 10: 48, *53,* 60–63
  red 10: 11, 48, 54–59, 60,
    63
  tree (Goodfellow's tree)
    10: 48, 51, 52, 66–67
  western gray **10:** 60, (62)
kangaroo rat 7: 13, 17
  bannertail **7:** 18–19
  Ord's 7: 24–25
Kannabateomys amblyonyx
  8: 30
Karroo desert **2:** 77
keratin **5:** 10, 29, (37); **6:** 60;
  8: 20
Kerodon rupestris **8:** 30
keystone species **5:** 26; **6:** (68);
  7: 32, 93
khur *see* ass, Asian wild
kiang *see* ass, Asian wild
kinkajou **1:** 20, *21*
klipspringer **5:** *8;* **6:** 60, 62
koala 10: (10), 77, (77),
  92–97
kob **6:** 62
Kobus
  K. ellipsiprymnus **5:** *75;*
    6: 62, 92–93
  K. ellipsiprymnus defassa
    6: 92–93
  K. ellipsiprymnus
    ellipsyprymnus **6:** 92–93
  K. kob **6:** 62
  K. leche **6:** 92
  K. vardonii **6:** 62
Kogia
  K. breviceps **3:** 55
  K. simus **3:** 55
korrigum **6:** 88
Kruger National Park **2:** 31
kudu, greater 6: 78–79
kulan *see* ass, Asian wild
kultarr **10:** *25,* 27

L

laboratory animals **4:** 40, 87;
  7: 15, 66, (75), 83, 86;
  8: (41)
  see also medical research
Lagenodelphis hosei **3:** 71
Lagenorhynchus
  L. acutus **3:** 71
  L. albirostris **3:** 71
  L. cruciger **3:** 71
  L. obliquidens **3:** 55, 70–71
  L. obscurus **3:** 71
Lagidium peruanum **8:** 30
lagomorphs **1:** *10;* **8:** 61–63
Lagostomus maximus **8:** 30
Lagostrophus fasciatus
  10: 48
Lagothrix
  L. flavicauda **4:** 72
  L. lagotricha **4:** 72, 82–83
Lama
  L. glama **5:** 92, 104–107
  L. guanicoe **5:** 92, 108–109
  L. pacos **5:** 92, (106)
Langorchestes
  L. conspicillatus **10:** 48
  L. hirsutus **10:** 48
langur 4: 42
  Hanuman 1: *12–13;* **4:** 40,
    41, 64–67
  Malabar **4:** 40
Lariscus insignis **7:** 36
Lasiorhinus
  L. krefftii **10:** 74, (101)
  L. latifrons **10:** 74, (101)
lassa fever **7:** 14
Laurasia **9:** 10
lechwe **6:** 92
lemming 2: 72; **7:** 13, 17, 65
  collared **7:** 9
  Norway 7: 66, 90–91
lemmus lemmus **7:** 90–91
lemur 1: 96; **4:** 96–97
  bamboo **4:** 96, 97
  black **4:** 96, *96*
  black-and-white ruffed
    4: 104, *105*
  brown **4:** 97
  brown mouse **4:** 96
  Coquerel's dwarf **4:** 96
  crowned **4:** 96
  dwarf **4:** 97, *97*
  eastern woolly **4:** 96
  fat-tailed dwarf **4:** 96
  flying **8:** 108
  fork-marked **4:** 96
  giant sloth **4:** 96
  golden bamboo **4:** 96
  gray mouse **4:** 96
  greater bamboo **4:** 96
  greater dwarf **4:** 96
  hairy-eared dwarf **4:** 96
  indri **4:** 96, 97
  Milne-Edwards's sportive
    4: 96, 97
  mongoose **4:** 96, *96*
  mouse **4:** 97, *97*
  pygmy mouse **4:** 8, 96, 97
  red ruffed **4:** 104, *105*
  ringtailed 4: 9, 96, 97,
    98–101
  ruffed 4: 96, 104–105
  sportive **4:** 97
  weasel sportive **4:** 96
  western woolly **4:** 96
Lemur catta **4:** 96, 98–101
Leontopithecus
  L. caissara **4:** 88
  L. chrysomelas **4:** 88
  L. chrysopygus **4:** 86, 88
  L. rosalia **4:** 86, 88–91
leopard 2: 9, 10, 13, 30–33
  black **2:** 30, *31*
  clouded **2:** 9, 10
  melanistic **2:** 30, *31*
  snow 2: 10, 13, 34–35
Lepilemur
  L. edwardsi **4:** 96
  L. mustelinus **4:** 96

Leporidae (leporids) **8:** 60, 64,
  67
leprosy **9:** (76)
Lepticidium **1:** *8*
leptospirosis **1:** 87; **7:** 14
Lepus
  L. alleni **8:** 64
  L. americanus **8:** 64, 74–79
  L. arcticus **8:** 82–85
  L. californicus **8:** 64, 80–81
  L. europaeus **8:** 64, 86–89
Lestodelphys halli **10:** 14
Lestoros inca **10:** 14
leverets **8:** 88
Liberiictis kuhni **1:** 98
lice, whale **3:** *57,* 92, 102, 108
Limnogale mergulus **9:** 24
linsang **1:** 89, 90, 91
  African **1:** 88, *90*
  banded **1:** 88
  spotted **1:** 88
lion 1: 15; **2:** *8–9,* 9, 10, *13,*
  14–19; **6:** 82; **8:** *18–19*
  Asian **2:** (15)
  Barbary **2:** 17
  mountain *see* puma
Lipotes vexillifer **3:** 55, (61)
Lipotyphla **9:** 10
Litocranius walleri **6:** 62,
  98–99
lizard, Caribbean ground
  1: 109
llama 5: 12, 92, 93, *93,*
  104–107
Lobodon carcinophagus
  3: 9, 36–37
lobtailing **3:** 96, 109
locomotion, plantigrade **9:** 8,
  12, 22, 68
logging **1:** 51, 77; **2:** 21; **6:** 20
Lonchothrix emiliae **8:** 30
Lontra
  L. canadensis **1:** 32, 64–67
  L. felina **1:** 32
Lophiomys imhausi **7:** 66
Lophocebus
  L. albigena **4:** 40
  L. aterrimus **4:** 40
loris 4: 106–107
  pygmy **4:** 106
  slender **4:** 106, *106*
  slow 4: 106, 108–109
Loris tardigradus **4:** 106
love charms **3:** 61
Loxodonta
  L. africana **5:** 14, 16–21
  L. cyclotis **5:** 14
lucky charms **8:** 67; **9:** 79
Lutra
  L. lutra **1:** 32, 58–63
  L. maculicollis **1:** 32
  L. sumatrana **1:** 32
Lutreolina crassicaudata
  10: 14
Lutrogale perspicillata **1:** 32
Lycaon pictus **2:** 50, 78–79
Lyncodon patagonicus **1:** 32
lynx 2: 10, 12, 38, 40–41;
  8: 76–77
  Canadian **2:** 40, 41
  Eurasian 2.40 **2:** 41
  Iberian **2:** 40, 41

M

Macaca
  M. fuscata **4:** 40, 48–49
  M. nigra **4:** 40, 52–53
  M. silenus **4:** 40
  M. sylvanus **4:** 40, 50–51
macaque 4: *8,* 40, 42, 43, 66
  Barbary 4: 40, 42, 50–51
  black 4: 40, 52–53
  Celebes (black) **4:** 40, 52–53
  Japanese 4: 40, 42, 48–49
  lion-tailed **4:** 40, *41*
  Sulawesi crested (black)
    4: 40, 52–53
Macrogalidia musschenbroekii
  1: 88

Macropodidae **10:** 48, 50
Macropus
  M. fuliginosus **10:** (62)
  M. giganteus **10:** 48,
    60–63
  M. parryi **10:** 48
  M. robustus **10:** 48
  M. rufogriseus **10:** 48,
    64–65
  M. rufus **10:** 48, 54–59
Macroscelidea **1:** *10;* **9:** 58
Macroscelides proboscideus
  9: 59
Macrostylus **9:** 86
Macrotis
  M. lagotis **10:** 27, 44–45
  M. leucura **10:** 27
Madagascar, carnivores in
  1: 90, 96–97
Madoqua
  M. kirkii **6:** 62
  M. saltiana **6:** 62
Makalata armata **8:** 30
mammals 1: 8–17
  changing species **1:** 15–16
  diversity of **1:** (11), 14–15
  evolution **1:** *10*
  major groups **1:** 11
  origin **1:** 8
  reproduction **1:** 12–14
mammoth **5:** 8
Mammuthus **5:** 8
manatee 1: *10;* **3:** 46–47;
  5: (10), (12)
  Amazonian **3:** 47
  Caribbean (West Indian)
    3: *46, 47,* 48–51
  West African **3:** 47
  West Indian 3: *46, 47,*
    48–51
mandrill 4: 40, 42, 60–61
Mandrillus
  M. leucophaeus **4:** 40
  M. sphinx **4:** 40, 60–61
mangabey **4:** 40, 42, 43
  agile **4:** 40, 42
  black **4:** 40, 42
  gray-cheeked **4:** 40, *40,* 42
  white **4:** 40, 42
mangrove swamps **4:** 71
Manis
  M. gigantea **9:** 65
  M. temminckii **9:** 65
  M. tricuspis **9:** 65
mara 8: 8, 30, 32–35
Marmosa
  M. mexicana **10:** 14
  M. murina **10:** 14
marmoset
  common 4: 86, 92–93
  dwarf **4:** 86
  Geoffroy's **4:** 86, *87*
  marmoset family 4: 86–87
  pygmy **4:** 86
  silvery **4:** 86
Marmosops
  M. dorothea **10:** 14
  M. fuscatus **10:** 14
marmot 7: *16,* 35, 36
  alpine (European) **7:** 34,
    52–53
  European 7: 34, 52–53
Marmota **7:** 34
  M. marmota **7:** 34, 52–53
  M. monax **7:** 34, 50–51
marsupials 1: *10;* **10:** 8–13
  Australian carnivorous
    10: 24–27
  other plant-eating
    10: 74–77
marten 7: 36
  American 1: 48–49
  American pine (American)
    1: 48–49
  pine **1:** 32, *35*
  yellow-throated **1:** 32
Martes
  M. americana **1:** 48–49
  M. flavigula **1:** 32

M. martes **1:** 32
M. pennanti **1:** 50–51
masseter muscles **7:** 16–17,
  64; **8:** 12, *12*
Massoutiera mzabi **7:** 108
Mazama americana **6:** 10
meat trade *see* bushmeat
  trade
medical research **4:** 13, 32, 63,
  78, 93; **7:** 15, (75); **8:** (41);
  9: 77, 97
  see also laboratory animals;
  surgery
medicine **6:** 51; **7:** (31)
  body parts for **2:** 21, 33,
    (97), 100; **6:** 107; **7:** 63; **8:**
    41; **9:** 91
  Chinese **5:** 37
meerkat 1: 19, 98, 99,
  100–105
  gray (meerkat) **1:** 19, 98,
    99, 100–105
  slender-tailed (meerkat)
    1: 19, 98, 99, 100–105
Megachiroptera **9:** 80, 86
Megaderma lyra **9:** 98–99
Megadermatidae **9:** 87, 98
Megaptera novaeangliae
  3: 55, 102–105
Megatherium **9:** *64*
Meles meles **1:** 32, 78–81
Mellivora capensis **1:** 32,
  82–83
Melogale personata **1:** 32
Melursus ursinus **2:** 82
Menotyphla **9:** 10, 58
Mephitidae **1:** 32, 84
Mephitis
  M. macroura **1:** 32
  M. mephitis **1:** 32, 84–87
Meriones unguiculatus
  7: 88–89
mermaids **3:** 53
Mesechinus
  M. dauricus **9:** 12
  M. hughi **9:** 12
Mesocapromys auritus **8:** 30
Mesocricetus auratus
  7: 86–87
Mesomys hispidus **8:** 30
mesonychids **3:** 56
Messelobunodon **1:** *8*
Metachirus nudicaudatus
  10: 14
Metatheria **10:** (10)
miacid **1:** *9*
Miacoidea **1:** 88, 98
mice *see* mouse
Mico
  M. argentata **4:** 86
  M. humilis **4:** 86
Micoureus
  M. alstoni **10:** 14
  M. constantiae **10:** 14
Microcavia australis **8:** 30
Microcebus
  M. coquereli see *Mirza*
    coquereli
  M. murinus **4:** 96
  M. myoxinus **4:** 96
  M. rufus **4:** 96
Microchiroptera **9:** 80, 86
Microgale
  M. melanorrachis **9:** 24
  M. parvula **9:** 24
Microperoryctes
  M. longicauda **10:** 27
  M. murina **10:** 27
Micropotamogale
  M. lamottei **9:** 24
  M. ruwenzorii **9:** 24
Microtus agrestis **7:** 92–93
migration **3:** 82, 85, 87,
  93–94, 103, (105), 109;
  5: 18, 109; **6:** 17, 23, 37,
  84–85, 96, 101; **7:** 91;
  9: (83), 102, (103),
  106–107
milu *see* deer, Père David's

miner's cat *see* raccoon,
  ringtail
mink 1: 35
  American 1: 32, 35, *35,*
    52–55, 62; **7:** 99; **9:** 53
  European **1:** 54, (55)
Miopithecus talapoin **4:** 40
Mirounga
  M. angustirostris **3:** 9,
    32–35
  M. leonina **3:** 32
Mirza coquereli **4:** 96
moldewarp *see* mole,
  European
mole 1: *10;* **9:** 9, (10), 11
  coast **9:** 40, *41*
  desert (Grant's) golden
    9: 56–57
  European 9: 40, 42, 44–47
  giant golden **9:** 40
  golden **5:** (10); **9:** 9, 10–11,
    11, 40, 41, 42, (42)
  golden mole family
    9: 40–43
  Grant's desert golden **9:** 40
  Grant's golden 9: 56–57
  hairy-tailed **9:** 40, *42*
  Japanese **9:** 54
  Juliana's golden **9:** 40, *43*
  marsupial 10: (10), 26, 27,
    42–43
  mole family 9: 40–43
  northern marsupial **10:** 43
  northwestern marsupial
    10: 27
  Persian **9:** 40, 43
  small-toothed **9:** 40, 43
  star-nosed 9: 40, 42,
    48–51
  see also shrew mole
molehills **9:** 43
mole rat 7: 15, 18, 65; **8:** 9
  African **7:** *12;* **8:** 56
  Balkan blind (lesser blind)
    7: 100–101
  blind **7:** 12–13, 15, 18;
    8: 57
  Cape **7:** *10;* **8:** 56
  Cape dune **8:** 56
  common **8:** 56, 57
  Damara **8:** 56, *57*
  dune **8:** 57
  Ehrenberg's **7:** *18*
  giant **8:** 57
  giant Angolan **8:** 56, 57
  lesser blind 7: 100–101
  Mechow's **8:** 56, 57
  mole rat family 8: 56–57
  naked 1: (11), 14; **7:** 13;
    8: 10, 56, 57, 58–59
  Namaqua dune **8:** 56
  silvery **7:** 9; **8:** 56
  southern dune **8:** 56
mollusks **3:** 25
Monachus schauinslandi
  3: 9, 30–31
mongoose
  Alexander's **1:** 98
  Angolan **1:** 98
  banded 1: *18–19,* 98,
    103–104, 110–111
  broad-striped **1:** 98
  brown **1:** 98
  bushy-tailed **1:** 98, *99*
  common Bengal (Indian
    gray) **1:** 108–109
  common gray (Indian gray)
    1: 108–109
  common Indian (Indian gray)
    1: 108–109
  dwarf 1: 98, 99, *99,*
    106–107, 111
  Egyptian **1:** 98, *99*
  Gambian **1:** 98
  giant-striped **1:** 98
  Indian (Indian gray)
    1: 108–109
  Indian gray 1: 108–109

Jackson's **1:** 98
Liberian **1:** 98
long-nosed **1:** 98
Madagascan **1:** 98
marsh **1:** 98, *99*
Meller's **1:** 98
mongoose family
  1: 98–99
  narrow-striped **1:** 98, *99*
  Pousargues' **1:** 98
  ringtailed **1:** 98, *99*
  Selous' **1:** 98, *99*
  slender **1:** 98
  white-tailed **1:** 98, *99*
  yellow **1:** 98, 101
monito del monte **10:** 11, 16,
  (16)
monkey
  Allen's swamp **4:** 40, *41*
  black-handed spider
    4: 72, 76–77
  Bolivian squirrel **4:** 72
  brown howler 4: 72,
    74–75
  Central American spider
    (black-handed spider)
    4: 72, 76–77
  cheek-pouch **4:** 40, 42
  cloaked *see* colugo
  common squirrel **4:** 72, 78
  common woolly
    (Humboldt's woolly) **4:** 72,
    82–83
  De Brazza's **4:** 40, *42–43*
  dusky-leaf **4:** 40
  golden leaf **4:** 40
  golden snub-nosed **4:** 40
  green (vervet) **4:** 40, 42,
    44–47
  grivet (vervet) **4:** 40, 42,
    44–47
  guenon (vervet) **4:** 40, 42,
    44–47
  Hanuman langur **6:** *13*
  howler **4:** 10, 72, 83
  Humboldt's woolly 4: 72,
    82–83
  leaf **4:** 40, 40–42
  leapers **4:** 72
  long-haired spider **4:** 72
  mantled howler **4:** 72
  mustached **4:** 40, *41*
  New World monkey
    family 4: 72–73
  night (northern night) **4:** 72,
    73, 84–85
  northern (northern night)
    4: 72, *73,* 84–85
  northern night 4: 72, *73,*
    84–85
  Old World monkey family
    4: 40–43, 72
  owl (northern night) **4:** 72,
    73, 84–85
  patas **4:** 40, *41,* 42, 43
  proboscis 4: 40, 41, 70–71
  red howler **4:** 72
  rhesus **4:** 42
  savanna (vervet) **4:** 40, 42,
    44–47
  snow *see* macaque,
    Japanese
  southern night **4:** 72
  spider **4:** *8,* 72, 75
  squirrel 4: 72, 78–79
  swingers **4:** 72
  thumbless **4:** 40
  vervet 4: 40, 42, 44–47
  woolly **4:** 72
  yellow-tailed woolly **4:** 72
Monodelphis
  domestica **10:** 14
  kunsi **10:** 14
Monodon monoceros **3:** 55,
  84–85
Monotremata **1:** *10;* **10:** 104
monotremes, spiny **8:** 12
moonrat 9: 9, 11, 12, 13
  Dinagat **9:** 12

greater 9: 12, 22–23
lesser **9:** 12
Mindanao **9:** 12, *13*
moose 6: 10, 12, 14–19,
  21–22
  Alaskan **6:** 14–15, *17*
  eastern **6:** 15
  northwestern **6:** 15
  shiras **6:** 15
moose disease **6:** 18
Mormoopidae **9:** 87
morrillo **8:** 51
Moschidae **6:** 10
Moschiola meminna **6:** 10
Moschus
  M. berezovskii **6:** 10
  M. chrysogaster **6:** 10,
    50–51
  M. fuscus **6:** 10
  M. moschiferus **6:** 10
mosquitoes **6:** (22)
mouflon **6:** 62, 63
mouse 7: *10,* 12
  African climbing **7:** 64
  birch **7:** 17
  coarse-haired pocket (desert-
    pocket) **7:** 22–23
  Costa Rican harvest **7:** 80
  Cozumel Island harvest **7:** 80
  deer 7: 64, 82–83
  desert **7:** 65
  desert pocket 7: 22–23
  field (wood) **7:** 13, 78–79
  hairy harvest **7:** 80
  harvest **7:** 64
  house 7: 13, 14–15, 65–66,
    68–71
  jumping **7:** 17, 19
  kangaroo **7:** 17
  long-clawed marsupial
    10: 27
  long-tailed field (wood)
    7: 13, 78–79
  marsupial **10:** (25), 27, 40
  meadow jumping **7:** *16*
  mole **7:** 65
  mouse family 7: 64–67
  New World **7:** 14, *64,* 65
  Nicaraguan harvest **7:** 80
  Old World **7:** 14, 65, *65*
  pencil-tailed tree **7:** 65
  pig mouse **8:** 38
  plains **7:** 65
  pocket **7:** 12, 18
  pygmy **7:** *64*
  shaker **7:** (69)
  singing **7:** (69)
  spiny **7:** 65; **8:** 11, 12
  three-striped marsupial
    10: *25,* 27
  waltzing **7:** (69)
  western harvest 7: 80–81
  West Indian key **8:** 11
  white-footed (deer) **7:** *64,*
    82–83
  wood 7: 13, 78–79
mouse-hare *see* pika
mouselike rodents 7: 16–19
muktuk **3:** 85
mulgara **10:** 27
multituberculates **7:** 10
Mungos
  M. gambianus **1:** 98
  M. mungo **1:** *18–19,* 98,
    110–111
Mungotictis decemlineata
  1: 98
Muntiacus
  M. crinifrons **6:** 10
  M. muntjak **6:** 10
  M. reevesi **6:** 46–47
muntjac 6: 12, 46–47
  Chinese **6:** 46–47
  hairy-fronted **6:** 10
  Indian **6:** 10
  Reeves's **6:** 46–47
Murexia
  M. longicaudata **10:** 27
  M. rothschildi **10:** 27

Muridae **7:** *12*, 65
Murinae **7:** 14
muriqui **4:** 72
Mus
　M. musculus **7:** 68–71
　M. musculus brevirostris
　　7: 71
　M. musculus domesticus
　　7: 71
　M. musculus musculus
　　7: 71
　M. musculus wagneri
　　7: 71
　M. porcellus **8:** 38
Muscardinus avellanarius
　7: 102, 106–107
musk **1:** 85; **6:** 51
muskox 6: 62, 104–105
muskrat 7: 13, 65, 96–97
　common 7: 96–97
mustang 5: 42, 58–61
Mustela
　M. erminea **1:** 32, 36,
　　40–43
　M. frenata **1:** 32, 36
　M. lutreola **1:** 54, (55)
　M. nigripes **1:** 32, 46–47
　M. nivalis **1:** 32, 36–39
　M. putorius **1:** 32, 44–45
　M. vison **1:** 32, 52–55
mustelids **1:** 32–35
Mydaus
　M. javanensis **1:** 32
　M. marchei **1:** 32
Myocastor coypus **8:** 30,
　44–47
Myocastoridae **7:** *12*; **8:** 31
myoglobin **3:** 11, 87
Myoictis melas **10:** 27
Myomimus
　M. personatus **7:** 102
　M. roachi **7:** 102
　M. setzeri **7:** 102
Myomorpha **7:** (8)
Myoprocta exilis **8:** 30
Myosciurus pumilio **7:** 34
Myosorex varius **9:** 28
Myotis lucifugus **9:** 104–105
Myoxidae **7:** *12*
Myrmecobiidae **10:** 24
Myrmecobius fasciatus
　10: 27, 34–35
Myrmecophaga tridactyla
　9: 65, 68–71
Mysateles prehensilis **8:** 30
Mystacinidae **9:** 87
Mysticeti **3:** 54
myxomatosis **8:** 72, 93
Myzopodidae **9:** 87

N

Nandinia binotata **1:** 88
Nannosciurus exilis **7:** 36
Nannospalax leucodon
　7: 100–101
narwhal 3: 55, 84–85
Nasalis
　N. concolor **4:** 40
　N. larvatus **4:** 40, 70–71
Nasua
　N. narica **1:** 20
　N. nasua **1:** 20, 28–29
Nasuella olivacea **1:** 20
Natalidae **9:** 87
national parks/nature reserves
　2: (15), 16, 31; **5:** 34,
　(102), 103
Neamblysomus julianae
　9: 40
nectar **4:** 105
Nectogale elegans **9:** 28
Nemorhaedus goral **6:** 62,
　108
Neofelis nebulosa **2:** 10
Neomys fodiens **9:** 28
Neophascogale lorentzi
　10: 27
Neophoca cinerea **3:** 9
Neotoma lepida **7:** 84–85

Neotragus
　N. batesi **6:** 62
　N. pygmaeus **6:** 62
Nesolagus
　N. netscheri **8:** 64
　N. timminsi **8:** 64
Neurotrichus gibbsii
　9: 54–55
New Zealand, mammals
　introduced into **1:** 43;
　10: (80)
nictitating membrane **7:** 28
nilgai **6:** 62
ningaui **10:** (24)
　Pilbara **10:** *25*, 27
　southern **10:** 27
Ningaui
　N. timealeyi **10:** 27
　N. yvonneae **10:** 27
Noctilio
　N. albiventris **9:** 108
　N. leporinus **9:** 108–109
Noctilionidae **9:** 87
noise pollution **3:** 88, 95
noolbenger *see* possum,
　honey
Notoryctemorphia **10:** 24
Notoryctes
　N. caurinus **10:** 27, 43
　N. typhlops **10:** 27, 42–43
Notoryctidae **10:** 24, 26
numbat 10: 13, 24, 25, 26,
　34–35
nutria *see* coypu
nyala, mountain **6:** 62
Nyctereutes procyonoides
　2: 50
Nycteridae **9:** 87
Nycticebus
　N. coucang **4:** 106,
　　108–109
　N. pygmaeus **4:** 106

O

ocelot 1: *17*; **2:** 10, *12*, 44–45
Ochotona
　O. alpina **8:** 94
　O. collaris **8:** 94, 98
　O. himalayana **8:** 94
　O. princeps **8:** 94, 98–101
　O. pusilla **8:** 94
Ochotonidae **8:** 60
Octodon bridgesi **8:** 30
Octodontidae (octodonts)
　7: *12*; **8:** 29–31
Octodontomys gliroides
　8: 30
octodonts **7:** *12*; **8:** 29–31
Odobenidae **3:** 8
Odobenus rosmarus **3:** 9,
　24–29
Odocoileus
　O. hemionus **6:** 10, 34–37
　O. virginianus **6:** 10, (36)
Odontoceti **3:** 54
oil **3:** 22, 34, 52, 58, 85, 89,
　91, 101
okapi **6:** 52, 52–53, 58–59
Okapia johnstoni **6:** 52,
　58–59
Olallamys edax **8:** 30
olingo **1:** 20, 21
Ondatra zibethicus **7:** 96–97
Onychogalea
　O. fraenata **10:** 48
　O. unguifera **10:** 48
opossum 1: 87
　agile gracile mouse **10:** 14
　Alston's woolly mouse
　　10: 14
　American 10: 14–17
　bare-tailed woolly **10:** 14
　black four-eyed **10:** 14
　black-shouldered **10:** 14,
　　16, *17*
　brown four-eyed **10:** 14
　bushy-tailed **10:** 14

Central American woolly
　10: 14, *17*
Chilean shrew **10:** 14
common (Virginia) **10:** *8*,
　13, 14, 15, 16, 17, 18–23
Dorothy's slender mouse
　10: 14
elegant fat-tailed **10:** 14
gray-bellied shrew **10:** 14
gray-bellied slender mouse
　10: 14, *15*
gray four-eyed **10:** 14, *17*
gray short-tailed **10:** 14
Incan shrew **10:** 14
lutrine **10:** 14
Mexican mouse **10:** 14, *17*
murine mouse **10:** 14
pale-bellied woolly mouse
　10: 14
pallid fat-tailed **10:** 14
Patagonian **10:** 14
pygmy short-tailed **10:** 14
shrew **10:** 16
silky shrew **10:** 14
Virginia 10: *8*, 13, 14, 15,
　16, 17, 18–23
water **10:** 13, 14, 16, *17*
white-eared **10:** 14
wood spirit gracile mouse
　10: 14
woolly **10:** 16
orangutan 4: *8*, 10, 12, 13,
　14–19
　Bornean **4:** 12, 14–15, 18,
　　18–19
　Sumatran **4:** 12, 14–15, 18
orca **3:** 55, (57), 62–65
Orcinus orca **3:** 55, 62–65
Oreamnos americanus **6:** 62,
　108–109
Oreotragus oreotragus **6:** 62
oribi **5:** *11*; **6:** 61, 62
Ornithorhynchus anatinus
　10: 106–109
Orycteropus afer **9:** 65,
　78–79
Oryctolagus cuniculus **8:** 64,
　68–73
oryx
　Arabian 6: 62, 90–91
　scimitar-horned **6:** 62
　white (Arabian) **6:** 62,
　　90–91
Oryx
　O. dammah **6:** 62
　O. gazella **6:** 62
　O. leucoryx **6:** 62, 90–91
Oryzorictes tetradactylus
　9: 24
Osbornictis piscivora **1:** 88
Otariidae **3:** 8
Otocyon megalotis **2:** 50,
　76–77
Otolemur
　O. crassicaudatus **4:** 106
　O. garnettii **4:** 106
otter 1: 19, 35, 54; **8:** 48
　Cape clawless **1:** 32
　Congo clawless **1:** 32
　European 1: 58–63
　European river **1:** 60
　giant **1:** 18, 32
　giant river 1: 68–69
　hairy-nosed **1:** 32
　Indian smooth-coated **1:** 35
　marine **1:** 32
　North American river
　　1: 32, 64–67
　northern river (North
　　American river) **1:** 32,
　　64–67
　sea 1: 19, 32, 72–75
　short-clawed 1: 32, 70–71
　smooth-coated **1:** 32
　spot-necked **1:** 32, 35
otter shrew **9:** 11, 24, 25
　giant **9:** 24, *25*
　Ruwenzori **9:** 24, *25*
ounce *see* leopard, snow

Ourebia ourebi **6:** 62
Ovibos moschatus **6:** 62,
　104–105
Ovis
　O. aries **6:** 62
　O. canadensis **6:** 100–103
　O. musimon **6:** 62
　owl **7:** (37); **9:** 33
　snowy **7:** (14)
oxpeckers **5:** 38; **6:** (73)
Ozotocerus bezoarticus
　6: 10

P

paca **7:** *12*; **8:** 11, 28, 30, *30*
　mountain **8:** 30
pacarana **7:** *12*; **8:** 28, 31
pademelon
　red-legged **10:** 48, *51*
　red-necked **10:** 48
Pagophilus groenlandica
　3: 44–45
Paguma larvata **1:** 88
Pan
　P. paniscus **4:** 12, 34–35
　P. troglodytes **4:** 12, 28–33
panda
　giant 2: 82, 98–101
　lesser (red) **1:** 20, 21,
　　30–31; **2:** (99)
　red 1: 20, 21, 30–31;
　　2: (99)
panda bear *see* panda, giant
pangolin 1: *10*; **9:** 64–67
　African **9:** 66
　armored **9:** *64*
　Asian **9:** 66
　giant **9:** 65, 66
　ground **9:** 64–65, 65
　tree **9:** 65
panther
　black **2:** 30, *31*
　see also leopard; puma
Panthera
　P. leo **2:** 10, 14–19
　P. leo persica **2:** (15)
　P. onca **2:** 10, 36–37
　P. pardus **2:** 10, 30–33
　P. tigris **2:** 10, 20–25
　P. uncia **2:** 10, 34–35
Pantholops hodgsoni **6:** 62
pantotheres **7:** 10, 11
Papio
　P. cynocephalus **4:** 40,
　　54–57
　P. hamadryas **4:** 40, 58–59
Paracynictis selousi **1:** 98
Paradoxurus
　P. hermaphroditus **1:** 88,
　　94–95
　P. jerdoni **1:** 88
　P. zeylonensis **1:** 88
Parantechinus
　P. aplicalis **10:** 27
　P. bilarni **10:** 27
parapox virus **7:** 44
Parascalops breweri **9:** 40
parasites **9:** 84
Paroodectes **1:** 9
Pasteurella tularense **8:** 81
patagium **8:** 108; **10:** (76), 84,
　86
Patagonia **5:** 108
Pecari **5:** 88
　P. tajacu see Tayassu
　tajacu
peccary 5: *8*, 12
　Chacoan **5:** 88, 89, *89*
　collared 5: 88, 89, 90–91
　peccary family 5: 88–89
　white-lipped **5:** 88, 89, *89*
Pectinator spekei **7:** 108
Pedetes capensis **7:** 20–21
Pedetidae **7:** *12*
Pelea capreolus **6:** 62
penguin **3:** 38–39
Pentalagus furnessi **8:** 64
Peramelemorphia **10:** 24
Perameles

P. bougainville **10:** 27
P. nasuta **10:** 27
Peramelidae **10:** 24
perfume industry **1:** (91);
　7: (31)
Perissodactyla **1:** *10*; **5:** 10, 12,
　43
Perodicticus potto **4:** 106
Peromyscus
　P. leucopus **7:** 83
　P. maniculatus **7:** 82–83
Peroryctes
　P. broadbenti **10:** 27
　P. raffrayana **10:** 27
Peroryctidae **10:** 24
Petauridae **10:** (76)
Petaurista
　P. elegans **7:** 36
　P. petaurista **7:** 36
Petauroides volans **10:** 74
Petaurus
　P. breviceps **10:** 74, 86–87
　P. gracilis **10:** 74
Petinomys crinitus **7:** 34
Petrodomus tetradactylus
　9: 59
Petrogale
　P. persephone **10:** 48
　P. xanthopus **10:** 48, 70–71
Petromuridae **7:** *12*; **8:** 31
Petromus typicus **8:** 30, 54–55
Petropseudes dahli **10:** 74
pets **1:** 22, 29, 35, 45, 95,
　109; **2:** 75; **4:** 53, 78, 81,
　83, 85, 87, 88, 101; **7:** 15,
　(69), 83, 86; **8:** 39, 42,
　(72); **9:** 13, 21
　see also cat, domestic; dog,
　　domestic
Phacochoerus
　P. aethiopicus **5:** 74
　P. africanus **5:** 74, 80–83
Phalanger **10:** 82
　P.carmelitae **10:** 74
　P.gymnotis **10:** 74
Phalangeridae **10:** 76
Phaner furcifer **4:** 96
phascogale **10:** (25)
　brush-tailed **10:** *26*, 27
　red-tailed **10:** *25*, 27
Phascogale
　P. calura **10:** 27
　P. tapoatafa **10:** 27
Phascolarctos cinereus
　10: 74, 92–97
Phascolosorex
　P. doriae **10:** 27
　P. dorsalis **10:** 27
pheromones **7:** 66, 70
Philander
　P. andersoni **10:** 14
　P. opossum **10:** 14
Phoca
　P. groenlandica **3:** 9, 44–45
　P. sibirica see Pusa sibirica
　P. vitulina **3:** 9, 40–41
Phocarctos hookeri **3:** 9
Phocidae **3:** 8
Phocoena phocoena **3:** 55,
　78–79
Pholidocercus **1:** 9
Pholidota **1:** *10*; **9:** 64
Phyllostomidae **9:** 87
Physeter catodon **3:** 55, 86–89
pig 5: *8*, 10, 12
　bearded **5:** 74, *75*
　bushpig **5:** 74, *75*
　lard pig **5:** (78)
　pig family 5: 74–75
pig fish **3:** 78
pig mouse **8:** 38
pika 8: 60, 62
　Alpine **8:** 94
　American 8: 67, 94, 96,
　　98–101
　Asian **8:** *97*
　collared **8:** 94, *97*, 98
　common (American) **8:** 94,
　　96, 98–101

Eurasian **8**: 98, 100
Himalayan **8**: 94, 96
pika family 8: 94–97
Rocky Mountain (American)
8: 94, 96, 98–101
Russian steppe **8**: 94, 97
Sardinian **8**: (96)
pingers **3**: 79
Pinnipedia **1**: 10; **3**: 8–13
pinto **5**: 59
pipistrelle **9**: 87
Pithecia
P. albicans **4**: 72
P. irrorata **4**: 72
P. monachus **4**: 72
P. pithecia **4**: 72
placental mammals **10**: 8, 9–11, 13
Plagiodontia aedium **8**: 30
plague **7**: 14, 76–77
planigale **10**: (24)
common **10**: 25, 27
Papuan **10**: 27
Planigale
P. maculata **10**: 27
P. novaeguineae **10**: 27
Platanista
P. gangetica **3**: 55, (61)
P. minor **3**: 55, (61)
platypus 1: 14
duck-billed 10: 105, 106–109
platyrrhines **4**: 11
Plecotus auritus **9**: 110–111
Pliohippus **5**: 42
poaching **4**: 24, 27; **5**: 39, (102)
Podogymnura
P. aureospinula **9**: 12
P. truei **9**: 12, 13
Poecilictis libyca **1**: 32
Poecilogale albinucha **1**: 32
Poelagus marjorita **8**: 64
Poiana richardsoni **1**: 88
polecat 1: 44–45
European **1**: 32, 34, 35, 35
marbled **1**: 32, 34, 34
pollution **1**: 61, 62, 64, 69, 71, 75; **2**: (88); **3**: 12, 41, 59, 61, 65, 67, 74, 79, 83
noise pollution **3**: 88, 95
Pongo
P. abelii **4**: 12, 14–19
P. pygmaeus **4**: 12, 14–19
Pontoporia blainvillei **3**: 55, (61)
pony
Falabella **5**: (43)
feral *see* mustang
Welsh **5**: 42–43
wild *see* mustang
porcupine 1: 50–51; **7**: 8; **8**: 10, 12–15
African **8**: 10, 12, 12–13, 14, 16–19
African brush-tailed **8**: 12
American **8**: 10
American tree **8**: 9
Asian brush-tailed **8**: 12
bahia hairy dwarf **8**: 12
bicolored tree **8**: 27
Brazilian tree **8**: 12, 13
brown hairy dwarf **8**: 12
brush-tailed **8**: 14, 16
Cape **8**: 12, 15
crested (African) **8**: 10, 12, 12–13, 14, 16–19
in Europe **8**: (19)
hairy dwarf **8**: 12
long-tailed **8**: 12, 14, 16
Malayan **8**: 12, 12, 14
Mexican tree (tree) **8**: 12, 13, 14, 26–27
New World 7: 12; **8**: 12–15
North African (African) **8**: 10, 12, 12–13, 14, 6–19

North American 7: (8); **8**: 10, 12, 13, 14, 20–25
Old World 7: 12; **8**: 12–15
South African **8**: 19
tree 8: 12, 13, 14, 26–27
upper Amazon **8**: 12
porcupinelike rodents 8: 8–11
Porcus piscus **3**: 78
porpoise
common (harbor) **3**: 55, 78–79
harbor 3: 55, 78–79
porpoising **3**: 69
possum 10: (10), 75–77
Arnhemland **10**: 80
brush-tipped ringtail **10**: 74
common brushtail 10: 10, 74, 76, 78–81
common ringtail **10**: 74, 76
copper ringtail 10: 74, 90–91
Daintree River ringtail **10**: 74
eastern pygmy **10**: 74
feathertail **10**: 74
green ringtail **10**: 74
honey 10: 8, 74, 75–76, 102–103
Leadbeater's 10: 74, 76, 77, 88–89
marsupial gliding **7**: (37)
mountain brushtail **10**: 74
mountain pygmy **10**: 74, 76, 77, (77)
ringtail **10**: (77)
rock ringtail **10**: 74
scaly-tailed **10**: 74
striped **10**: 74, 76
western pygmy **10**: 74
Weyland ringtail **10**: 74
see also opossum, Virginia
Potamochoerus
P. larvatus **5**: 74
P. porcus **5**: 74
Potamogale velox **9**: 24
Potamogalidae **9**: 11
potoroo 10: 48, 50, 51, 72–73
Gilbert's **10**: 73
long-footed **10**: 48
long-nosed (potoroo) **10**: 48, 50, 51, 72–73
Potorous
P. longipes **10**: 48
P. tridactylus **10**: 48, 72–73
Potos flavus **1**: 20
potto **4**: 106, 106–107
golden **4**: 106
Martin's false **4**: 106
pouches **10**: (10)
prairie dog 1: 46–47; **7**: 13, 15, 18, 36
black-tailed 7: 34, 56–59
plains (black-tailed) **7**: 34, 56–59
Utah **7**: 58
white-tailed **7**: 58
Presbytis **4**: 41
P. comata **4**: 40
P. femoralis **4**: 40
primates 1: 10; **4**: 8–11
higher **4**: 11
lower 4: 11, 106–107
Priodontes maximus **9**: 65
Prionodon
P. linsang **1**: 88
P. pardicolor **1**: 88
Proboscidea **1**: 10; **5**: 14
Procapra picticaudata **6**: 62
Procavia capensis **8**: 103, 106–107
Procaviidae **8**: 102
Procolobus **4**: 41–42
P. badius **4**: 40
Procyon
P. cancrivorus **1**: 20
P. gloverellani **1**: 26

P. lotor **1**: 20, 22–27
P. pygmaeus **1**: 26
Procyonidae **1**: 20–21
Proechimys semispinosus **8**: 30
Prolagus **8**: (96)
pronghorn 6: 60, 62, (63), 110–111
American **2**: 26; **6**: 63
pronking **6**: 97
Pronolagus
P. crassicaudatus **8**: 64
P. randensis **8**: 64
P. rupestris **8**: 64
Propaleotherium **1**: 8
Propithecus
P. diadema **4**: 96
P. tattersalli **4**: 96
P. verreauxi **4**: 96
protection, legal **1**: 35, 47, 51, 62, 69, 74; **2**: 21, 28, 33, 35, 39, 44, 49, 55, (97), 100; **3**: 12, 19, 59, 74, 107; **5**: 41, 60; **9**: 85; **10**: 28, 32, 37, 43, 71, (95)
Proteles cristata **2**: 102, 110–111
Prototheria **10**: 104
pseudantechinus
fat-tailed **10**: 25, 27
Woolley's **10**: 27
Pseudantechinus
P. macdonnellensis **10**: 27
P. woolleyae **10**: 27
Pseudocheiridae **10**: (76)
Pseudocheirus peregrinus **10**: 74
Pseudochirops
P. archeri **10**: 74
P. cupreus **10**: 74, 90–91
Pseudochirulus
P. caroli **10**: 74
P. cinereus **10**: 74
Pseudois nayaur **6**: 62
Pseudopotto martini **4**: 106
pseudoruminants **5**: 70
Pseudoryx nghetinhensis **6**: 62
Pteronura brasiliensis **1**: 32, 68–69
Pteropodidae **9**: 86
Pteropus **9**: 86
P. giganteus **9**: 88–91
Ptilocercus lowii **9**: 59
pudu **6**: 10, 12
northern **6**: 10
southern **6**: 10, 12
Pudu
P. mephistophiles **6**: 10
P. pudu **6**: 10
puma 2: 10, 13, 42–43
punare **8**: 30
Pusa sibirica **3**: 9
Pygathrix roxellana **4**: 40

Q

quagga **5**: 45, 48
quillpig *see* porcupine, North American
quills **8**: 12, (14), 16–17, (21)
see also spines
quokka 10: 48, 52, 68–69
quoll 10: (25), 27
New Guinea **10**: 25, 27
northern 10: 27, 32–33

R

rabbit 1: 43; **8**: 61, 62
Amami **8**: 62, 64
American swamp **8**: 66
annamite **8**: 64
brush **8**: 64
bunyoro **8**: 63, 64
bush *see* hare, snowshoe
chocolate Dutch **8**: 72–73
cottontail **1**: 87
desert **8**: 66

domestic (European)
8: 60–61, 62, 64, 68–73
European 8: 60–61, 62, 64, 68–73
forest **8**: 66
marsh **8**: 65
Mexican volcano **8**: 64
Old World (European)
8: 60–61, 62, 64, 68–73
pygmy **8**: 64, (93)
rabbit family 8: 64–67
riverine **8**: 62, 64
rock *see* pika
snowshoe *see* hare, snowshoe
Sumatran **8**: 63, 64
Sumatran short-eared **8**: 64–66
swamp **8**: 62
volcano **8**: 63, 64
see also cottontail
rabbit hemorrhagic disease **8**: 72
rabbit warrens **8**: 70–71
rabies **1**: 26, 87; **2**: (67), 77, 79; **7**: 14, 74; **9**: 84, 97, 103
raccoon
Barbados **1**: 26
common 1: 20, 21, 22–27
Cozumel Island **1**: 26
crab-eating **1**: 20
raccoon family 1: 20–21
ringtail **1**: 20, 20, 21, 21
Rangifer tarandus **6**: 10, 20–25
Raphicerus campestris **6**: 62
rat 1: 15; **7**: 12
African marsh **7**: 65
Amazon bamboo **8**: 30
armored **8**: 30
armored spiny **8**: 30
Asian climbing **7**: 64
Atlantic bamboo **8**: 30
Australasian water **7**: 65
Australian water **7**: 9, 17, 65
bamboo **8**: 31
black (ship) **7**: 11, 13, 14–15, 72, 75, 76–77
bristle-spined **8**: 30
broad-headed spiny **8**: 30
brown 7: 14–15, 72–75, 77; **8**: 10; **10**: 11
brush-furred **7**: 65
cane **7**: 12; **8**: 31
Central American climbing **7**: 64
Central American vesper **7**: 64
Chilean rock **8**: 30
chinchilla **7**: 12
common (brown) **7**: 14–15, 72–75, 77; **8**: 10; **10**: 11
dassie **7**: 12; **8**: 31, 54–55
desert wood 7: 84–85
golden-backed tree **7**: 67
greater cane **8**: 30
greedy olalla **8**: 30
house (ship) **7**: 11, 13, 14–15, 72, 75, 76–77
Indonesian key-footed **7**: 64
Kenyan crested **7**: 66
lesser cane **8**: 30
Natal multimammate **7**: 65
New World **7**: 64
Norway (brown) **7**: 14–15, 72–75, 77; **8**: 10; **10**: 11
Old World **7**: 14, 65
Owl's spiny **8**: 30
pack (desert wood) **7**: 84–85
painted tree **8**: 30
Panama spiny **8**: 30, 31
plague (ship) **7**: 11, 13, 14–15, 72, 75, 76–77
plain brush-tailed **8**: 30
plains viscacha **8**: 30
pouched **7**: 18

rat family 7: 64–67
rock **8**: 29
roof (ship) **7**: 11, 13, 14–15, 72, 75, 76–77
rufous tree **8**: 30
ship 7: 11, 13, 14–15, 72, 75, 76–77
smooth-tailed giant **7**: 65
South American climbing **7**: 64
spiny **7**: 12; **8**: 31
spiny tree **8**: 30
trade (desert wood) **7**: 84–85
tuft-tailed spiny tree **8**: 30
viscacha rat **8**: 29, 30
vlei **7**: 65
water *see* vole, water
see also chinchilla rat; kangaroo rat; mole rat; viscacha
rat-bite fever **7**: 74
ratel *see* badger, honey
rat-kangaroo **10**: 51, 52
desert **10**: 48
musky **10**: 48, 72
rufous **10**: 48, 51
see also potoroo
Rattus
R. norvegicus **7**: 72–75
R. rattus **7**: 76–77
ratufa *see* squirrel, Indian giant
Ratufa
R. affinisi **7**: 36
R. bicolor **7**: 36
R. indica **7**: 34, 62–63
recolonization **3**: 14, 35; **7**: 33
red ape *see* orangutan
Red Lists of Threatened Species (IUCN) **1**: 16
Redunca
R. arundinum **6**: 62
R. fulvorufula **6**: 62
R. redunca **6**: 62
reedbuck
bohor **6**: 62
mountain **6**: 62
southern **6**: 62
reestablishment **3**: 31, 93
refection **9**: 29, 29
reforestation **4**: 91
regeneration, of land **10**: 89
reindeer 6: 10, 12, 20–25
reindeer moss **6**: 22–23
reintroduction **1**: 46; **2**: 41, (56), 69; **4**: 87, 88, 90–91; **5**: 34; **6**: 45, (66), 91; **7**: 29, 107
Reithrodontomys
R. hirsutus **7**: 81
R. megalotis **7**: 80–81
R. paradoxus **7**: 81
R. rodriguez **7**: 81
R. spectabilis **7**: 81
religious ceremonies **5**: 25
relocation **5**: 34
repopulation **1**: 61, 75
reproduction **1**: 12–14
see also embryonic diapause; implantation/fertilization; breeding
rhebok, gray **6**: 62
Rheithrosciurus macrotis **7**: 36
rhinoceros 5: 8, 8, 9, 11, 12
black 5: 28, 33, (34), 36–39
giraffe **5**: 8
grass (white) **5**: 28, 29, 30–35
greater Indian (Indian) **5**: 28, 40–41
Indian 5: 28, 40–41
Javan **5**: 28
northern white **5**: 34
rhinoceros family 5: 28–29
southern white **5**: 34, 35

square-lipped (white) **5:** 28, 29, <u>30–35</u>
Sumatran **5:** 28, *29*
white 5: 28, 29, <u>30–35</u>
woolly **5:** 28
Rhinoceros
 R. sondaicus **5:** 28
 R. unicornis **5:** 28, <u>40–41</u>
Rhinocerotidae **5:** 28
Rhinolophidae **9:** 87
Rhinolophus hipposideros
 9: <u>106–107</u>
Rhinopithecus roxellana see *Pygathrix roxellana*
Rhinopomatidae **9:** 86
Rhynchocyon
 R. chrysopygus **9:** 59, <u>62–63</u>
 R. cirnei **9:** 59
 R. petersi **9:** 59
Rhynchogale melleri **1:** 98
Rhynchocholestes raphanurus **10:** 14
Rhynchomeles prattorum **10:** 27
rinderpest **6:** 73, 77, 85
ringing of trees **7:** 37
ringtail *see under* possum; raccoon
rockhare *see* hare, greater red rockhare
Rocky Mountain tick fever **7:** 14
rodents 1: *10*; **7:** <u>8–15</u>
 cavylike 8: <u>8–11</u>
 evolution **7:** *12*
 expansion **7:** 11
 extinct **7:** 11–12
 mouselike 7: <u>16–19</u>
 porcupinelike 8: <u>8–11</u>
 squirrel-like 7: <u>16–19</u>
Romerolagus diazi **8:** 64
rorquals **3:** 55, 106, 107
Rousettus aegyptiacus **9:** <u>92–93</u>
rumen **6:** 8
ruminants 5: 11, 12; **6:** <u>8–9</u>
 pseudoruminants **5:** 70
Rupicapra
 R. pyrenaica **6:** 62
 R. rupicapra **6:** 62, 108
Rupicaprini **6:** 108

S
sable, American **1:** 48, 50
sacred animals **4:** 59, (66); **9:** 91
Saguinus
 S. fuscicollis **4:** 86
 S. imperator **4:** 86, <u>94–95</u>
 S. imperator imperator **4:** 94
 S. imperator subgrisescens **4:** 94
 S. oedipus **4:** 86
saiga **6:** 62
Saiga tartarica **6:** 62
Saimiri
 S. boliviensis **4:** 72
 S. sciureus **4:** 72, <u>78–79</u>
saki
 bald-faced **4:** 72
 bearded **4:** 72
 buffy **4:** 72
 Guianan **4:** 72, *73*
 monk **4:** 72
 white-nosed **4:** 72
Salanoia concolor **1:** 98
saliva **9:** 17, 21
 poisonous **9:** 8, 11, (32), 39
sand puppy *see* mole rat, naked
saola **6:** 62
Sarcophilus
 S. harrisii **10:** 27, <u>28–31</u>
 S. laniarius (*harrisii*) **10:** 27, <u>28–31</u>
Scandentia **1:** *10*; **9:** 58
Scapanus orarius **9:** 40

Scelidotherium **9:** *64*
Sciuridae **7:** *12*
Sciurognathi (sciurognaths) **7:** (8), *12*, 16–19; **8:** 8
Sciuromorpha **7:** 8
Sciurus
 S. carolinensis **7:** 34, <u>38–41</u>
 S. niger **7:** 34, <u>46–47</u>
 S. vulgaris **7:** 34, <u>42–45</u>
scorpion **1:** (102)
Scutisorex somereni **9:** 28
sea canary *see* beluga
sea cow
 Steller's **3:** 46, 47, *47*, 53
 see also dugong
sea grass **3:** 46, 52
seal 1: *10*; **3:** <u>8–13</u>, 64; **7:** 12
 Antarctic fur **3:** 9, 12
 Baikal **3:** 9, *10–11*
 Cape fur 3: 8, 9, <u>16–17</u>
 Caribbean monk **3:** 9
 circus tricks **3:** (23)
 common (harbor) **3:** 8, 9, <u>40–41</u>
 crabeater 3: 9, 11, <u>36–37</u>, 38
 eared **3:** 8, 9, *9*, 10, 11, *13*
 fur **1:** (11)
 gray 3: <u>42–43</u>
 harbor 3: 8, 9, <u>40–41</u>
 harp 3: 9, 12, <u>44–45</u>
 Hawaiian monk 3: 9, <u>30–31</u>
 leopard 3: 9, 11, 37, <u>38–39</u>
 monk **3:** 9
 northern elephant 3: 9, *12*, <u>32–35</u>
 northern fur 3: 9, 12, <u>14–15</u>
 phocid **3:** 9–10, 11
 ringed **2:** 86–87
 saddleback (harp) **3:** 9, 12, <u>44–45</u>
 southern elephant 3: 32
 southern fur (Cape fur) **3:** 8, 9, <u>16–17</u>
sea leopard *see* seal, leopard
sea lion 1: *10*; **3:** <u>8–13</u>, 64
 Australian **3:** 9, 11
 California 3: 9, *13*, 18, <u>20–23</u>
 Galápagos **3:** 9
 New Zealand **3:** 9, 12
 Steller's 3: 9, 12, <u>18–19</u>
Selvinia betpakdalaensis **7:** 102
Semnopithecus **4:** 40
 S. entellus **4:** 40, <u>64–67</u>
 S. geei see *Trachypithecus geei*
 S. hypoleucos **4:** 40
 S. obscurus see *Trachypithecus obscurus*
sengi **9:** 58
Serengeti Plains **6:** 84, (85)
serow **6:** 108
 Japanese **6:** 62
 mainland **6:** 62
serval 2: 10, <u>46–47</u>
servalines **2:** 46
Setifer setosus **9:** 24
Setonix brachyurus **10:** 48, <u>68–69</u>
sewellel **7:** (29)
sheep 1: 15; **5:** 11, *11*; **6:** <u>60–63</u>
 American bighorn 6: <u>100–103</u>
 barbary **6:** 62
 blue **6:** 62
 desert bighorn **6:** 100
 domestic **6:** 62, 63
 Orkney Island Soay **6:** *63*
 wild **6:** 63
shrew 1: *10*; **9:** 8, 9, (10), 11
 African forest **9:** 28
 American short-tailed 9: <u>30–33</u>
 American water 9: <u>36–37</u>

armored **9:** 28, 29
 desert **9:** 29
 elephant **9:** 10
 Etruscan **1:** (11); **9:** 28
 Etruscan white-toothed 9: 28, <u>38–39</u>
 Eurasian common 9: <u>34–35</u>
 Eurasian pygmy **9:** 28, *29*
 Eurasian water **9:** 28, *29*
 forest **9:** 28
 greater white-toothed **9:** <u>8–9</u>
 Indian house **9:** 28
 least **9:** 28
 northern (American) short-tailed **9:** 28, <u>30–33</u>
 piebald **9:** 28
 pygmy white-toothed **9:** 8, 28
 shrew family 9: <u>28–29</u>
 Tibetan water **9:** 28
 see also elephant shrew; otter shrew; tree shrew
shrew mole 9: 40, 41
 American 9: <u>54–55</u>
 Asiatic **9:** 42
 Gibb's (American) **9:** <u>54–55</u>
 inquisitive **9:** 40
shrew mouse **8:** 102
 branch **8:** 102
 variable **8:** 102
siamang **4:** *8*, 36, 37
Siebenschlafer **7:** 104
sifaka
 diademed **4:** 96
 golden-crowned **4:** 96
 Verreaux's **4:** 96
Sigmoceros lichtensteinii see *Alcelaphus lichtensteinii*
Sign Language, American **4:** 13, (16), 27
simakobu **4:** 40
Simias concolor see *Nasalis concolor*
Sirenia **1:** *10*; **3:** 47; **5:** (12)
sitting patches **4:** 39, 52, 58
skin trade **1:** (23), 69, 72, 74; **2:** 33, 36, 37, 39, 47, 100, 111; **3:** 12, *5*: 91; **6:** 66; **10:** 56, 91
 see also fur trade
skunk 1: 34
 Andes **1:** 32
 hooded **1:** 32
 pygmy spotted **1:** 32
 striped 1: 32, <u>84–87</u>
 western hog-nosed **1:** 32
 western spotted **1:** 32
sloth 9: 64–65, 65–66, 66, (66)
 brown-throated three-toed (three-toed) **9:** 65, <u>72–73</u>
 giant ground **9:** *64*
 Hoffmann's two-toed **9:** 65
 maned three-toed **9:** 65
 southern two-toed **9:** 65
 three-toed 9: 65, <u>72–73</u>
Smilodon fatalis **2:** 10
Sminthopsis
 S. aitkeni **10:** 38
 S. crassicaudata **10:** 27
 S. dolichura **10:** 38
 S. gilberti **10:** 38
 S. murina **10:** <u>38–39</u>
 S. virginiae **10:** 27
snakes **1:** (102), 109; **9:** 16
snares **4:** 24, 53
snowshoes **8:** (78)
solenodon **9:** 8, 9, (10), 11
 Cuban **9:** 9
 Hispaniola **9:** 9
Solenodon
 S. cubanus **9:** 9
 S. paradoxus **9:** 9
Solenodontidae **9:** 9
sonar **3:** 83

songs
 gibbons **4:** 36, 39
 whale songs **3:** 99–100, 105
Sorex
 S. araneus **9:** <u>34–35</u>
 S. minutus **9:** 28
 S. palustris **9:** <u>36–37</u>
Soricidae **9:** 9, 58
Spalacopus cyanus **8:** 30
Speothos venaticus **2:** 50
spermaceti **3:** 86, 87, 89, 91
Spermophilus tridecemlineatus **7:** 34, <u>54–55</u>
Sphiggurus
 S. insidiosus **8:** 12
 S. vestitus **8:** 12
Spilocuscus
 S. kraemeri **10:** 74
 S. maculatus **10:** <u>82–83</u>
 S. papuensis **10:** 74
Spilogale
 S. gracilis **1:** 32
 S. pygmaea **1:** 32
spines **9:** 13, 15, *16–17*
 see also quills
spiny mammals **8:** 12
springbok 6: <u>8–9</u>, 61, 62, <u>96–97</u>
springhaas *see* springhare
springhare 7: *12*, 18, <u>20–21</u>
spy-hopping **3:** 71, 96, 107
squid **3:** 87, (88), 91
squirrel 7: 11, *12*, 13, 15
 African ground **7:** 101
 African pygmy **7:** 34
 American gray (gray) **7:** 34, 36, <u>38–41</u>, 43–44, 47
 American red **7:** 42
 Arctic ground **2:** 65
 black flying **7:** 34, *36*
 black giant **7:** *36*
 black-striped **7:** *36*
 Cape ground **7:** *36–37*
 colonial ground **7:** 36
 eastern flying (southern flying) **7:** 34, <u>60–61</u>
 eastern fox 7: 34, <u>46–47</u>
 Eurasian red 7: <u>42–45</u>
 European red **7:** 34
 flying **7:** 8, 13, 17, 34, *37*, (37); **10:** (76)
 gray 7: 34, 36, <u>38–41</u>, 43–44, 47
 gray-cheeked flying **7:** *36*
 ground **7:** 18, 19, 34, 36
 Harris' antelope **7:** <u>8–9</u>
 horse-tailed **7:** *36*
 Indian giant 7: 34, <u>62–63</u>
 Javanese flying **7:** *36*
 Low's **7:** *36*
 Malabar (Indian giant) **7:** 34, <u>62–63</u>
 Mindanao flying **7:** 34
 northern flying **7:** 61
 northern striped palm **7:** 34, 35
 pale giant **7:** *36*
 plantain **7:** *36*
 Prevost's **7:** *36*
 pygmy **7:** *36*
 red **7:** 41
 red-cheeked flying **7:** 34, *36*
 red giant flying **7:** *36*
 scaly-tailed **7:** *12*, 17, (19)
 slender **7:** *36*
 South African ground **7:** *10*, *36–37*
 southern flying 7: 34, <u>60–61</u>
 spotted giant flying **7:** *36*
 squirrel family 7: <u>34–37</u>
 thirteen-lined ground 7: 34, <u>54–55</u>
 three-striped ground **7:** *36*
 tree **7:** 17, 34, 35, 36
 tufted ground **7:** *36*
 squirrel-like rodents 7: <u>16–19</u>
stances **5:** 9–10

steenbok **6:** *61*, 62
Stenella longirostris **3:** 55, <u>76–77</u>
stoat 1: 19, *32*, 34, 36, <u>40–43</u>
stomach stones **3:** (27), 91
stones
 as hammers **1:** (74); **4:** 31–32, (31)
 in the stomach **3:** (27), 91
stotting **6:** 35, 97; **8:** 32
strandings, on shore **3:** (59), 66, 67, 96
strepsirhines *see* primates, lower
stridulation **9:** 27
Strigocuscus
 S. celebensis **10:** 74
 S. pelengensis **10:** 74
styloglossus **5:** (12)
subungulates **5:** (12)
"sulfur bottom" *see* whale, blue
Suncus etruscus **9:** 28, <u>38–39</u>
Sundasciurus
 S. hippurus **7:** 36
 S. lowii **7:** 36
 S. tenuis **7:** 36
Supercohort **1:** *10*
sureli **4:** 41
 banded **4:** 40
 grizzled **4:** 40
surgery
 animal parts for human surgery **5:** 79
 testing surgical techniques **4:** 13
Suricata suricatta **1:** 98, <u>100–105</u>
suricate *see* meerkat
Sus
 S. barbatus **5:** 74
 S. scrofa **5:** 74, <u>76–79</u>
suslik, thirteen-lined *see* squirrel, thirteen-lined ground
swimming therapy **3:** 74
Sylvicapra grimmia **6:** 62, <u>80–81</u>
Sylvilagus
 S. aquaticus **8:** (93)
 S. audubonii **8:** 64, (93)
 S. bachmani **8:** 64
 S. dicei **8:** (93)
 S. floridanus **8:** 64, <u>90–93</u>
 S. insonus **8:** (93)
 S. palustris hefneri **8:** 64
 S. transitionalis **8:** (93)
symbiosis **6:** (73)
Syncerus caffer **6:** 62, <u>70–73</u>
syndactyly **10:** 75, (94)

T
Tachyglossus aculeatus **10:** <u>110–111</u>
Tadarida brasiliensis **9:** <u>100–103</u>
tahr, Himalayan **6:** 62
takh *see* horse, Mongolian wild
takin **6:** 62, 108
talapoin **4:** 40, *41*, 43
Talpa
 T. europaea **9:** 40, <u>44–47</u>
 T. streeti **9:** 40
Talpidae **9:** 9
tamandua **9:** 68
 southern **9:** 65
Tamandua tetradactyla **9:** 65
tamaraw **6:** 62
tamarin 4: *8*
 bearded emperor **4:** 94
 black-chinned emperor **4:** 94
 black-faced lion **4:** 88
 black lion **4:** 86, 88
 cotton-top **4:** 86, *87*
 emperor 4: 86, <u>94–95</u>
 golden-headed lion **4:** 88

golden lion 4: 86, 87, 88–91
lion **4**: 86
saddleback **4**: 86, 95
tamarin family 4: 86–87
Tamias
T. sibiricus **7**: 48
T. striatus **7**: 34, 48–49
tapetum lucidum **2**: 10–12;
4: 85, 106, 107
tapir 5: *8*, 11, 12
Baird's **5**: 62, *62*, 63
Brazilian 5: 62, 63, 64–65
Malayan **5**: 62, 63, *63*
mountain **5**: 62, *63*
South American (Brazilian)
5: 62, 63, 64–65
tapir family 5: 62–63
Tapirus
T. bairdii **5**: 62
T. indicus **5**: 62
T. pinchaque **5**: 62
T. terrestris **5**: 62, 64–65
tarsier **4**: 11, 106, 107
pygmy **4**: 106, 107
spectral **4**: 106, *107*
western **4**: 106, 107, *107*
Tarsipes rostratus **10**: 74, 102–103
Tarsius
T. bancanus **4**: 106
T. pumilus **4**: 106
T. spectrum **4**: 106
Tasmanian devil 10: (24), 27, 28–31
Taurotragus
T. derbianus **6**: 62, 76–77
T. derbianus derbianus
6: 76
T. derbianus gigas **6**: 76
T. oryx **6**: 62, 76
Taxidea taxus **1**: 32, 76–77
Tayassu
T. pecari **5**: 88
T. tajacu **5**: 88, 90–91
Tayassuidae **5**: 88
tayra **1**: 32; **4**: 89
teeth
aardvark **9**: 65, (66), 78–79
bats **9**: (85), (95)
selenodont **6**: 9
teledu **1**: 32
Telicomys **7**: 11–12
tenrec 8: 12; **9**: 8, 9, 11
aquatic **9**: 24, 25, *25*
common 9: 24, 26–27
four-toed rice **9**: *24*
greater (common) **9**: 24, 26–27
greater hedgehog **9**: *24*, 25
large-eared **9**: 24, 25
lesser hedgehog **9**: 24, 25
long-tailed **9**: *24*, 25
pygmy shrew **9**: 24
rice **9**: 24, 25
spiny **9**: 25
streaked **9**: 24, *24–25*
tailless (common) **9**: 24, 26–27
tenrec family 9: 24–25
Tenrec **9**: 9
T. ecaudatus **9**: 24, 26–27
Tenrecidae **9**: 9, 11, 24
termite mounds, as vantage
points **6**: 88, *88–89*
termites **2**: 50, 76, 110–111;
6: 87; **9**: 64, 66, 69;
10: 34
Tetracerus quadricornis
6: 62
Theropithecus gelada **4**: 40, 62–63
Thomomys talpoides
7: 26–27
Thrichomys apereoides **8**: 30
Thryonomyidae **7**: *12*; **8**: 31
Thryonomys
T. gregorianus **8**: 30
T. swinderianus **8**: 30

thylacine 2: 80; **10**: 24, 26, 28, 36–37
Thylacinidae **10**: 24, 26
Thylacinus cynocephalus
10: 27, 36–37
Thylamis
T. elegans **10**: 14
T. pallidior **10**: 14
Thylogale
T. stigmatica **10**: 48
T. thetis **10**: 48
Thyropteridae **9**: 87
tiang **6**: 88
ticks **6**: 18; **7**: 14
tiger 2: 10, 20–25
Bali **2**: 21
Bengal **2**: 21, *21*, *22*, *23*
Caspian **2**: 21
Chinese **2**: 20, 21
Indochinese **2**: 21
Javan **2**: 21
Siberian **2**: 20, 21, 22–23
Sumatran **2**: 21
Tasmanian *see* thylacine
white **2**: *23*, (23)
tiger-horses **5**: 52
titi
dusky **4**: 72
masked **4**: 72
yellow-handed **4**: 72
toddy **1**: 95
toddy cat *see* civet, common
palm
tommie *see* gazelle,
Thomson's
tool users **1**: (74); **4**: 10–11,
(16), 31–32, (31)
topi 6: 62, (85), 88–89
torpor **7**: 80; **9**: 20–21, 29, 38,
82, 102; **10**: 40, 85, 103
tourism **3**: 51, 71, (94), 95;
5: 39; **9**: 53, 101
whale watching **3**: (57),
71, 95, 104
Trachypithecus
T. geei **4**: 40
T. obscurus **4**: 40
Tragelaphus
T. buxtoni **6**: 62
T. scriptus **6**: 62
T. strepsiceros **6**: 78–79
Tragulidae **6**: 10
Tragulus **6**: 48
T. javanicus **6**: 10, 48
T. napu **6**: 10, 48–49
tree dwelling **2**: 31
tree shrew 1: *10*; **5**: (10);
9: 10, 58–59
common 9: 59, 60–61
pen-tailed **9**: 58, *58*, 59
Philippine **9**: *58*
pygmy **9**: *58*, 59
Tremarctos ornatus **2**: 82
tribal warfare **4**: 30
Trichechus
T. inunguis **3**: 47
T. manatus **3**: 48–51
T. senegalensis **3**: 47
Trichosurus
T. caninus **10**: 74
T. vulpecula **10**: 74, 78–81
Trichys fasciculata **8**: 12
triok, Tate's **10**: 74, (77)
truffles **5**: 79
Trypanosoma cruzi **8**: 27
tsessebe **6**: 88
tuberculosis, bovine **1**: 81;
10: (80)
Tubulidentata **1**: *10*; **5**: (12);
9: 65
tuco-tuco **7**: *12*; **8**: 9–10, 11,
28–29, *31*
forest **8**: 30
strong **8**: 30
tularemia **8**: 81, 93
tuna **3**: 69, 77
tunnels, foraging **7**: 15,
100–101
see also burrows

Tupaia
T. glis **9**: 59, 60–61
T. minor **9**: 59
tur
east Caucasian **6**: 106, 107
west Caucasian **6**: 106, 107
Tursiops truncatus **3**: 55, 72–75
tusks **3**: 26, 84–85; **5**: 14, 17,
26, 66, 72, 74, 80–81, 86,
87
see also ivory
Tympanoctomys barrerae
8: 30
typhus **7**: 14, 74

U

uakari
bald (red) **4**: 72, 80–81
black **4**: *9*, 72
black-headed **4**: 80
red 4: 72, 80–81
white (red) **4**: 72, 80–81
Umfolozi park **5**: 34
Uncia uncia **2**: 34–35
ungulates (hoofed mammals)
5: 8–13
even-toed **1**: *10*; **5**: 10, 88
odd-toed **1**: *10*; **5**: 10, *11*,
43
urchin *see* hedgehog,
European
Urocyon
U. cinereoargenteus **2**: 50
U. littoralis **2**: 50
Urogale everetti **9**: 59
Uropsilus investigator **9**: 40
Urotrichus **9**: 54
Ursus
U. americanus **2**: 82, 90–93
U. arctos **2**: 82, 92, 94–97
U. maritimus **2**: 82, 84–89
U. melanoleuca **2**: 98
U. thibetanus **2**: 82

V

vaccination, against rabies
2: (67)
Vampyrum spectrum **9**: 86
Varecia
V. variegata **4**: 96,
104–105
V. variegata rubra **4**: 104
V. variegata variegata
4: 104
Vespertilionidae **9**: 87
vibrissae **8**: 56
Vicugna vicugna **5**: 92,
110–111
vicuña 5: 92, 93,
110–111
viscacha **7**: *12*; **8**: 28
mountain **8**: 28
northern **8**: 30
plains **8**: 28, 30
viscacha rat **8**: 29, 30
plains **8**: 30
Viverra
V. megaspila **1**: 88
V. tangalunga **1**: 88
V. zibetha **1**: 88
Viverricula indica **1**: 88
Viverridae **1**: 18, 88, 98
vole 7: 13, 17, 65
bank **7**: *14–15*
field 7: 92–93
north European water
(water) **7**: 9, 98–99
short-tailed (field) **7**: 92–93
**southern red-backed
7**: 94–95
water **1**: 54; **7**: 9,
98–99
Vombatiformes **10**: 75
Vombatus ursinus **10**: 74,
98–101
vomeronasal organ **5**: 62, 65
Vormela peregusna **1**: 32

Vulpes
V. bengalensis **2**: 50
V. cana **2**: 50
V. chama **2**: 50
V. corsac **2**: 50
V. lagopus **2**: 50, 70–73
V. rüppelli **2**: 50
V. velox **2**: 50, 68–69
V. velox herbes **2**: 69
V. vulpes **2**: 50, 64–67
V. zerda **2**: 50, 74–75

W

Wallabia bicolor **10**: 48
wallaby 10: 48–53
banded hare **10**: 48, *51*
Bennett's (red-necked)
10: 48, 64–65
bridled nail-tailed **10**: 48, *50*
lesser forest **10**: 48
northern nail-tailed **10**: 48
Papuan forest **10**: 48
prettyface **10**: 48
Proserpine rock **10**: 48, *50*
red-necked 10: 48, 64–65
ringtailed rock (yellow-
footed rock) **10**: 48,
70–71
rock **10**: 51
rufous hare **10**: 48, *51*
spectacled hare **10**: 48
swamp **10**: 48, *49*
toolache **10**: 53
whiptail **10**: 48, *51*
**yellow-footed rock
10**: 48, 70–71
wallaroo **10**: 60–61
common **10**: 48, *50*, 60
hill **10**: 48, *50*
wallowing **5**: 38, 69, 71, *71*,
76–77, 83
walrus 3: *8*, 9, 10, 11,
24–29
want *see* mole, European
wapiti *see* elk
warthog 5: 75, 80–83
common **5**: 74
desert **5**: 74
washing bears **1**: (24)
Washington Convention *see*
Convention on
International Trade in
Endangered Species of
Wild Fauna and Flora
waterbuck 5: *75*; **6**: 62,
92–93
defassa **6**: 93
water reabsorption **5**: 96
weasel
African striped **1**: 32, *34*
European common (least)
1: 19, 32, 34, *35*, 36–39
least 1: 19, 32, 34, *35*,
36–39
long-tailed **1**: 32, 36
North African banded **1**: 32,
34
Patagonian **1**: 32, *34*
short-tailed *see* stoat
weasel family 1: 32–35
webbed fingers **4**: 71
Weil's disease **7**: 14, 74
wetlands **1**: 24
whale 1: *10*, (11), 14;
3: 54–59; **5**: (10), 66;
7: 12
baleen **3**: 54–55, 56, 58
blue 1: (11); **3**: 54, 55,
(57), 58, 98–101
bowhead **3**: 55, 108,
110–111
dwarf sperm **3**: 55
gray 3: 55, *57*, (57), *59*,
92–97
humpback 3: 55, (57), *58*,
102–105
killer 3: 37, 39, 55,
62–65, 83, 94, 96

long-finned pilot 3: 55,
66–67
minke 3: 55, 106–107
**northern bottlenose
3**: 55, 90–91
northern right **3**: 109
pygmy right **3**: *54*, 55
pygmy sperm **3**: 55
right **3**: 55
short-finned pilot 3: 66
southern right 3: 55,
108–109
sperm 3: 55, 57, 58,
86–89
white *see* beluga
whale meat **3**: 59, 67
whale songs **3**: 99–100, 105
whale watching **3**: (57), 71,
95, 104
whaling industry **3**: 58, 89, 91,
93, 101, 105, 107, 108
whistlepig *see* woodchuck
whiteness in mammals **8**: (84)
wildcat 2: 10, 13, 48–49
African **2**: *12*
European **2**: *12*
wildebeest 5: 12, 47; **6**: 95
black 6: 62
blue 6: 62, 82–85
wolf **2**: 9
Ethiopean **2**: 50, *52*
Falkland Island **2**: 50, 53,
(53)
gray 2: 50, 53, 54–57,
59
maned **2**: 50, 53
marsupial *see* thylacine
Mexican **2**: 54
red **2**: 59
Tasmanian *see* thylacine
timber (gray) **2**: 50, 53,
54–57, 59
wolverine 1: 18, 32, *35*,
56–57
wombat 10: (10), 77, 93
common 10: 74, 75,
98–101
northern hairy-nosed
10: 74, (101)
southern hairy-nosed
10: 74, *101*, (101)
woodchuck 1: 87; **7**: 34,
50–51
wool production **5**: 104, 105,
(106), 108, 111
World Conservation Union *see*
International Union for the
Conservation of Nature
worms **9**: (46)
Wyulda squamicaudata
10: 74

X

Xenarthra **1**: *10*; **9**: 64–66

Y

yak 6: 74–75
wild **6**: 75
yapok *see* opossum, water
Yellowstone National Park
6: 66, 67
Yersinia pestis **7**: 76

Z

Zalophus californianus **3**: 9,
20–23
zebra 2: *8–9*; **5**: 12, *12–13*;
6: (85), 95
Burchell's (plains) **5**: 42,
46–51
common (plains) **5**: 42,
46–51
Grèvy's 5: 42, (44),
52–53
mountain **5**: 42
plains **5**: 42, 46–51
zebra family 5: 42–45
zokor **7**: 15
zorilla **1**: 32, 34, *34*

Picture Credits

Abbreviations

FLPA   Frank Lane Picture Agency
NHPA   Natural History Photographic Agency
NPL   naturepl.com
OSF   Oxford Scientific Films

t = top; b = bottom; c = center; l = left; r = right

Jacket

tl caracal, Pete Oxford/naturepl.com; tr group of dolphins, Robert Harding Picture Library; bl lowland gorilla, Martin Rügner/Naturphotographie; br Rothchild's giraffe, Gerard Lacz/FLPA

8–9 Daniel Heuclin/NHPA; **10** P. Morris/Ardea; **13** Daniel Heuclin/NHPA; **14–15** E.A. Janes/NHPA; **16l** Daniel Heuclin/NHPA; **16r** Dietmar Nill/NPL; **16–17** B. Borrell/FLPA; **18–19** Foto Natura Stock/FLPA; **20–21** Jim Tuten/Animals Animals/OSF; **22–23** C. & R. Aveling/ICCE; **24–25** Pete Oxford/NPL; **26–27** Peter Steyn/Ardea; **28–29** Stephen Dalton/NHPA; **29** Barrie Watts/OSF; **30–31** Dan Griggs/NHPA; **32–33** Joe McDonald/Animals Animals/OSF; **34–35** Robin Redfern/OSF; **36–37** Marty Stouffer Prods/Animals Animals/OSF; **38–39** Daniel Heuclin/NHPA; **40–41** Darrell Gulin/Dembinsky/FLPA; **42** Bill Beaty/Animals Animals/OSF; **42–43** Peter Steyn/Ardea; **43** Tim Jackson/OSF; **44–45** John Mason/Ardea; **46** P. Morris/Ardea; **47** OSF; **48–49** Zig Leszczynski/Animals Animals/OSF; **50–51** Dembinsky Photo Ass./FLPA; **53** John Hartley/NHPA; **54–55** Ronn Altig; **56–57** Michael Fogden/OSF; **58–59** Bruce Davidson/NPL; **60–61** Marty Stouffer Prods/Animals Animals/OSF; **62–63** P. Morris/Ardea; **64–65** N. Dennis/Sunset/FLPA; **66** Foto Natura Stock/FLPA; **66–67** Kevin Schafer/NHPA; **68–69** Tom Brakefield/Corbis; **70** Kenneth W. Fink/Ardea; **70–71** Kevin Schafer/NHPA; **72–73** Luiz Claudio Marigo/Bruce Coleman Collection; **74–75** Silvestris/FLPA; **76–77** Haroldo Palo Jr./NHPA; **77** Jeff Foott/NPL; **78–79** Anthony Bannister/NHPA; **80–81, 82–83** Dietmar Nill/NPL; **84–85** Merlin D. Tuttle/Bat Conservation International; **85** David Thompson/OSF; **87** J.A.L. Cooke/OSF; **88–89** Daniel Heuclin/NHPA; **90–91** E. & D. Hosking/FLPA; **91** Silvestris/FLPA; **92–93** Gallo Images/OSF; **94–95** Jens Rydell/Bruce Coleman Collection; **96** Adrian Warren/Ardea; **96–97** J.W. Wilkinson; **98–99** Stephen Dalton/NHPA; **100–101** Silvestris/FLPA; **101** George Bryce/Animals Animals/OSF; **102–103** Stephen Krasemann/NHPA; **104–105** Joe McDonald/Animals Animals/OSF; **106–107** Dietmar Nill/NPL; **108–109** Stephen Dalton/NHPA; **110–111** John Daniels/Ardea

Artists

Denys Ovenden, Priscilla Barrett with Michael Long, Graham Allen, Malcolm McGregor

While every effort has been made to trace the copyright holders of illustrations reproduced in this book, the publishers will be pleased to rectify any omissions or inaccuracies.